The brand is the company driver
in the new value economy

Unique

now

...or never

FINANCIAL TIMES
Prentice Hall

An imprint of **PEARSON EDUCATION**
London · New York · New Delhi · Madrid · Paris · Toronto · Sydney · Tokyo
Singapore · Hong Kong · Cape Town · Amsterdam · Munich · Milan · Stockholm

Unique now ...or never
By Jesper Kunde

PEARSON EDUCATION LIMITED

Head Office:
Edinburgh Gate
Harlow CM20 2JE
Tel: +44 (0)1279 623623
Fax: +44 (0)1279 431059

London Office:
128 Long Acre
London WC2E 9AN
Tel: +44 (0)20 7447 2000
Fax: +44 (0)20 7240 5771
www.business-minds.com

First published in Great Britain in 2002

ISBN 0 273 65962 6

British Library Cataloguing in Publication Data
A CIP catalogue record for this book can be obtained from the British Library

This publication is designed to provide accurate and authoritative information
in regard to the subject matter covered. It is sold with the understanding that
neither the authors nor the publisher is engaged in rendering legal, investing, or
any other professional service. If legal advice or other expert assistance is required,
the service of a competent professional person should be sought.

The publisher and contributors make no representation, express or implied, with
regard to the accuracy of the information contained in this book and cannot accept
any responsibility or liability for any errors or omissions that it may contain

10 9 8 7 6 5 4 3 2 1

Designed and Typeset by Kunde & Co, Copenhagen, Denmark
Printed and bound in Italy by Rotolito Lombarda

The Publishers' policy is to use paper manufactured from sustainable forests.

Contents

Preface

Corporate Religion sparked a major movement because the book caught a trend in the market. I had many calls from companies wanting assistance in defining and articulating the essence of their enterprises. Corporate Religion revealed an unfulfilled demand for working on branding of corporations. So the outcome of all the religion talks, all the interviews that I gave to journalists, had to be writing a new book – a book about the transformation of a traditional production enterprise into a modern, brand-oriented corporation.

To me, it is crystal clear that in the future it will be the brand that drives the company. This book is meant to show top managers how to act successfully in the new value economy.

Thanks to my partner

I would like to thank the people who, in the past three years, have assisted me with this book. First and foremost, my partner, Gaute Høgh, and all the senior consultants at Kunde & Co. Their wise input has contributed to developing and throwing light on new ways of using the brand to direct the company.

Thanks for the readability

Great thanks to Anders Krag, who edited the entire book and made it most readable and came up with the title. Without Anders Krag, this book would not have been as easily accessible as it is, and consistently challenged me to articulate essences whenever I was on a dreary trail.

Thanks for the production

Niels Henrik Eriksen played an indispensable role in the making of this book. He put together all the case stories and kept control of all loose ends after Andres Krag and myself were on top of it content wise.

Our small book team owes great thanks to Helle Knutsen for keeping us on the track and for her sharp and constructive criticism, which is the reason why the book's message remain plain and clear.

Also great thanks to all the corporations which appear in the book and share their knowledge with the readers and us.

Thanks to the designers

Graphic designer Jan Andersen deserves a great many thanks for the design of the content and art director Anders Adolvsson for the design of the front cover of the book.

I thank Camilla Søfeldt, Dannie Søndergaard and Louise Riparbelli for desktop publishing and final polishing off. They often had to make changes to make the book really swing. And thanks to Eva Maria Nielsen for the design of the figures and to Jens Bjørn Flodin for his assistance.

Also, warm thanks to our faithful proofreader Axel Frissenette – called Frisse – to Charlotte Gottlieb and Pernille Bigum for the production and for co-ordination with the publisher. Thanks to Børsen Forlag for their understanding of our intention to make the ultimate book.

Thanks to the nearest

Last but not least, thanks to my wife and girlfriend Helle, and my two children Nynne and Nanna, for once again, having to do without their husband and father physically and mentally for long periods of time.

I will probably not be allowed to write more books.

Introduction

Brand-U-Nique

Ask yourself a question: How metaphysical is your company? The answer, I believe, holds the key to the future success of the business. Here's why.

We all recognize unique moments when we encounter them.

The intensity of childbirth. A key insight into a relationship. A sudden feeling of being at one with nature when a spectacular view comes into sight. Watching an animal in the wild. A particularly memorable concert or play. A sublime flash of talent from a top sports man or woman.

Big moments also occur in business. When you meet a major target. When a major project is an unconditional success. When your hopes for a brand are transformed into reality.

I believe that if you create unique moments involving the customer and your brand, the customer will form an intense and sincere relationship with the brand – and will remain loyal to it for years.

SAS achieved this under Jan Carlzon's leadership in the 1980s, providing customers with a powerful and satisfying sense of SAS being 'The Businessman's Airline'.

Michael Jordan did it for the Nike brand in the 1980s and 1990s with his flawless sporting performances. Sir Richard Branson made his big breakthrough in the early 1990s as the rebel challenging established conventions – an image he still cultivates. Bill Gates was hailed as a demigod in the early 1990s and his powerful position still rests on that status. Nokia established a close understanding with its customers in the late 1990s and quickly became a world leader.

In short, if a brand offers customers unique experiences,

the company that owns the brand can live off the perception of value this creates for a long time. In my opinion, companies should be seeking to bring about unique moments by migrating from the physical world to the realm of the metaphysical. And we should seek to generate as many of these unique moments as possible in order to renew regularly the values upon which the brand is based. In terms of Maslow's hierarchy of needs, this represents migration from the lowest subsistence level to the highest level of self-fulfilment.

The new value economy

Nowadays, young people entering the labour market for the first time already have two televisions, the latest mobile phone, a car, two boy/girlfriends and a wardrobe full of clothes. While these material values may be important, there is more to life – and the employee of the future knows that and will seek meaning and value.

I am convinced that this change in behaviour and attitudes will be the strongest driving force in the market of the future. It will also have a major effect on the economy, on companies, and on the way we live and work. Moving from the physical to the metaphysical world also entails moving from the old product-oriented economy to a new value economy.

In this new economy you will still have to supply products, of course, but the most important factor will be the (metaphysical) value that your products convey to the individual customer. People will seek out brands that fulfil some of our new and growing needs. We will demand the unique because, on the physical level, we can have anything we want. In a lot of companies this will require a dramatic change in the way of thinking. I do not believe that they will all survive because not all understand the nature of this social change and the influence it is having on their business.

Most managers have no idea how to add value in the

metaphysical world. But that is what the market will cry out for in the future. There is no lack of products to choose between.

The point of the brand

A new situation is beginning to emerge in which brands are extremely powerful and loom large in the popular consciousness. The demonstrations we used to see against the state will turn into demonstrations against brands that do not behave properly. Remember Nike and child labour? Or Shell and Brent Spar? It is no coincidence that Shell so unstintingly markets its brand on the basis of its visions and commitment to research into new sources of energy.

If we are to incorporate these new ideas into the organizations of the future, then the direction that the company takes has to be defined and determined by the brand and its values. Companies will have to accustom themselves to giving of themselves, to doing good deeds, and to being human in every sense of the word.

Unique now or never ...

One reason some companies are starting to respond to these changes is the popularity of the 'branding' concept. The problem is that they tend to equate branding with marketing. Design a sparkling new logo, run an exciting new marketing campaign, and voilà – you are back on course.

This is a misconception widespread among company executives, communications companies and advertising agencies.

They are wrong, so wrong.

The task is bigger, much bigger. It is about the company fulfilling its potential, not about a new logo. What is my mission in life? What do I want to convey to people? And how do I make sure that what I have to offer the world is actually unique? In other words, the task is developing and transforming the concept of the company in the meta-physical world to boost the unique aspects of the brand.

Companies have to offer consumers something special and that implies targeting the chosen few instead of the masses. You simply cannot be all things to all men without watering down your message. The brand has to give of itself, the company has to give of itself, and management has to give of itself. Above all, it is a matter of providing people with something of great value, otherwise you will vanish in the new value economy. To put it bluntly, it is a matter of whether you want to be unique NOW ... or never.

CHAPTER 1

Believe or leave

If you want to keep running a good company, you need to know what's special about your business. You have to understand what it stands for in the marketplace. It's now or never. And it's all about being unique.

The purpose of this book is to drive companies towards a brighter future. It was devised and written to explain to you why branding is the only way forward. In every industry.

Perhaps you manufacture paperclips, notch grinders or 9 mm bolts and believe that branding doesn't matter. You're wrong. The world will flock to buy your paperclips or bolts if you brand them well.

All Nike does, after all, is manufacture trainers and some sports gear. Nothing else. What makes Nike special is the way it sells its products. It doesn't actually sell train-ers at all. It sells the experience of using Nike, the feeling of being a winner. And it condenses its whole philosophy into three words: Just Do It.

What you offer the market can never be 'just' a product. Any company can make a product. But the unique way a product is presented must always originate from intangible concepts. It has to represent a personality, a value, an attitude – in short, a brand.

We are leaving the product economy behind – leaving behind the days when everything could be measured, weighed, counted and entered into the accounts. Intangible values make the world go round and attract customers. The future belongs to brand experts. Those who have not

Intangible values make the world go round and attract customers. The future belongs to brand experts. Those who have not yet made brands the absolute focal point in their companies must learn to do so quickly. The value economy is here to stay.

yet made brands the absolute focal point in their companies must learn to do so quickly. The value economy is here to stay.

What do you want to bring to the world?

This book is aimed at company executives, whether in large multinationals or smaller companies. I have extensive experience of both types of company and I want to make one point forcibly: stop whatever you are doing and do something radical instead. You can't just go on forever floating with the tide, monitoring the competition and conducting surveys to find out what your customers want now. What do you want? What do you want to communicate to the world?

What do you want to communicate to the world?

If the answer is 'nothing in particular' then you might as well go straight home and stay there. You need to find out what your company has to offer that will, in some way, enrich the world. And you must believe in that. Believe so strongly that you become unique at what you do.

If you think that sounds impossible then you will be forced out of the market sooner rather than later. In the future there will be no room for ten-a-penny 'me-too' companies.

Today the western world is over-supplied. There is an over-abundance of everything. There are too many shops, too many advertising messages, too many TV channels, hamburgers, cars, clothes and just about anything else you care to think of. We live in an era of excess. Offering more of the same is not a viable option. It is no longer enough to pile your product higher than your rivals'. In such a crowded market there is no point in competing for shelf space or simply making more noise. You have to differentiate your offering. There is only one place in which you are (or should be) interested in being taken seriously, being heard, noticed, registered, remembered, used. That place is the human mind. That is where you must strive to grab some space.

Without this mind space there is no room for your company in the market. How then do you guarantee your survival in the new value economy? By living up to the definition of a brand in the new value economy:

The definition of a brand in the new value economy is: A brand that has a unique value that can be communicated globally and multiplied repeatedly.

> *A unique value that can be communicated globally and multiplied repeatedly.*

How would you like to make your breakthrough?

In recent years, market noise has increased exponentially. The scramble for customers has increased the volume of information directed at the individual consumer. Research shows that an ordinary citizen in the western world now receives 3,000 marketing messages each and every day. The consumer has to sort through a jumble of advertising slogans, films, TV news, quiz shows, traffic chaos, football matches, delayed flights and all the rest. The noise is deafening.

This is the reality that companies face. This is the white noise in which they must attempt to transmit their marketing messages.

Over-communication does something to the society we live in. Any company that is serious about what it does must learn to live with this communications reality. How? The answer is surprisingly simple, yet incredibly difficult to live up to. To be heard above the cacophony of noise, the company needs its own signature tune. To make itself heard, a company has to offer the market something unique.

To offer something unique, the company has to focus its activities. It has to appeal to narrower segments and then compensate for ignoring the broad segments by marketing its brand globally. This means more communication to penetrate more markets and to reach more of these narrow segments – and that means more focus on building values. It is a bit like a centrifuge – and it is the centrifugal effect that will propel companies into the new value economy.

Would you like to be unique?

The new value economy has its own rules. You must have either a unique product, a unique shop, a unique service or a unique brand. If you have none of these, you will vanish into the grey mass of companies that fail to stand out from the crowd.

There are so many products to choose between and they are so similar in terms of quality that the customer craves something extra, something that appeals to him or her and adds value to the product. This implies a migration from a product world to a brand world.

Figure 1.1 Capture a place in an over-communicated reality

Can you capture a place here?

In the west, every day of our lives we are bombarded with more than 3,000 marketing messages.
This makes it even more vital to be able to cut through and capture a place in the minds of the consumer.
Rather a unique brand, which cuts through to a particular target group, than a broad and undefined
brand for everybody.

Today, anything and everything can be a brand. Products, companies, people, countries, organizations, even animals are being transformed into brands with specific values. This constitutes a dramatic social change and has far-reaching implications for the way we live, think and act.

Think about it. The natural disaster that attracts most media coverage also receives most emergency aid. The policies that are best presented in the media win elections. The brand that is marketed best sells most. The country that sees itself as a brand and uses every means at its disposal to market itself efficiently pulls in the most tourists and attracts the most investment.

Take Sir Richard Branson as an example. The chairman of the Virgin Group is a walking brand, with enormous value. So too is the Formula 1 driver Michael Schumacher. Anybody who is interested in brands knows how people can build brands. In the US, the basketball player Michael Jordan's enormous popularity and cult status played a decisive role in building up the Nike superbrand.

Brands are bigger than nation states

The biggest international brands are bigger than many nation states. These new brand states transcend national boundaries and exert greater influence on public opinion than the old institutions of the nation states. Brands are the world's new opinion makers. Because they are so meaningful customers often buy into their values to such an extent that they read more into the brand than it can possibly live up to. They expect brands to be even better than they really are. Customers are so deeply involved that they look beyond the surface of the brand and notice everything about it. They also continually reassess its credibility. This presents a future challenge for every brand – for a brand to be credible, regardless of where in the world the customer happens to run into it, will require genuine consistency.

For a brand to be credible, regardless of where in the world the customer happens to run into it, will require genuine consistency.

Mistakes will be punished promptly. Unlike real nation states, where you cannot refuse to pay your taxes, customers can, and do, simply stop buying a brand if it loses its credibility.

A future without USPs

Today, the greatest value is generated by brands. And the companies that flourish are the ones that have successfully established their ownership of a customer group, a group that shares the company's basic (brand) values. These customers will follow the brand even into other product categories so long as the brand continues to live up to its values. That is why I think value positions will separate winners and losers in the future.

The companies that flourish are the ones that have successfully established their ownership of a customer group, a group that shares the company's basic (brand) values.

Product USPs (unique selling propositions) are less important than they used to be. Product life cycles are becoming shorter. Innovations are rapidly imitated by competitors. Markets are no longer static. Product innovation is faster and more regular and markets merge. So owning a specific product segment is of less value than it used to be.

Something more lasting is needed. In the future, sustainable competitive advantage will come from a company's unique value proposition (UVP). Without a value position, which can be moved from one market segment to another, you will be unable to capture and hold mind space – see the horizontal arrow in Figure 1.2.

Figure 1.2 illustrates how the new reality will look for companies. Whereas they used to be viewed in relation to a product-oriented market and it was important to own a product USP (indicated by the vertical line in the diagram), the value economy ushers in a much more chaotic situation.

Companies now transcend product categories with their strong value positioning. They are able to do this because they own strong brands with unique values and a distinct direction that a certain group of customers is willing to buy into.

Figure 1.2 Market borders become multi-dimensional in the new value economy

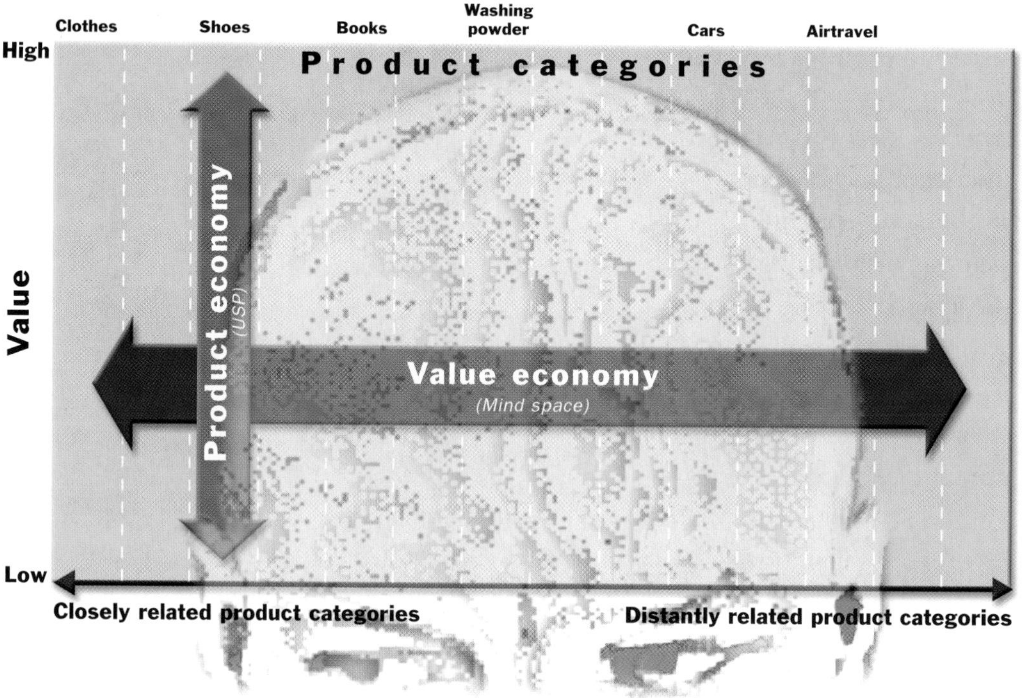

Within the old product orientation, market boundaries are often defined by the product category in which you have chosen to place your product. If, in contrast, you understand the ideas within the new value economy, you can diversify your brand into a series of categories and fields. It is then going to be harder to anticipate who your future competitors will be, which radically changes the rules of the game for the corporation.

Richard Branson is able to diversify his Virgin brand into airlines, banking, cola, bridal wear and a whole host of product categories because they live up to the ultimate Virgin brand value of 'confronting convention'.

In much the same way, the Nike brand 'owns' young people, so Nike is unlikely to restrict itself to sports products in future. It will exploit its 'winner' value to sell all sorts of products to the young. The only requirement will be that the new products live up to the Nike brand value. This process will accelerate as companies start to realize what the new value economy is all about, what dangers it holds – and the huge opportunities it presents.

Mobile phone manufacturers such as Nokia and Sony Ericsson will soon have their market blown wide open by the new UMTS licences, which will create the mobile Internet market. All of a sudden they will have to compete with brands like Philips, Siemens and Panasonic. As if that were not enough, they can also expect competition from IBM, Apple, Toshiba, Compaq, Psion and all sorts of other as yet unknown competitors (see Figure 22.4).

As soon as the struggle comes down to value positioning, claiming to be the 'original' mobile phone producer will be pointless because all the others will be able to make mobile multimedia terminals. In this context, only values and brand power will count. They are the currency of the new value economy.

Only values and brand power will count. They are the currency of the new value economy.

Change your way of thinking now

To get on board the new growth train, companies have to react right away. But how can a company react if it has not yet redefined itself in the light of the new reality?

Figure 1.3 attempts to illustrate how management must reallocate resources and switch focus from internal production to external brand building. The figure follows the path of the brand. It moves from management, through the company and its culture (depicted by the first oval to the left), into external positioning among customers (the second oval) and out into value positioning (on the extreme right). Value positioning is the key to the development of the company and the brand.

Most companies in the old product-oriented economy waste too much of their resources on product development, management systems and logistics. They could achieve much more by investing in the strength of the brand and positioning in the market.

For example, Philips has a great track record in product innovation but does not sell enough of its new products because its brand lacks the requisite strength. The Dutch company launched a unique flat screen TV to hang on the wall. If Sony had been first on the market with the flat-screen TV, it would have sold in greater numbers. Sony has the value positioning to sell unique innovations. Philips does not. Its value message is too diffuse. Because the company manufactures everything from light bulbs to high-tech products, the brand lacks focus. It has not defined a value proposition that would enable it to sell chic, state-of-the-art technology. The point is not that Philips should necessarily stop making light bulbs (although that is something it might consider) but that it should define its distinctive brand value in terms of its uniqueness.

Lots of companies make light bulbs; few are genuinely at the leading edge of technology innovation. When they think of Philips, consumers should know what is unique about the company. That uniqueness could imbue its products with a meaning that goes beyond the product. This focusing of company activities means that the only products marketed are those that promote the desired value and brand position. The marketing effort should concentrate only on the activities that support that message.

In the new reality of the value economy, there is no room for redundant, hard-to-use or unnecessary functionality. In how many households around the world does the clock on the VCR just flash away because no one knows how to set it properly? The resources freed by cutting out superfluous non-brand products increase real market access. This is illustrated in Figure 1.3.

The resources freed by cutting out superfluous non-brand products increase real market access.

Porter is right

In the new value economy, you build your company around the brand and the value positioning to which you

Figure 1.3 Optimization of resources in the new value economy

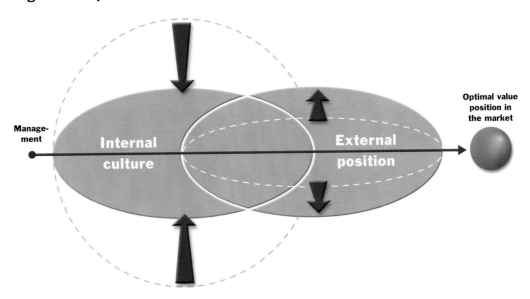

Many corporations experience instability because of the prevailing product fixation. The corporation is then unrealistically inflated in relation to the capability of the external value position in the market. The imbalance in the division of the resources needs to be adjusted for the new value economy.

wish to stake a claim in the market. Differentiating the company's value proposition is the only strategy that makes sense because products and markets change all the time and innovations come on stream more and more frequently.

Figure 1.4 presents a list of things that companies have to redefine in the switch from the old economy to the new value economy. The most important thing to change is the company's way of thinking. Otherwise it is impossible to devise a proper strategy. There is no point in restructuring and optimizing processes – that is not how a strategy is drawn up – or in optimizing the product value chain, as many have done over the past decade. Professor Michael Porter of Harvard Business School, who developed the concept of the company value chain, says management consultants

Figure 1.4 Redefine your company

From the old economy → to the new value economy

1. Redefine the idea of company strategy (Chapter 18)

From optimizing the product value chain ⋯⋯⋯→⋯⋯⋯ to optimizing the brand value chain

2. Redefine your idea of value (Part 1)

From product ⋯⋯⋯→⋯⋯⋯ to value position in the market
From product brands ⋯⋯⋯→⋯⋯⋯ to the company as a brand
From logo and design ⋯⋯⋯→⋯⋯⋯ to brand systems

3. Redefine your idea of the company's way to the market (Chapter 19)

From long distribution chains ⋯⋯⋯→⋯⋯⋯ to short distribution chains
From physical distribution ⋯⋯⋯→⋯⋯⋯ to mental distribution
From customer relations ⋯⋯⋯→⋯⋯⋯ to brand relations

4. Redefine your idea of the company organization (Chapter 20)

From international and local domains ⋯⋯⋯→⋯⋯⋯ to global domains in specific segments
From product organization ⋯⋯⋯→⋯⋯⋯ to brand culture
From hierarchical organization ⋯⋯⋯→⋯⋯⋯ to a horizontal knowledge organization
From control and administration ⋯⋯⋯→⋯⋯⋯ to articulation and communication
From systems excellence ⋯⋯⋯→⋯⋯⋯ to innovation excellence
From titles ⋯⋯⋯→⋯⋯⋯ to actual knowledge and generating value

5. Redefine your idea of leadership (Chapter 21)

From product management ⋯⋯⋯→⋯⋯⋯ to brand management
From top-down ⋯⋯⋯→⋯⋯⋯ to team values
From management ⋯⋯⋯→⋯⋯⋯ to innovator
From administrator ⋯⋯⋯→⋯⋯⋯ to communicator
From tight management ⋯⋯⋯→⋯⋯⋯ to broad management
From rules and regulations ⋯⋯⋯→ to the management of ideas, brand and culture

6. Redefine your idea of market boundaries (Chapter 22)

From local ⋯⋯⋯→⋯⋯⋯ to global
From product barrier ⋯⋯⋯→⋯⋯⋯ to brand barrier
From product value ⋯⋯⋯→⋯⋯⋯ to brand value

Within the new value economy, you must settle accounts with the product fixation. You can then free up resources for investments in a stronger, external value position. In other words, it is the value that you wish to capture, which is to be your guide, when optimizing the corporation. This calls for radical changes in the ways of running large corporations in the future.

have defined so much best practice that companies are now more or less identical.

The important thing will be to define unique value positioning for the company. And you can't find that out by asking customers who you are – customers have never developed anything. Like everyone else, they are afraid of change – inertia feels safe, cozy and warm. If companies base their future on the apparent needs of their customers, there will be no one left to communicate anything new and unique to the world.

The brand value chain of the future

As a result, executives have to be capable of deciding what to do, what to do without, what to cut back. They must believe in something and pursue it relentlessly. This ultimate belief then has to be disseminated throughout the company – that has to be their goal.

In future instead of optimizing the product value chain, you will have to optimize the 'brand value chain', i.e. optimize the company in relation to its brand.

Figure 1.5 shows (from left to right) progress from management, through the company and its corporate culture, to the customers, the market, the company's external positioning in the market, and the desired value positioning in the market.

This value positioning has to be the standard by which you attempt to optimize your company. (See Figure 18.2.)

I believe companies will be forced to think radically to survive in the new value economy. They will have to take chances, make choices, and prioritize. This will require totally different skills and systems than the ones used to manage and administer a product organization.

The companies that successfully manage the brand value chain will be the winners in the value economy. Defining and communicating a unique value proposition,

If companies base their future on the apparent needs of their customers, there will be no one left to communicate anything new and unique to the world.

I believe companies will be forced to think radically to survive in the new value economy.

Figure 1.5 The brand value chain

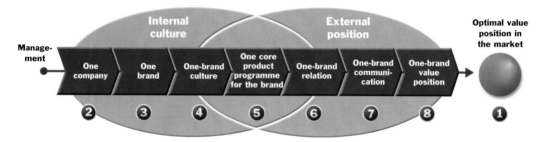

For a successful transition into the new value economy, the corporation must optimize its brand value chain. Only then can it achieve the optimal value position in the market. The entire corporation must be structured and trimmed according to the brand, which must pervade everything. (See Figure 18.2 for a closer examination.)

I believe, will create a centrifugal force – the value centrifuge – which will generate a virtuous spiral, or vortex, that will enable them to enjoy rapid growth and outperform their competitors.

This book describes how you can acclimatize your company to the new value economy and position it to take advantage of the enormous opportunities.

The three parts of the book

Chapters 2 to 4 deal with the transition from the old product-oriented economy to the new value economy.

After that, the book is divided into three parts dealing with the main aspects of a company's transformation from the old economy to the new value economy.

Part 1, from Chapter 5 to Chapter 7, describes how the company has to create high and unique value in a brand with a clear direction that can be communicated globally. I describe how to develop this value by referring to the value positionings of major international companies.

Part 2, from Chapter 8 to Chapter 16, deals with some of the obvious problems companies encounter when expanding into new product groups and customer segments but still keeping the growth within the remit of the brand and not diluting it. I have compiled numerous examples of international companies that have successfully controlled growth, often within the confines of a single brand. I have devised my own brand system as a modest contribution to the subject of brand strategy. Case studies include LEGO, Danone, Virgin, Heinz, Audi, Mercedes, SAS, Levi's, Giorgio Armani, VW, Nestlé and Unilever.

Part 2 also looks at the art of merging brands when companies acquire, merge or are taken over. This involves more than designing new logos and headed notepaper. It requires uniting two company cultures, two external positionings, and two optimal value positionings in the market. It requires in-depth analysis and insight into the two companies' values and what each of them has brought to the new unit.

Part 3, from Chapter 17 to Chapter 22, is concerned solely with the redefinition of the company – and the brand value chain. Figure 1.5 is one of the main models.

Whereas physical distribution was crucial in the past, the critical type of distribution in the future will be the mental communication of your brand. This is not to say that you no longer have to ship goods to your customers. It just means that mental distribution is what will make the products indispensable and win mind space. You will have to transform the organization in such a way that you establish direct contact with the most important decision makers for the brand in the market.

This has important, sometimes paradoxical, implications for managers. For example, hierarchical management may have passed its sell-by date, yet companies need to be disciplined enough to bring some form of unique value to the market consistently.

When organizations change, executives have to change too in order to play a new role. The executive has to come out of his or her closet and play an active and highly visible role in the company. They have to be able to formulate the company's idea, its mission and visions, and be able to communicate this set of basic values to the staff and to the market. So how do we cope with the volume of information and knowledge in the future?

Stop whatever you are doing

Right now, companies are busy implementing IT structures and CRM (customer relationship management) systems in order to improve co-ordination of all their activities. But there is no point in these things for their own sake. You have to stop and define the essence of the company – and concentrate instead on what is unique about your company. That is what you need to communicate.

An IT infrastructure is an empty shell – it does nothing on its own. It is the content that flows through the structure that is interesting. You have to put the brand to work throughout the company. This will be the executive's most important role after the metamorphosis from administrator to communicator.

You have to put the brand to work throughout the company. This will be the executive's most important role after the metamorphosis from administrator to communicator.

Instead of a sterile IT infrastructure, the company should concentrate on a 'brand communication infrastructure' and make it the new backbone for the whole organization. It should be the core, the heart, of all the activities in a major international company. The next challenge is to identify people in vital departments who are good at collating and disseminating information and knowledge about the market and information and knowledge passed on by the senior management.

I envisage a transitional phase between the old and the new value economies during which companies will find themselves running two parallel management systems

– the old one that moves products and the new one that communicates knowledge and provides direction.

Sub-optimization is dead

Sub-optimization is a thing of the past. The only protection against sub-optimization is a very tight internal chain and a management that is good at formulating and communicating the brand's values and direction. Management has to be on its toes all the time, ever ready to explain market developments and how they affect the brand and the individual within the company. You cannot leave that to an information department or a staff magazine. Managers can no longer hide.

The market demands something unique from companies. Customers want to be surprised and enriched, otherwise they will go elsewhere. Employees demand the same. They want to be part of something unique on the mental level. They want to understand the brand and be proud of it. Otherwise they will find a new employer. *Unique now ... or never.* Welcome to the new value economy.

Beyond the product economy

Confusion is spreading through the world of business. Are we moving towards a new economy – and what kind of economy is that?

As we have seen, the new economy is not the Internet, although we know that it has radically changed the industrial economy. Consequently, we are moving away from markets dominated by products to a situation where value is perceived differently.

Attractively valuable

In the past the physical product was all important. It was the repository of value. Today that is changing. Increasingly, the end products are simply the tip of the iceberg, the physical manifestation of the value chain.

What matters now is less what a product can do and much more the value embedded in it. This includes all the activities that surround it. Naturally, value lies in the processes involved in its production, but also in a host of other activities. These include the way products are marketed; what ownership says about the consumer. Value comes directly from what the company stands for in the world, the way it treats its employees, the way it defines itself. Value resides in who the company is and who its customers are. In short, the value of the brand.

The fact is that in our globalized, affluent society we can all have everything. The choice is between a little more or a lot more. There is an almost infinite number of products, services, businesses and communication methods to choose from. This places enormous demands on companies that want to attract customers. They must be visible and heard.

If they cannot cut through the noise and make consumers use their freedom of choice to pick out their particular products from the bulging shelves, they might as well pack up and go home.

To stand out in the market, companies must offer something so individually attractive and so valued that it transcends being merely a product. They must break through and capture a position in the minds of fickle and choosy consumers. Simply winning a position in a market is no longer enough to occupy space in the minds of customers. I work with many brands that cannot record particularly noteworthy sales curves even though they are well known. In future, you must be indispensable. And in order to become so, you must offer your customers a unique value. I call this imperative 'value positioning'.

Companies must break through and capture a position in the minds of fickle and choosy consumers.

How wise is your brand?

If just being known in the market is no longer enough, what should you aim for? I suggest sharpness – because the more intelligent your profile, the better the chance that your customers will get involved with your brand. The Internet has made the need for a sharper profile and a consistent brand experience particularly urgent. Using it, consumers can very easily get closely in touch with a brand and see whether the company behind it actually stands for what they want.

The traffic the other way – from company to customer – is just as immediate, down to earth and simple. But even though it appears obvious (to me at any rate) that the most important task in the new value economy is to own the customer, most companies are lagging behind in their understanding of the new market mechanisms.

Top management must find a way of operating both economies at the same time if they want to be efficient and enrich the future of their companies.

Top management must find a way of operating both economies at the same time if they want to be efficient and enrich the future of their companies.

Figure 2.1 The traditional company system

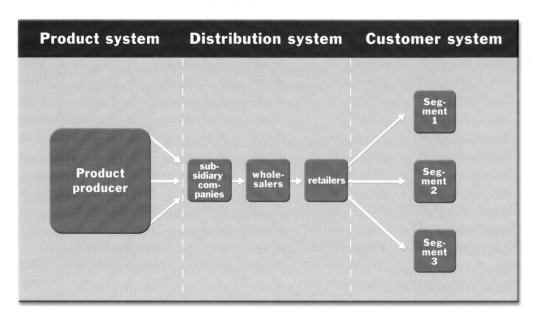

The company's main focus in the traditional company system is the development of products that are sold through a sales and distribution system, which ends up having a certain customer mass.

The old focus

Within the traditional market structure, the focus – both mentally and in terms of resources – was placed on the product system. It was, primarily, a matter of making a product, then of distributing it and, in the end, of market orientation. This means that most of the resources were spent on the left side of Figure 2.1. Figure 2.2 shows the product life curve (PLC) that determined value development for a company in relation to the traditional market structure. A characteristic of this period – which I call the industry economy – was that if you were in an entry phase with a new product you could command a high price. In a mature market, there were more suppliers and profits were correspondingly lower.

Figure 2.2 The industry economy

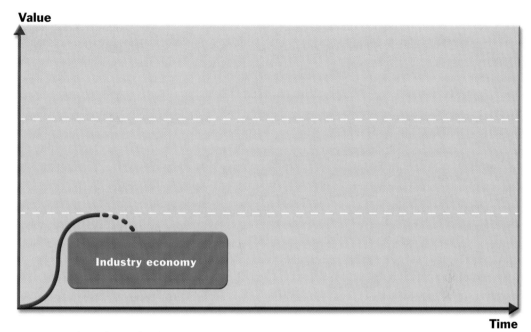

Figure 2.2 shows the product life curve (PLC) that determined value development for a company.

However, the main focus was still on the product and its unique selling proposition. At a later stage, brands had to differentiate further and many saw the opportunities of building positions based on a well-defined target group and its core values. This meant that the traditional PLC curve no longer stood up – your brand became the new value factor. As it appears in Figure 2.3, a new curve is placed above the normal product life curve.

Most brands grew out of a strong product with a strong USP. When their USP stopped being unique and other producers made equally good products, product strength was replaced by brand values.

Figure 2.3 The marketing economy

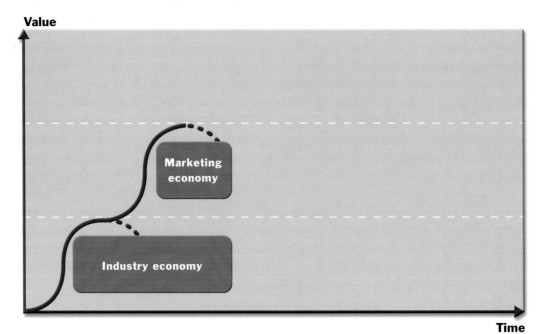

In the marketing economy the brand's path of development goes beyond that of the traditional PLC path. The brand takes over the value and products are ongoingly shifted out so that the curve continues to grow for as long as the brand develops itself in a positive way.

The car that would not die

The story of the Volkswagen Golf model is a good example of what this development is about. In the car industry manufacturers regularly launch new models and they typically follow the PLC curve. The Golf did not do this. It did not accept being just another model under a corporate brand. Golf wanted to be a brand itself.

This caused a dilemma for Volkswagen. Should it replace the popular car with a new model, and thus throw a lot of excellent Golf value in the bin? Or should it acknowledge consumer desire for a Golf brand side by side with the Volkswagen brand? VW chose the latter. Golf continued its career in a brand life curve shown in Figure

2.3. The development of the Golf represents the common course of most brands today.

In the beginning, the brand is synonymous with a certain product. Then it moves on to a certain product category, with some brands ending up owning a certain target group. Compared with the development in Figure 2.1, this means that while the focus used to be on the optimization of the product system to the left of the figure, we later became more interested in marketing and distribution in the middle of the figure. Today, it has become solely a matter of who is best at positioning themselves with the customers. There are many ways to do so – see Figure 2.4.

VW's Golf has survived the traditional PLC curve and has gone from being merely a product to now being a strong brand.

How do you want to own the customer?

Whoever has the greatest brand power owns the customer – and there are many people battling for this ownership. There are several routes to achieving superlative brand power. It could be by starting off with a unique product, unique distribution – or a unique communication.

Figure 2.4 shows the historical development of brand powers and gives an overview of those elements within the market that are battling over the customer's favours, both by fighting against each other and by working together.

For example, Nike has its own flagship stores – Nike Town – that both compete with ordinary shops selling Nike shoes and clothes and yet contribute to increasing the Nike value by giving their customers a special Nike experience. Nevertheless, traditional shops try to conquer enough brand power to turn product brands – such as Nike – into sub-suppliers.

At the top of the figure is a product that is sold as a result of its product power. During this period, companies would generally have a set-up as shown in Figure 2.1. Coca-Cola is a typical product brand. The company spends enormous sums on advertising, partly to ensure a high

The special Nike Town experience builds even more value into the Nike brand. Here you can watch spectacular sporting moments and see famous athletes' sportswear, like Tiger Woods' shoes.

Figure 2.4 Brand power

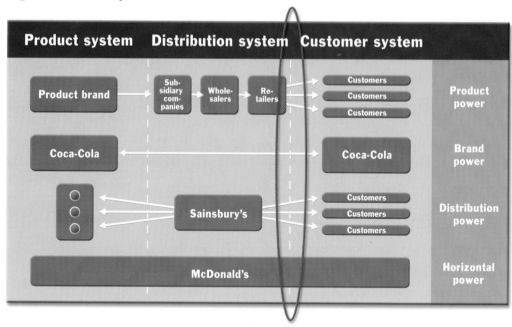

The one who owns the customer has the power, illustrated by the vertical oval. The way to own the customer is via product power, brand power, distribution power or by being a horizontal brand, which controls everything.

awareness so that consumers buy the product, partly in order to own the customer, and partly to keep a hold on distributors so that they do not move to selling competing colas.

This product brand way of thinking contributed to the expansion of the communication industries of advertising and public relations. This can be seen as a vicious spiral. More brands, tougher competition and more marketing led to a situation where the distributors had to fight back to regain control over their customers. The counter move was for them to develop their own brands – the so-called private labels – which provided the communication industries with even more work.

Today, product brands compete with distribution brands over the ownership of the customer.

Today, product brands compete with distribution brands over the ownership of the customer. From the very moment a product brand loses its ownership, it becomes a sub-supplier – and then the distributor can force down the price by choosing between several suppliers.

Shelf wars

Anyone who has visited the UK supermarket chains Tesco and Sainsbury's will have seen how hard they work to make their own names the most important brand for their customers.

The war between product brands and distribution brands has given rise to a new form of branding – the horizontal brand (illustrated by McDonald's in Figure 2.4). Horizontal brands are characterized by covering a whole supply chain. They must be good both at optimizing the product and the distribution system, taking care of retail problems, and at marketing the brand. This is quite a lot of things to handle simultaneously. But companies such as Ikea, Gap and McDonald's seem to have a talent for being horizontal.

New brand forms that mix everything together are emerging, such as Nike and its flagship stores. Nike is only horizontal in big cities; the major part of its distribution still goes through traditional retailers. Nike reasons that flagship stores are a part of its total marketing. The same methods are used in the fashion industry, where Giorgio Armani and others have their own shops in big cities at the same time as selling their products through traditional clothes shops. Armani has taken this strategy a step further by using shops to differentiate the brand, with Giorgio Armani shops for the exclusive, rich clientele and Emporio Armani shops for the younger segment.

Internet brands

Figure 2.4 becomes really interesting when we include the bottom box about the structure of the Internet. The prevailing opinion sees the Internet as a special market with its own rules. But it seems to me that the mechanisms that rule the traditional market also control the Net.

High value for the few

Without a strong brand you can forget all about getting the customer's attention, both in the physical world and on the Internet.

Whether it is in the physical world or in cyber-space, the same rules apply. You can forget about getting the customer's attention if you do not have a strong brand. To attract customers you must use the same communication methods for both channels.

But the era of scattershot marketing is over. Now, the only thing that matters is to create high value for the few rather than aiming for awareness and poor value for the many.

Creating relationships of trust

The alternatives are stark. You must either burn yourself into consumers' consciousness and leave behind a warm glow – or drop abruptly out of the market. In the wealthy parts of the world, scarcity of goods is history. Now the precious resource is the space in the minds of consumers. If you can also win their hearts, your message will be really engaging. If customers identify with your messages, you will gain impact. This is the prerequisite for a long-term relationship of trust.

Trust creates a foundation for growth for both parties. And several companies have realized that their value positions are so strong that they can encompass much more than a production company has to offer the market.

The three steps in Figure 2.5 represent a typical brand company's progress over time. It begins with the development of a unique product, which leads to the creation of a company (Step 1). In Step 2, the product accumulates further value and becomes a brand. Step 3 shows how the way the brand is worked becomes decisive.

Figure 2.5 The new value economy

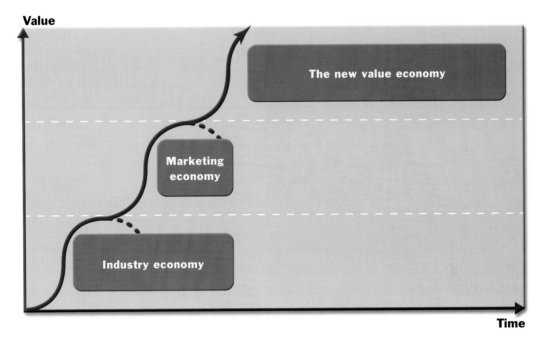

In future, mind space will become a scarce resource, which makes it essential for companies to build up value positions in the minds of a particular customer group. We are moving towards a new value economy where you must have unique value and stand out from the rest.

Figure 2.6, which is put together from Figures 2.1 and 2.5, illustrates how a typical company starts off at the left with a product-oriented mindset. The company renews its products and, with time, optimizes its sales and marketing system in order to grow, both in single markets and globally. The company moves up to Step 2 in Figure 2.6 and towards the right at the bottom of the figure but continues to think only in product terms. This means that resources are spent on the development of new products and on sales and distribution systems. But to what purpose if the battle of the customers is the most important one to win?

Figure 2.6 From product to value

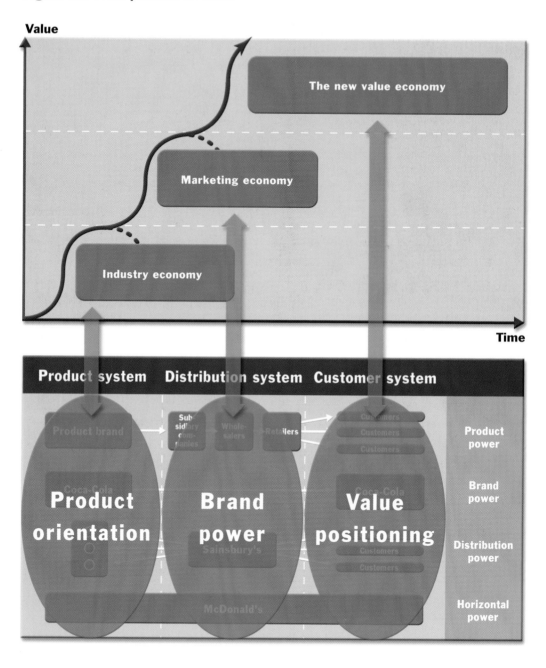

Figure 2.6 illustrates how we have moved from an industry economy to a value economy. This places a demand on companies to shift focus from product orientation and optimizing the distribution and customer systems to capturing value positions in the market.

Figure 2.7 The strategic dilemma of the resources

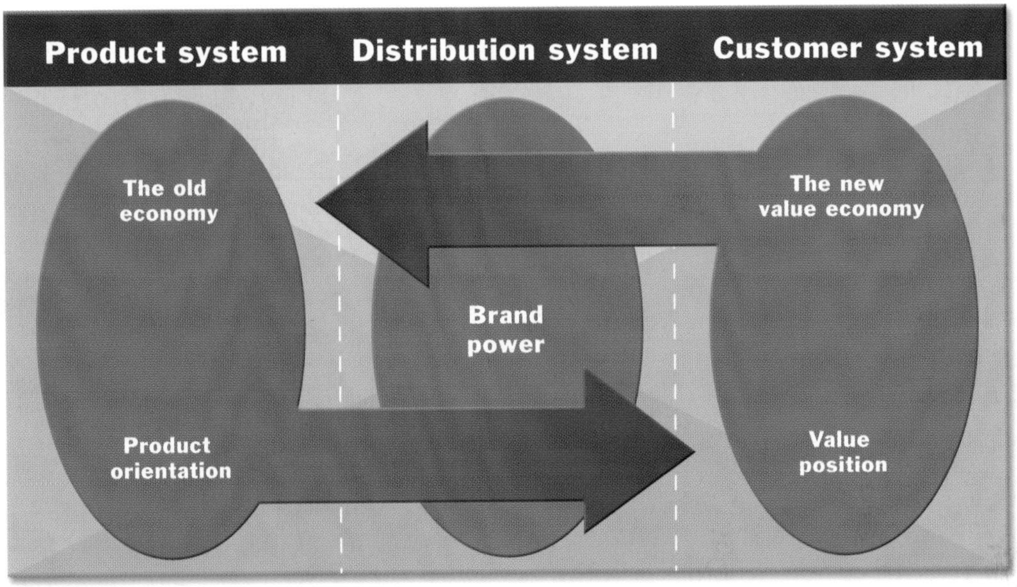

In the old economy, companies spent most resources on the product system, less on the sales and distribution system, and almost nothing on winning customers. This is illustrated by the blue triangle dropping from the left towards the right in the background of the figure. But companies should spend the majority of their resources on capturing a value position in the market in order to ensure a future in the new value economy. Their resources should be distributed as illustrated by the blue triangle dropping from the right towards the left.

The strategic dilemma appears in Figure 2.7, where a traditional company avoids becoming involved in the creation of high value and building strong relationships with customers.

Within the old economy, in keeping with the product orientation, most of the resources were spent on the product and on distribution systems. Next to nothing was spent on winning customers. This is illustrated by the blue triangle dropping from the left towards the right in Figure 2.7. But the new value economy demands more resources be spent ensuring the value position in the market – owning the customers. This is illustrated by the blue triangle dropping from the right towards the left in Figure 2.7.

Of course, no company can spend all its resources on capturing customers. A product still has to be delivered, so the truth is probably to be found some place in between. I am simply trying to put a new perspective on the battle for customers. In order to achieve a strong value position you must deal with cost-heavy systems and liberate finances that will enable you to get closer to the customer.

Dell Computers has built direct relationships with customers and now holds an incredibly strong position because it is able to invest in value for those customers. The Ferrari Formula 1 driver Michael Schumacher, with his extremely high value, is another example. And so is the US film director Steven Spielberg. He has reached mega-high

The Formula 1 driver Michael Schumacher represents great value for his sponsors, such as Shell and Marlboro.

brand value because he delivers unique films. He is able to leverage a brand position created in the new value economy along with the mechanisms of the old economy.

However, there is clearly a difference between a Schumacher or a Spielberg and a marketing message. While we can choose to go and see a car race or a movie, advertising messages are forced upon us whether we want them or not.

My point is: be aware of the movement from rational to irrational value; from quantitative value to qualitative; from material to immaterial – and learn the new rules of the game.

The misery of Levi Strauss

When strong brands with sharp value positions suddenly venture into new areas and capture large market shares from, usually, other strong companies it is a sign of the power of the new value economy. This development could not have taken place within the old economy. There you would build up your product brand, own your product category, and optimize the distribution system, erecting barriers to entry. But within the new economy, brands can establish an ownership built on quite different values to those traditionally important to a particular product category. Levi's did not believe this.

How to divide the resources?

Levi Strauss owns the original American jeans concept, with its roots in the Californian gold rush of the mid-1800s. This means that it owns the entire consumer segment that buys denim jeans.

But shouldn't I really be writing in the past tense? Because fashion brands such as Armani, Donna Karan, Hugo Boss, Calvin Klein and Ralph Lauren have built incredibly strong brand positions in the market. At some

The classic red tab from Levi's.

point their relevant value position pulled the rug from underneath Levi's. And Levi's customers were gone. It was no good that Levi's had the best product and the best global sales system to deliver denim jeans. The customers were gone.

Didn't Levi's have a strong brand? Yes, if it had continued to maintain its position as 'The Original'. But to what avail if the market has been redefined by fashion brands which operate at the far right of Figure 2.7? They have built up such incredibly strong value for their customers that they are prepared to follow them into any product category.

Towards the end of the 1990s, Levi's recognized that its real potential was in an area where it had been spending little of its resources. Even though it had a strong brand, Levi's was incredibly product oriented. It tied up large sums in factory systems to produce excellent jeans. Levi's was operating according to an allocation of resources shown at the top of Figure 2.8 – from the left towards the right as a product-oriented company.

Levi's went through a major restructuring, realizing it had to develop and distribute brands to younger customer segments globally. The company invested more in a brand- and detail-oriented organization and closed several factories. It recognized that it had to get closer to customers and create high involvement to become attractive and fashionable again – and win back deserting customers. Now Levi's distributes new sub-brands to fashion shops. One of these is Red, a rethinking of the original denim jeans.

The interesting point in this little case study is that Levi's became aware that its product-oriented mindset was leading it off the rails. Viewed in relation to the upper part of Figure 2.8, Levi's has moved its resources to the right.

Figure 2.8 Levi Strauss from product orientation to value orientation

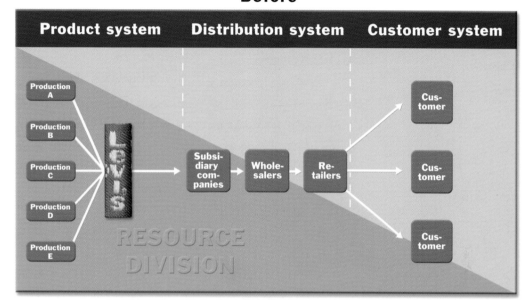

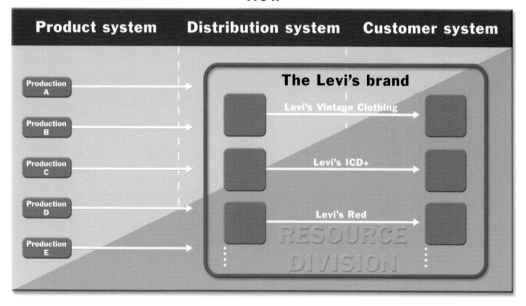

Levi Strauss has restructured to adjust the allocation of resources to match the new value economy. It has moved the emphasis from production to the sales system and branding. New sub-brands that have been specially developed for particular customer segments should create new dynamics for the brand. (See also the Levi's case study in Chapter 10.)

Be open

If the customer believes in your brand and its value position you can sell almost anything – just think of Richard Branson's Virgin (see also the case study in Chapter 11). So, look behind you regularly. When competition is about value positions, your new competitors may turn up from anywhere. Another tip: keep your eyes wide open, look ahead, drop your prejudices, be receptive to all input available. For companies that use a little imagination, there is an abundance of inspiration.

Entering the value economy

Why is there an increasing focus on value today?

I think an explanation can be found in Figure 3.1, which shows how we move from an industry economy to a marketing economy. Three strong factors – communication, value and globalization – increase the speed of development dramatically. It is a spiral, which is automatically drawn faster and faster towards its centre.

A good example is buying a mobile phone. At least ten companies making handsets pump advertising into the market to sell their products. There are ten operators, which also market themselves, and there will be at least 30 retailers, which also pour communication into the market with the aim of selling you a mobile phone.

This creates a huge amount of noise in the market. To stand a chance of being heard everyone has to have a sharper focus. They have to differentiate in some way. This places more emphasis on the content of the messages that are used to win over customers. These messages must also be delivered globally, which leads to still more communication.

Products must shout louder and louder to get attention. When higher value is the only thing that can produce real customer involvement, companies must become very good at one thing instead of being reasonably good at many. Making unique brands and products implies concentrating on narrow segments. But companies must go global in these segments so that they can create a critical mass of customers. In other words, they must live up to the definition of the new value economy: to have a unique value that can be multiplied many times and be communicated globally.

To stand a chance of being heard everyone has to have a sharper focus. They have to differentiate in some way.

Figure 3.1 The value centrifuge gives rise to the new value economy

Value

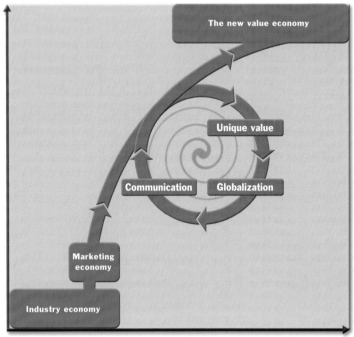

Time

The value centrifuge accelerates the old product oriented economy into a new value economy. The abundant society has created hugely increased communication, which at the same time, because of the increased noise, makes it harder and harder to get through to the market. This means that companies must have a unique value. They must focus. And when they grow, they must grow globally.

The media is the message

Global media such as CNN, CBC Worldwide, Eurosport, MTV and CNBC control opinion forming in the global society. Companies are consequently forced to try to get the media interested in their brands.

Global communications place increased demands on the values companies communicate if they are to stand a chance in a world of very similar products where unique product advantage is short-lived.

Messages about personalities, sport, music, business or product ideas travel around the world rapidly and have a higher credibility than advertisements. This places increased demands on the values companies communicate. In a world of very similar products, unique product advantage is short-lived. Sustainable competitive advantage, then, can only come from communicating something that transcends individual products, a unique set of brand values. A company's brand must stand for something that differentiates all its products from the competition – now and in the future.

Values must carry unique messages. If they do, they can push through the media noise and achieve staying power in the minds of consumers. Never forget: we fight for memories and for brain hemispheres. If we can engage them fruitfully, market share will follow.

Nike (the name is a Greek goddess of victory) is a unique brand. It has long since captured a 'winner' position in the market. For years it has been synonymous with the greatest and most successful sports stars and, as Figure 3.2 shows, it centrifuges this winner position into the minds of consumers all over the world.

Global sporting events, such as the football World Cup and the Olympics, are broadcast to hundreds of millions of sport lovers. Because Nike's 'swoosh' symbol is printed on football boots, running shoes, T-shirts and so on, its symbolic value position is stamped onto TV screens around the world. As a result, Nike builds up high value in the minds of consumers, which it can convert later into sales of sports products.

Nike invests its profits in sponsoring even more sports stars who, thanks to the omnipresent communication society, immediately have a global impact. The Nike brand can also, via the centrifuge effect, expand into related categories if they also bring the brand position 'winning' with them. And which category wouldn't like to be driven by 'winning'?

Figure 3.2 Nike's centrifuge effect within the new value economy

Value

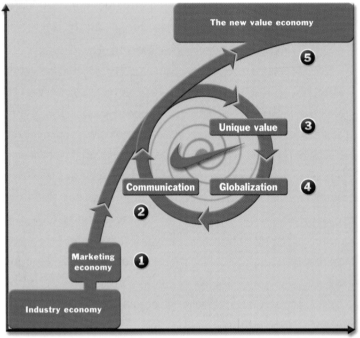

Time

1. Nike invests in world sports stars in order to create as strong a brand position as possible.

2. The global communication of major sports events accelerates Nike's brand position as 'the winning company' around the world.

3. Because the target group sees the winning stars wear Nike products, a unique value and positioning of Nike as 'the winning brand' is established.

4. The global media coverage of sports events accelerates the effect of Nike's sponsorship of world stars. This is reinforced by its own global marketing of the same stars.

5. The number of countries that follow sports events on TV controls the global demand for Nike's products. This leads to a situation where global communication forces Nike to become ever more global, which again leads to more communication – the centrifuge will spin faster and faster.

Nike exploits the mechanisms in the new value economy highly effectively. Its challenge will be to determine how to maintain this winner position.

The night-and-day wide-open world

If we place the Internet in the value centrifuge of Figure 3.1 we will see an interactive communication channel that means the world is wide open day and night. Contrary to classic interruption marketing you don't need to passively receive everything it has to say. And you can answer back.

Many people thought the Internet was simply a matter of putting up a homepage and waiting for customers to find their way to it. Of course, this did not happen. Fundamentally, the Internet is a completely anonymous space. In spite of thousands of dot-com meltdowns, it has become easier to find proverbial needles in haystacks than for customers to find you on the Net.

There are, of course, search engines, but so far none of them has registered all existing pages – far from it. The situation is just like the old economy, where distribution brands help to run the traffic.

The one sense in which the Net is unsurpassed is in its ability to build relations between consumers and brands. It is a powerful tool that combines the important factors in the value centrifuge – communication, high value and globalization – with the possibilities of a radical individualization.

The one sense in which the Net is unsurpassed is in its ability to build relationships between consumers and brands. It is a powerful tool that combines the important factors in the value centrifuge – communication, high value and globalization – with the possibilities of a radical individualization (Figure 3.3).

Shorter chains

We need to understand that it is not enough just to be on the Net. You must deliver high value in the form of individual service and knowledge for the customer.

All customers split into three camps: those who want high quality and pay for it, those who will pay a little less for an adequate quality, and those who just want the products

Figure 3.3 The value leap of the future

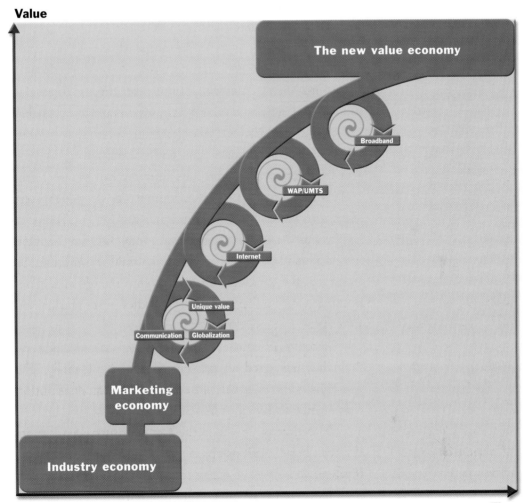

The Internet contributes to a major centrifugal effect from the old economy to the new value economy. With the Internet it is possible to communicate a unique value globally, which makes it an important part of the development of the new value economy. Before, business-to-business corporations had no global communication channel, but all that has changed with the Internet. New technologies, such as UMTS – mobile Internet – and broadband net, will cause major centrifugal effects and move us even faster into the new value economy.

New technologies, such as UMTS – mobile Internet – and broadband net, will cause major centrifugal effects and move us even faster into the new value economy.

We are facing an incredible technological development that will revolutionize our ways of thinking and acting. But we must always remember that our ability to adapt to a new situation is a key factor.

as cheaply as possible. Obviously, this pattern also applies to the Internet. A good example of this is Dell, who, with its web-based sales, has redefined the price structure of PCs. But the Net will unquestionably also redefine the general price level of many sectors. This is because in future it will contribute to the restructuring of the value chain. This won't happen overnight since most industry structures are locked into existing power structures between producers, wholesalers, retail chains and so on. It will be a slow process that will take many different forms but it only escalates the power struggle for customers – see the brand power model in Figure 2.4.

In a short while almost everybody will have digital TV, which will provide consumers with 300 individually customized channels. Individualization will be total. And as a result each TV channel – and particularly TV ads – will find it increasingly difficult to get through to consumers. TV advertising is more effective where there are fewer channels. It is easier to reach consumers when they have less choice about what they view. US research has shown that no matter whether there are 200 or 300 TV channels available, even the TV addict will only watch around seven.

We are facing an incredible technological development that will revolutionize our ways of thinking and acting. But we must always remember that our ability to adapt to a new situation is a key factor. That is why progress is normally made at a slower pace than technology allows. We will welcome the new if we can discover the value, otherwise we will reject it. Even if the human brain is open to sudden change, there is still a limit to the rate at which it can adjust to quantum leaps and paradigm shifts. I already notice an early consumer reaction when we test development concepts. When everything is moving a little bit too fast people begin to daydream, start talking about having peace of mind, of returning to nature. With time, this dream will become an undeniable need and it will turn consumers away from speed and technology. That is why I am convinced that future development will depend on whether we can see the attraction in all the new things that we are constantly being offered.

Valuable visions

The communication society has speeded up our common experience of globalization because major media events concern us all. Companies and their brands have flooded our homes and have unified us, whether we want it or not.

In 1962, Herbert Marshall McLuhan launched the vision of the global village in his book *The Gutenberg Galaxy* (University of Toronto Press, 1967). The concept of the global village gave the Canadian professor of literature immediate status as the original media guru. The book, which has been translated into 12 languages including Japanese and Serbo-Croatian, is about how the printed word brought Europe into the era of technological progress, and it looks ahead towards the electronic revolution.

McLuhan's argument is that when Gutenberg introduced printing, Europe moved into an era where change became the norm. This is not so very different from the principle of the value centrifuge: constant change and renewal created by communication, value and globalization.

That world, which McLuhan could only imagine, is the world in which we live today. Brands are ruling with powerful value positions. Companies that want to grow would be wise to narrow their activities to core business – i.e. to their value positions, which, as mentioned before, does not mean that they cannot sell many different types of products.

From Timbuktu to Tølløse with one click

When McLuhan wrote *The Gutenberg Galaxy*, the 100 largest economies in the world were nation states. Today, half of the world's largest economies are international companies which are striving to become even more powerful. They can only do that via globalization.

One example of the forces of globalization is the Olympic Games. For three weeks the whole world is subjected to a 24-hour, seven-days-a-week media bombardment. The multinational companies' sponsorship millions are well spent. People watch TV, drink Coca-Cola and eat McDonald's while walking round in Nike shoes. When they have to go to work they switch on their IBM-PCs and open a Microsoft program, fetch a Sprite from a soft drinks dispenser and absent-mindedly turn the pages of an issue of *Red Herring* or *Fast Company*.

When they go home again to watch more of the Olympics they get into cars made by Mercedes, Audi, BMW, Ford, Toyota, VW, Fiat and Renault, while prattling on mobile phones from Nokia, Panasonic, Siemens, Ericsson and Motorola. Before leaving the car in the garage, they check the latest stock exchange quotations on a WAP phone and note some important things to remember on a Palm Pilot or a Psion. Nobody can say that they do not feel closer to everything, thanks to interactive communication. Regardless of age, status and interests, anybody can move from Siberia to Tierra del Fuego in a single mouse click.

Information moves around the world instantaneously. We expect to be able to respond in seconds. Yet it still takes several hours to travel physically from Scandinavia to the US.

The world will never be the same again

Thanks to the Internet the world will never be the same again. With ever increasing speed, news flows faster and faster. It is no longer possible to hold back international communication. But just as the Net opens a wealth of opportunities and global freedom of communication, it also makes it harder to get through to the customer. Branding becomes an even more essential issue. The Net may not be a suitable tool for building a new brand but it represents an amazing opportunity to create high involvement with specific target groups for an already well-established brand.

However, we need to understand that the Net will have an impact on the way companies function. The centralized model of corporations is in decline and we will see companies develop via network organizations into new, non-hierarchical structures. The Net will contribute significantly to the faster movement of communication around the global network corporation, as illustrated in Figure 3.4.

The Net may not be a suitable tool for building a new brand but it represents an amazing opportunity to create high involvement with specific target groups for an already well-established brand.

Figure 3.4 The Internet has set communication free

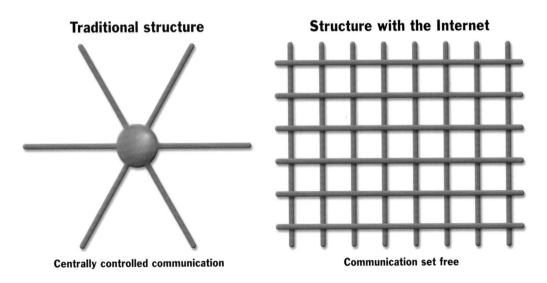

Traditional structure

Centrally controlled communication

Structure with the Internet

Communication set free

Before the Internet was introduced it was easier to control communication from a central point. But with the Internet communication is set free and can no longer be controlled in the same way. Communication has been given the freedom of movement across borders and continents.

CNN delivers the world's best news coverage across the globe.

Living with the new value economy

Would you rather see your local football team play on the pitch around the corner or watch Manchester United versus Barcelona on a multinational sports channel? Not a very hard choice, particularly as it is on several channels at the same time.

Why go to your local bar and see a local band when you can watch Madonna on MTV? Why use a locally developed operating system for your computer when you can just as easily have the best Microsoft has to offer?

Why watch the news on the local TV station when you can have CNN? Why eat hotdogs at a local grill-bar when you can have a Big Mac at McDonald's?

Why go to your local bookshop when you can buy the book you want online from Barnes & Noble, or download electronic books from www.bn.com? No added tax, no trouble – you don't even have to bother to get up from your armchair.

Why spend your time going round to lots of different car dealers to find out which car you want when you can get all the information you need straight away on the Net?

The effects of mass communication and globalization are plain to see. The value centrifuge is already changing our lives as consumers. It is also changing the way that companies have to operate. Today they have to deliver more and more value to capture consumer mind space. We are rapidly moving to a value economy. 'Why make do with the ordinary when I can have the world's best?' will be the consumer mantra of the future.

'Why make do with the ordinary when I can have the world's best?'

Why make do with English cooking if you can have French or Italian food? When I look at my eating habits and compare them with the food of my childhood, a lot has changed. Previously, a week's menu would be different types of Danish dishes; now it comprises the best from all over the world. One day sushi, another day the best Italian, then a burger from McDonald's, a pizza, and the following day, a French meal. At other times I eat Thai food or wok dishes from Asia. In the mornings I'll sometimes have Danish cheese and yogurt, at other times a Swiss Emmental. The cheese I sprinkle on pasta is, of course, an Italian Regianio Parmiggiano. This is globalization on a plate. Within the value economy there is no room for mediocrity.

Dreams work

The value centrifuge – Figure 3.1 – will change reality for companies. But what is it that companies must do to respond? Though value can originate from many places, the most important thing to acknowledge is that you must be unique in one way or another. You can develop a unique technology like WAP or software like Microsoft, but it is, and always will be, the brand that differentiates your offering. You could develop a communication channel such as CNN or an Internet portal such as Yahoo. Both have uninterrupted, omnipresent accessibility. The same goes for Amazon.com and freight companies UPS, DHL and TNT. It applies just as much to the singer Madonna and the film director Steven Spielberg, whose corporation, DreamWorks SKG, says more than anything about what makes a great brand. Dreams work.

The value centrifuge will change reality for companies.

Are you good at explaining your dream?

You can create attractive value in many different ways. The crucial point is that you create what no one else has – something unique.

This requires knowledge within the organization. Without branding expertise it is impossible to direct the company properly into the value economy and then stake your unique value position in the minds of customers. Companies must therefore be consistent in everything they do because they will become as transparent as clingfilm.

Procter & Gamble is the corporation behind strong, independent brands such as Ariel, Pampers, Oil of Ulay and Pringles.

How will many of Procter & Gamble's customers feel when one day they find out that the corporations behind brands such as Ariel, Pampers, Oil of Ulay and Pringles are purely fictional? Disappointed, perhaps.

Modern brand corporations are involved in fruitful dialogues with their customer segments and deliver further involvement via the Internet. It takes a lot of adaptability and willingness to change in order to define your company to customers, employees, recruits and others.

Mind space – not awareness

What impact will the new value economy have on the way that a company acts? The unique value that consumers will demand will cause a fossilization of marketing techniques we have been used to. It makes little sense, for example, to be chasing quantity within the new value economy.

What use is an enormous consumer awareness of our products when, as it so often turns out, 100 per cent awareness rarely results in more than a 25 per cent market share? However, there is a paradox here. In future, customer involvement in the corporation will be decisive for its visibility.

Fifty per cent market share is a disadvantage

A market share of 50 per cent doesn't necessarily give customers metaphysical value and well-defined individuality. This is bad news for those companies – and that is the majority – that have put all their efforts into dominating their product categories.

The scary truth within the value economy is that brands such as Levi's and Coca-Cola risk getting killed by their own success. As I write, Coca-Cola is experiencing a decline in many markets. The question is, in a value economy sense, whether it can continue to grow by capturing dominant market shares.

Figure 3.5 Mind space

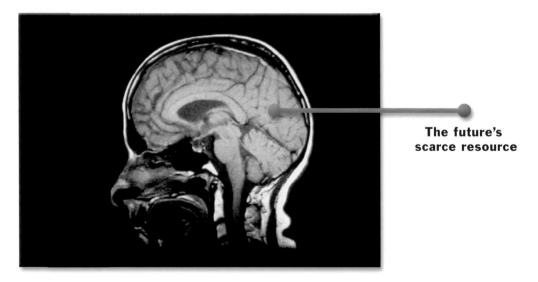

**The future's
scarce resource**

Within the new value economy, the capturing of mind space will become crucial. This is the conclusion two Swedes, Jonas Ridderstråle and Kjell Nordström, reach in their book Funky Business, from which this illustration is taken.

What is the matter with the Coca-Cola brand? Nothing within the old economy and everything within the new. When a brand is broadly marketed it tends to become bland and therefore without value.

Soon, when the value economy dominates, we shall all have to find out how we can maintain a dominant role within a product category at the same time as building a stronger and more meaningful value position. If your communication with consumers operates on a generic level rather than being directly related to the product you are trying to sell, what are customers supposed to get involved with? What do they engage with?

Coca-Cola's wrong conclusion

From the outside, it seems as if Coca-Cola is trying to get in touch with several target groups and that its communication

is too heterogeneous. Coke says it wants to both remain global and communicate locally. In my opinion, it would be a disaster for Coca-Cola to give up a homogenous global value position that consumers can understand. It is this immediate plainness of approach that has been behind its success so far. It is making wrong assumptions about globalization if it is planning to
fragment its approach to the market. Coke will become vulnerable to brands that have understood the ability of a strong value position to expand beyond a product category.

Coca-Cola must accept that in order to involve customers there is an upper limit to the market share it can have. Instead it must try to win fewer, but more solid, market shares in several markets. In other words: globalize.

Within the new value eco-nomy there is one com-mandment that cannot be repeated often enough: you must be able to cap-ture mind space – and thereby mind share – by cutting through to one well-defined target group.

Within the new value economy there is one command-ment that cannot be repeated often enough: you must be able to capture mind space – and thereby mind share – by cutting through to one well-defined target group (see Figure 3.5).

An acid rain of communication

Each day we are bombarded with messages, symbols, sounds, images and music. There is no end to the products, shops, services and entertainment. There is no certainty in this disturbed world, and how we all wish we could find peace, quiet and security.

Society is changing rapidly. Old, unshakable institu-tions are crumbling. Families are breaking up. It is hard to find a politician you can trust. Education is out of date in a shorter time than it takes to deliver a lecture on economics.

Within this mass-commu-nicated disruption and confusion a strong, consistent brand has a unique chance to replace lost security.

Within this mass-communicated disruption and con-fusion a strong, consistent brand has a unique chance to replace lost security (Figure 3.6). Finally, the consumer will say, here is something I can trust. That is why it is so crucial that corporations realize their true potential within the new value economy. They must understand what they have to live up to when their customers buy them.

Picture this all-pervading fragmentation as a brand mosaic, a picture put together by all sorts of different brands and expressing how people invent themselves via their choice of labels.

Personal brand mosaics

Public opinion polls try to map the brand mosaic from the point of view of universal values such as the family, value for money, premium price, discount segments and so on. But in vain. There is no specific way of telling what importance people place on different product categories. For a woman walking her rottweiler, dog food means the whole world. A dog hater could not care less. Others can't find

Figure 3.6 Capture a place in an over-communicated reality

In the western world we are bombarded with more than 3,000 marketing messages a day. This places demands on the ability of companies to cut through the noise and capture consumers' mind space. A unique brand that cuts through to a particular target group is better than a broad and unclear brand for everyone.

toilet paper posh enough. Some people express their souls, their strength and social status through a car. But social status can also be expressed via more intimate values such as the make of a kitchen appliance. The assertion that we are all the same is untrue. We are just as different as the enormous range of goods we buy. Within one product category we demand the very best; within another we go for the very cheapest.

What am I, as the manager of a company, to make out of a brand mosaic? It can indicate something about the consumer images your brand appeals to. You need to have your label placed in their personal brand mosaic. If your product ends up on the bottom shelf, where you are chosen just for your price, then you need to get a grip.

Different brands are discovered at different phases of life. Beer brands are chosen when we are young, the suit brand joins when we start our careers (Figure 3.7). When we start a family, brands attach to children's clothes and toys.

Reactionary methods leave room for the brave

It makes no sense to try to systematize the way different brands should handle this situation. Try to perceive it as a cultural battle that your company is fighting in the market. There is not much point in trying to make rules for when you should deliver product advantages and when you should deliver values based on lifestyle and attitudes.

One thing is certain, though. In order to get in touch with a certain group of people in the market and engage them in a stimulating dialogue, you must deliver a unique product with a unique value. It is alarming how many companies just go on building brands with reactionary methods. That is, they put more focus on the product than on the brand value. This leaves plenty of room and possibilities for those who dare to work with brands on a value economy basis.

Figure 3.7 The personal brand mosaic

Our personal brand mosaic consists of our individually preferred brands. Those brands to which we are indifferent end up in the box below, where only the price matters.

The brave don't care about awareness and analysis of brand choice. They know that they cannot make a living out of awareness. They must create involvement to capture that mind space, which, along with time, is the world's scarcest resource.

The vital mind space

I do not belong to those who think that customers will provide us with the answers through a perpetual dialogue. Customers have rarely created anything at all. They are conservative and they prefer to keep what they have already got. They know what they like and they like what they know. The only way companies can move customers is by launching unique products which customers can get involved in. Companies must educate customers to use the new and they must incorporate the products into a value system that makes the launch of new things logical and relevant. They should not promote insecurity with a relentless flood of new things that nobody can put into context.

At the moment the buzzword is innovation. This contradicts the customer's desire for stability. Companies should respect the customer's desire for stability by building brands with consistent values. Consistent brands justify their value position in the market by ensuring a product development is in line with brand values.

The mindset in which the brand controls the company in order to capture consumer mind space demands an internal revolution. The alternative is a mindless launching of more and more new products. I hope only a minority will opt for that.

CHAPTER 4

Navigating from the old to the new

Within the value economy, companies often have a much higher market value than accountants can spot. This is because brands are becoming increasingly valuable in their own right.

American Airlines (AA) illustrates the difference between the old economy and the new. The company introduced a software booking system, Sabre, which allowed consumers to book flights on both AA and competing airlines. In October 1996, AA's parent company, AMR Corp, sold 18 per cent of its shares in Sabre to the public. Very soon, the value of the remaining Sabre shares amounted to 50 per cent of the assets of the whole AMR group. So, in one of the largest airline companies in the world, a software system is worth more than 700 airplanes and over 100,000 employees. The difference between a plane and a booking system is that a plane can only be used once on a journey from St Louis to Boston; Sabre can be multiplied over and over again before the plane has landed in Massachusetts.

This example clearly illustrates the difference in valuations within the old economy and the new. The new management challenge is to devise strategies that take as their starting point how to use a brand in the development of new business areas and to communicate that to customers.

If you can master this exercise, your company is well on the way from the old economy to the new, particularly if you are able to weed out the multitude of brands. In future, one-brand companies will win.

The new management challenge is to devise strategies that take as their starting point how to use a brand in the development of new business areas and to communicate that to customers.

A gradual transition from old to new

Few corporations are natural heirs to the new economy and able to build their brands to fit the new conditions. For the majority, what matters is becoming good at working within the two economies simultaneously. American Airlines combines the two economies cleverly. It has its main business, air transport, within the old economy and has a stake in the new economy with Sabre.

Figure 4.1 illustrates what is important to a company in the transition from the old economy to the new.

Figure 4.1 From the old economy to the value economy

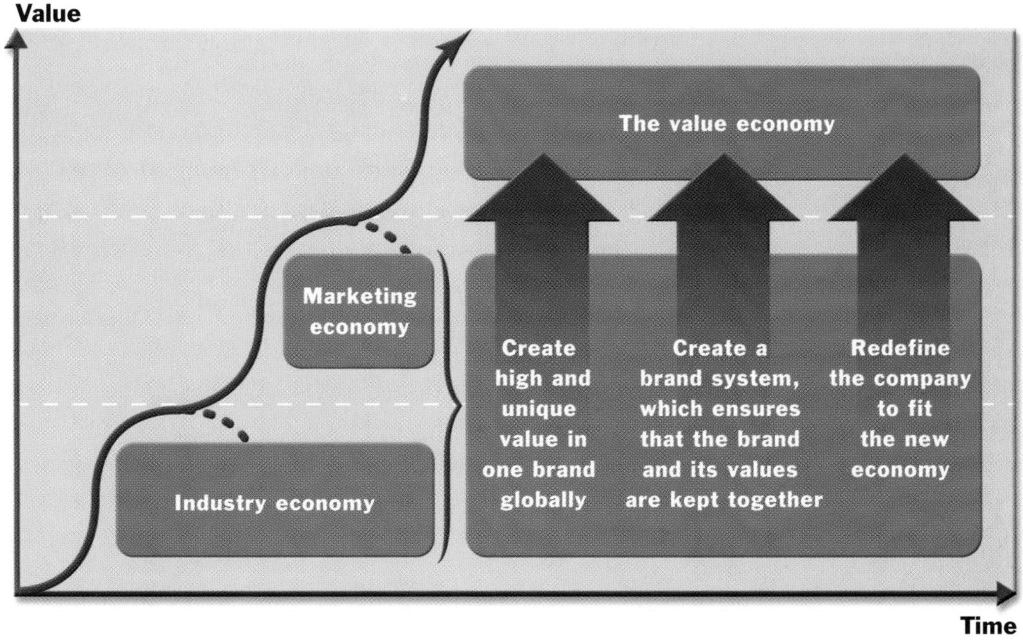

Three factors are important for a successful transition from the old economy to the value economy.

1. Creating a global brand with a unique value.

2. Ensuring that the brand grows within a brand system that can hold it and its values.

3. Redefining the company to enable it to work within the new value economy by changing the corporate mindset from a product orientation to a value orientation.

The protagonist of the old economy has always been the product. If you cannot stay within the old economy and concentrate on the development of unique products and sell them, it is high time you entered the value economy.

A slow transition is taking place. The old economy and the new are running simultaneously, though sometimes at different speeds depending on the marketplace. I am sure that certain companies can continue with the old economy for some time yet. But if your company is 'middle of the road' you must watch out. No one is interested in me-too companies that don't inject unique value into their brand.

No one is interested in me-too companies that don't inject unique value into their brand.

There is nothing new in demanding that corporations redefine themselves and adapt to changes in the market, whether they are due to social changes, competition or technological innovation. What is new is the speed of these changes. Spotting competitors used to be easy – they were in the same category as your own company in the Yellow Pages. In future, it will be much harder to keep track. Your greatest enemy could appear from a line of business that you have never competed with before if that company has the right value positions and ownership of the right customer groups.

Just take a look at the mobile phone market. It is now so mature that established handset suppliers such as Nokia and Ericsson could easily find themselves in competition with brands new to the market that hold unexpected value positions.

These could include fashion brands such as Prada, Armani and Nike. Their customers don't need technical specifications and 24 ringing tones just so long as it says Prada or Nike on the phone.

Razor-sharp value positions

Borders within the value economy are unclear and it will be difficult to manoeuvre with a traditional technological business view. Companies will have to monitor the strongest brands and read the market from the point of view of who has access to which customer groups. Never forget that he who owns the customer also owns the power (see Figure 2.4).

Borders within the value economy are unclear and it will be difficult to manoeuvre with a traditional technological business view.

Apart from mastering product development, production, and distribution, your company must become an expert in branding. You can leave production and distribution to others, as Coca-Cola has done for years.

Let us consider Figure 4.1 – the simplified model for the old economy and the new – and which three factors are important for the building up of a brand.

You have to know the answers to some essential questions in order to build up a strong brand: Who are we? What is it that we can offer our customers and does it represent high value to them?

Few companies are prepared to grow into the value economy. This is because they have invested too few resources on building structured value into their brands. Their brands are puny reeds, swaying in the wind, and little more than a logo stuck onto a product as a futile badge of quality. Just take, for example, Philips, which covers acres of all sorts of electronic products at all prices and all levels of quality.

Few companies are prepared to grow into the value economy because they have invested too few resources on building structured value into their brands.

This is not unlike the global food group Nestlé, which produces all types of foodstuffs across a wide spectrum of quality and prices. But for Philips there is no direction or any promise to the confused consumer – in other words: no value.

Some of the most razor-sharp brands of our times are LEGO, Nike, Virgin, Mercedes, Bang & Olufsen, Microsoft, McDonald's, Ikea and The Body Shop. Their

The strongest brands of our times all have razor-sharp value positions to offer the market.

Mercedes-Benz

common denominator is that they have built up high value for their customer segments under a meaningful consumer promise. They own their customer segments and this ownership is worth more than their entire production system. They can easily encompass several product areas because they work in a clear direction and keep their promises. That is value positioning.

I would go so far as to assert that the companies that will be most successful in this new millennium will be those that have built their organization around one internationally strong superbrand.

We need to find a way to create growth globally with one strong brand while expanding into new product and customer segments without watering down that brand. Within the old economy this is not possible; within the value economy it is. I have developed a brand system that allows corporations to both expand and strengthen their brands, which is the second factor in Figure 4.1.

Break the branding law

For my branding system to be useful, forget classic brand ideas.

For my branding system to be useful, forget classic brand ideas. It is a matter of building up value in the market for only one brand and to have this as a large, unifying force. The customers must be able to understand what a brand stands for – so forget the dictate of the logo.

Does this sound liberating? Good, then come up with a brand system of your own. The classic design manual has ceased to be the answer to everything in the dynamic world in which we live.

When Giorgio Armani developed the sub-brand Emporio Armani to cover the younger segment with cheaper products, was he breaking the branding laws? Yes. He developed a new logo for his sub-brand. Traditionally, he should have used the corporate brand name Giorgio Armani in the context of another name. But he is cheeky, so he didn't. I believe this is a brilliant way of differentiating your brand. The new sub-brand moves in a clear direction for the younger segment, while keeping a connection with the corporate brand.

Older customers spending a lot of money on a suit won't feel that their brand is devalued just because a few younger people can buy Armani products at a fifth of the price. But Armani succeeds only because he is using a very progressive branding for this differentiation.

I am convinced that this is the way forward when you want to create growth beyond product areas and customer segments but still keep your values under one corporate brand.

GIORGIO ARMANI

EMPORIO ARMANI

With the Emporio Armani brand, Giorgio Armani has broken the traditional branding laws in a brilliant way.

Redefine the company

The third important factor, decisive for a successful transition from the old economy to the new, is that you redefine your company.

You should be aware of what it is that you are good at and which position you own with your customers. You must be open to a redefinition of this value position according to new ways of distribution, communication or new competitors.

You should be aware of what it is that you are good at and which position you own with your customers.

When market situations change, companies often find themselves facing the dilemma of having to make most of their money on the 'old' company system at the same time as they are building up the new. But companies face a larger change than they have ever done before because they have been running according to a company structure and system dictated by the old product-oriented economy. Within this old system there has been no need to keep an eye on what it takes to be cutting edge.

Redefining your company and your brand to give it a strong profile in the market calls for knowledge of what is happening in your customer segment.

Redefining your company and your brand to give it a strong profile in the market calls for knowledge of what is happening in your customer segment. You must also be able to communicate with customers directly so that you can change their perception of what is possible. You must abandon the mindset that sees the world as a product value chain and, instead, see the world in the light of the brand value chain.

To illustrate what I mean by the brand value chain perspective, I have found a company that has followed the development of Figure 2.5 from being a product-oriented corporation, established within the industry economy, through the phase of brand building, and into the value economy.

LEGO – Who are we?

LEGO has built up a strong international brand centred on a unique play system. The company has been through a long series of internal evaluations and each time redefined what LEGO is and what the brand means for the company's growth.

LEGO has struggled to strategically optimize itself within the old economy while trimming the brand to adapt to the new value economy. The company has been in a unique position, where management has been spending a lot of resources on an analysis of who they are and which values they appreciate.

LEGO has been lucky that its value position has created a basis for a major leap in growth within the value economy (see figure 4.1). It has built the company around a strong brand and has been working on the systematic development of the management of the brand in order to keep growth within one large corporate brand – LEGO.

At the turn of the millennium, however, LEGO went through a minor crisis as growth and earnings came to a halt. Had it reached the limits of the potential of the LEGO brand? Not at all. The solution to the crisis turned up when management realized that their value position 'stimulating play' could create growth in product areas that need not be closely related to a rectangular plastic brick. The articulation of this value position is the latest outcome of the dynamic process, which started with 'play well', through 'LEGO system in play' to 'just imagine …'.

So LEGO possessed the third factor of Figure 4.1, which is about organizing to control and develop your brand while

It all began with a LEGO brick.

Since the beginning, the LEGO motto has been 'The best is not good enough'.

entering new product areas where production, distribution and, most of all, know-how are missing.

LEGO – expert in its brand

As LEGO owner Kjeld Kirk Kristiansen once said: 'It is the crises in LEGO that have forced us to constantly reassess who LEGO is.' Kristiansen continued: 'We have had an ongoing movement towards finding the core of LEGO but the crises have given us the necessary focus, which has meant that we have been able to give the company a boost and a leap into a new phase of growth.'

This realization meant that LEGO put its efforts into making the company and the organization within the old economy as efficient as possible. It was then feasible to liberate sufficient resources to invest in new business areas within the new economy, where the value of the LEGO brand can be multiplied almost perpetually. Consequently, LEGO has ventured into children's clothes, computer games, watches and LEGO systems, which can be programmed and built from

An example of LEGO BABY – products for the youngest that replaced LEGO PRIMO.

your computer. In addition, it is moving into entertainment with its own TV programmes, magazines, the Internet and other media – typical areas for the new economy.

Today, the biggest challenge for LEGO is how the company will continue to operate within two different economies at the same time. In the old economy, it is a matter of optimizing production and distribution; within the new economy, it is a case of building up a value position and a matter of alliances and the outsourcing of production, logistics and sales.

LEGO is only an expert in its brand. For everything else it must find partners. And as a brand expert, LEGO must monitor its new working partners and make sure they don't cause any damage to the brand, which could impede the corporate brand for life. It must also ensure that the new products live up to the corporation's brand values about stimulating creative play.

Soon, many questions arise. Should the company franchise or use the different producers as sub-suppliers? Who is to market the new areas – LEGO itself or each individual company that it enters into business relations with? Will LEGO end up being torn in several directions by a lot of companies that all have their own agenda?

LEGO BABY – former LEGO PRIMO – address the youngest.

LEGO has already been trying to get some of the products that are marketed as sub-brands closer to its corporate brand. One example is the sub-brand LEGO PRIMO, bricks for children aged 0–24 months. The name has been changed to LEGO BABY because the term 'BABY' is generic and is a clearer denomination. LEGO BABY is a sub-brand with close relations to a corporate brand.

I think LEGO is a prime example of a corporation that is conscious of the importance of its brand, and of a top management that puts a lot of effort into a development led by the brand. It is an example to follow because it is becoming increasingly important to understand who you are and what it is you actually own in the market.

LEGO's four eras

In 1932, the toy production began under the motto 'the best is not good enough'. Two years later, the name LEGO was introduced. Since then, the corporation has been through four eras during which its value position has been established.

1934–1955 The era of plastic

After having produced wooden toys for more than ten years, LEGO saw the possibilities of plastic. In 1947, it bought one of the first plastic injection moulding machines in Denmark. Shortly afterwards, it developed the forerunner of the world-famous LEGO brick.

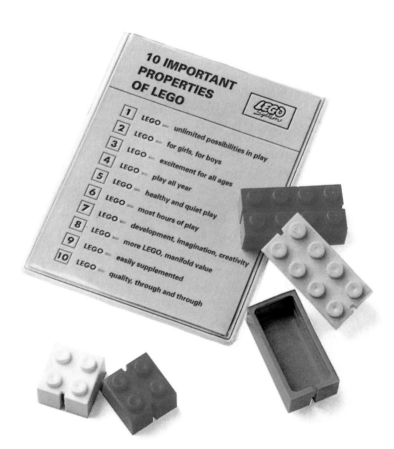

Godtfred Kirk Christiansen's ten product properties for the LEGO system products.

1955–1978 The era of LEGOLAND and DUPLO

In 1955, Godtfred Kirk Christiansen, the son of the founder, put the bricks into a system. Mass production of plastic made it possible to produce in bulk at reasonable prices. By changing the name to 'LEGO System in Play' the foundation was laid for a brand that was to become one of the strongest in the world.

In the wake of each crisis in LEGO's life, a stronger corporation has appeared. In 1960, when a great fire destroyed most of the production, Godtfred Kirk Christiansen cut out the production of wooden toys, which did away with 50 per cent of the turnover in one go. But focusing on plastic bricks gave the corporation a major boost that resulted in 15 years of uninterrupted growth.

In 1963, Godtfred Kirk Christiansen summed up ten product properties which in future were to define the LEGO system products. Two years later, in 1965, a decision was made to ensure growth by an ongoing development of the product and consequently the product development department, LEGO Futura, was formed.

In 1969, during the period of growth, a new plastic brick was invented which was twice as big as the original LEGO brick. It was particularly suited for smaller children, who could not manage LEGO's other products, and it was named DUPLO. The year before, 1968, had seen the opening of LEGOLAND as a showcase for the toys. It was not until 1997, however when the decision was made to focus on building up a strong LEGO brand, that LEGOLAND began to carry the LEGO brand. Until then, the coloured bricks, which at the time were part of the LEGO brand logo, had been contained in the LEGOLAND logo.

1978–1992 The era of the idea system

During the third era it took another crisis to boost LEGO onwards when growth rates came to a halt in 1976. It was around this time that the founder's grandchild, Kjeld Kirk Kristiansen, returned to Denmark after having completed his

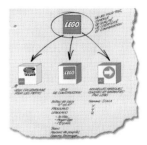

Kjeld Kirk Kristiansen's brand model from 1968, where he divides the brand into three brand classes. One is the corporate brand with various themes – for example LEGO Pirate and LEGO Castle. Another class is sub-brands, such as LEGO DUPLO, LEGO PRIMO and LEGO TECHNIC. A third class is new areas, where, for example, LEGO SCALA, a play system for girls, ended up.

Figure 4.2 LEGO's historical development – the four eras

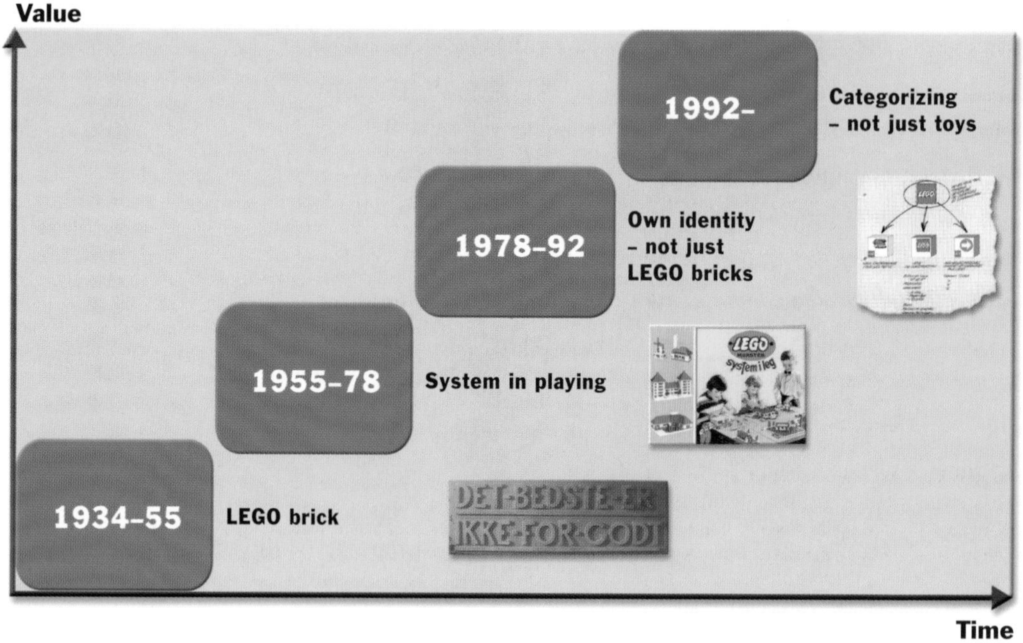

Value

Time

LEGO has gone through four eras. Each time the corporation has been through a crisis, it has asked itself the question: Who are we? By finding the essence of who the LEGO company is, it has created new growth each time.

education in Switzerland. His overall idea was to try to see LEGO as a brand that need not be restricted by the LEGO brick. This led to an expansion of the product development that saw LEGO as an idea system with different product lines.

It also meant that the products were organized thematically under the LEGO brand and presented with various degrees of independent identity. The philosophy was that 'LEGO was a brand' which could offer different themes. The model, which was to control the brand in future, was a marketing model that Kjeld Kirk Kristiansen had developed. The brand core was the box in the middle, where thematic lines, such as a castle line, a pirate line, etc., were developed – a pure LEGO brand. In another box they began to develop sub-concepts. In here were products such as LEGO PRIMO and LEGO TECHNIC. In other words, LEGO plus sub-brands.

The third box was to contain new products that did not necessarily build on the LEGO building system, but would still be based on LEGO's fundamental values about stimulating creative play. This is where new product lines, such as LEGO SCALA, a play system for girls, ended up.

During this process, the company worked intensively on finding out what the LEGO brand was. In order to be able to expand beyond the LEGO brick system, the management had to be fully aware of the core of the brand. They described the brand as 'a symbol of creative and challenging quality toys for

Figure 4.3 The LEGO brand system

Corporate brand	Corporate brand with graduation	Corporate brand with denomination	Corporate brand with differentiation	Combined brand	Endorsing brand	One-product, one-brand

Here the LEGO branding has been put into a system, which is defined in part 2 of this book (Chapters 8–16). The figure shows how the LEGO brand is kept together around the corporate brand. As far as possible, the company tries to use generic descriptions of sub-brands, so they do not become brands in their own right. When making sub-brands, it ensures they are combined with the LEGO brand in order to establish a clear link, thereby ensuring a unified brand construction in the LEGO brand.

Since LEGO has defined what the brand stands for and what it can manage, it has begun to address girls with products such as LEGO BELVILLE and LEGO SCALA.

children of all ages'. In other words, a value position. I am quite convinced that this has contributed to the fact that LEGO has ended up as one of the strongest brands in the world.

However, LEGO, like so many others, did make some mistakes during the branding process, for instance by placing DUPLO outside of the LEGO brand. And many of the new projects, such as SCALA, were thought of as concepts outside of the LEGO brand. This was completely wrong, because the sub-brands were based on the LEGO values. But, as shown in the brand system in Figure 4.3, LEGO has placed different sub-branding concepts as far to the left as possible, so that they get very close to the corporate brand LEGO.

During the same period, the corporation experienced major growth, and even though a few concepts missed the corporate brand LEGO, the major growth was here. It succeeded in creating growth on the basis of the core position within the customer segments – boys aged 4–9 years.

A classical problem for corporations is to handle a further development of the brand to contain new customer segments without watering down the existing. Via an intelligent sub-branding, LEGO succeeded in reaching the infants with LEGO PRIMO, while DUPLO did not make it into the family during the first round. LEGO TECHNIC expanded the customer segments to older children and the girls were approached with sub-brands such as LEGO BELVILLE and LEGO SCALA. It has usually been in this phase of growth that other corporations have failed, because they are so brand overloaded that they have neglected the building up of a strong position in the market.

1992 The relieving era of crisis

Major growth continued right through to the beginning of the 1990s, when another stagnation phase for the turnover again made the management focus even more. Had they reached the limit for the LEGO brand and how should they develop the corporation?

Typically for this period, they were still safeguarding the identity. The major brand corporations viewed their brand one-dimensionally, and the design manual was also God in LEGO. Most important was whether the logo was put in the right place. We must remember that at that time LEGO Company was still not using its logo on LEGOLAND, which most people would probably find rather incredible, since this place is both the ultimate playground for children and a unique value maker. However, the LEGOLAND name was printed along with the LEGO logo in some places. The management were once again, forced to ask themselves the same questions that they had asked before. Who are we? If we are a universal concept, then what does our brand signify? They tried to speed up product development and the sales system, but that only caused more problems and low profits for the corporation. What the management could not quite grasp at the time was that their unique value position, to stimulate creative play, allowed them to expand the brand to cover entirely new product areas. This in return called for a redefinition of the corporation.

LEGO understood what represented high value for most kids in its target group – football – and transformed that into a product in connection with the European Championships 2000.

LEGO is made for the new value economy, which requires the ability to multiply the brand value many times all over the world. LEGO is easily communicated, because it already has a strong profile and a brand value. LEGO had all the prerequisites. The management's task was to optimize the 'old corporation' within the old economy to liberate resources for entering the new value economy.

Towards the end of the 1990s, LEGO formed a crisis group, which was to make an in-depth investigation of its turbulent business and come up with an idea for a new LEGO. I was called upon by this group – they must have read *Corporate Religion* – and asked to say something about the corporation as a brand. The debates were centred on two issues: how to achieve a new and more streamlined sales organization and how to use the brand for increasing growth.

The first issue was a major problem for LEGO, because the organization had run away in all directions. Each country had huge organizations that were based on the premises of the old economy with many different product organizations and headquarters. Nothing was really moving, because the employees were busy justifying their individual positions. The second issue simply dealt with finding product areas which could instigate new growth and fit the brand values that LEGO had built up in the market.

The new LEGO, which was formed at the beginning of the new millennium, is based on a thorough rationalization of the entire product, sales and marketing system. A matrix organization has been formed to control the different business areas globally. This global management has been placed in some business centres, each of them specializing in one area. Like Shell, IBM and other major international corporations throughout the 1990s, LEGO sacked the kings in each country and replaced them with new competence centres, where the main challenge is to control the brand across the borders.

This process of self-awareness also led to a new and stronger self-perception, where the brand came out even more clearly as the crux of the corporation. New growth is to be

Figure 4.4 LEGO's historical brand development for age groups

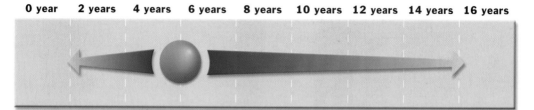

The LEGO brand sprang from play products for boys aged 4–9 years. Since then, it has expanded to meet younger age groups with LEGO PRIMO and older age groups with LEGO TECHNIC and LEGO MINDSTORMS. Simultaneously, it has expanded with products for girls, such as LEGO SCALA.

created by the brand and the value position: 'to stimulate creative play'.

The realization led to even greater variety in the efforts
put into the product range and the management decided to
upgrade the software programs in the sub-brand LEGO MIND-
STORMS. Even more efforts are put into the LEGOLAND parks
and the new children's clothes sub-brand has been promoted
from experiment to implementation. The aim is ambitious: to
hold a place among the five strongest children's clothes
labels in the year 2005. Finally, interactive media, one of the
major exponents of the new economy, has been chosen as a
new area for investment.

Figure 4.5 Concentration of the LEGO brand in a time perspective

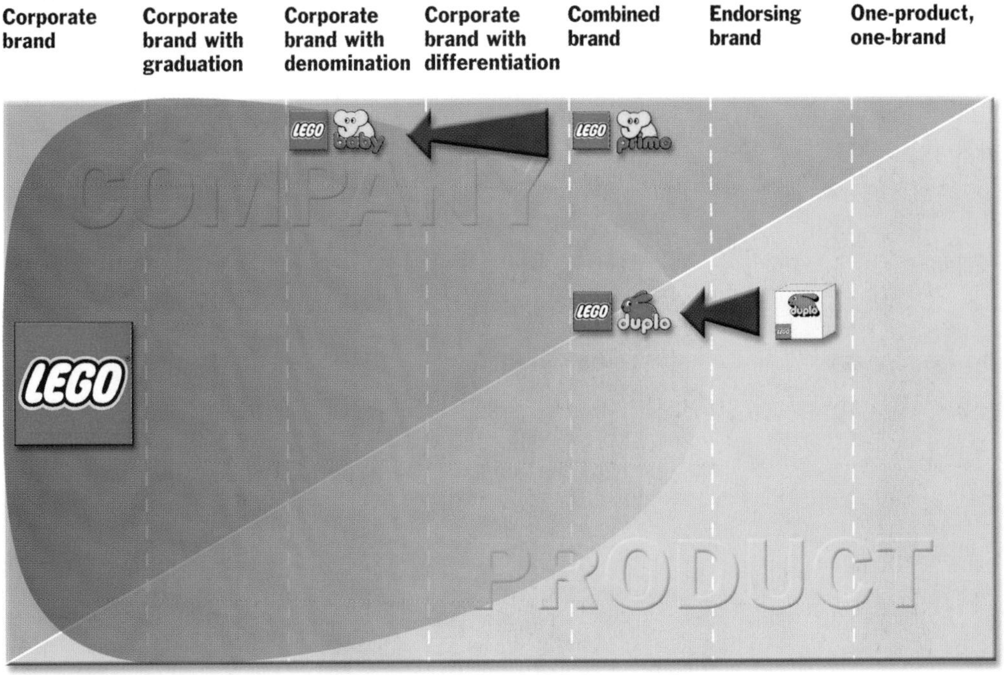

Corporate brand	Corporate brand with graduation	Corporate brand with denomination	Corporate brand with differentiation	Combined brand	Endorsing brand	One-product, one-brand

The figure shows the attempts at moving the two sub-brands LEGO PRIMO and LEGO DUPLO closer to

LEGO's brand core. LEGO PRIMO was renamed LEGO BABY to ensure unambiguous brand building, and

LEGO DUPLO moved from being endorsed by LEGO to being a combined brand with the LEGO corporate brand.

LEGO is still aimed mainly at boys but is trying to cover both sexes from the age of 0–16, as it appears from Figure 4.4 – For example, in the LEGO brand stores, where the whole brand is on display, and on the Internet, from which the company has taken up direct sales.

While the corporation is growing in all directions, the management focuses on keeping the brand together. Within the brand system they work on placing different sub-brands close to the LEGO brand and building up as strong a corporate brand as possible. Therefore, LEGO is trying to find descriptive denominations for the various sub-brands, which means that the brand value enhances the LEGO brand, as shown in Figure 4.3.

LEGO PRIMO, for instance, has been moved to the left in the brand system (see Figure 4.5) and it has been made more descriptive by a name change to LEGO BABY. This way, there should be no risk of BABY becoming an independent brand, which could steal value from the corporate brand. Also, DUPLO has been changed from an endorsement by LEGO to a combined brand, LEGO DUPLO. The same goes for LEGOLAND, which previously made do with an endorsement.

I think concentration of the LEGO branding is a wise move, which can ensure the maintenance of the LEGO brand as one of the strongest in the world.

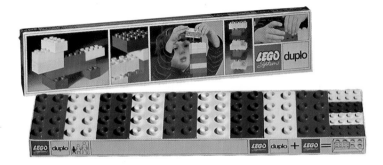

At first, DUPLO was endorsed by LEGO.

Safeguarding the future

LEGO is a prime example of what it takes for a corporation to be successful. It works on a systematization of its brand and on redefining itself as an ongoing process. It has built up the corporation around a strong corporate brand and worked on the articulation of a fixed set of values that are the basis of the development of products and brand. The brand is the driver because the company has acknowledged that it is its value position that is to safeguard its future – not just some product category or other.

One of the huge best sellers during the past years is LEGO Star Wars.

Facts

Take six single coloured bricks and you have 102,981,500 different ways of combining them. This is one of the main reasons for LEGO's worldwide success. More than 6.5 million traditional LEGO bricks have been produced – and that is actually just a fraction of the 203 billion LEGO parts that have been sold all over the world since 1932. In 1934, the word LEGO was put together from the words 'leg godt' – play well – and it was adopted as a company name two years after the carpenter, Ole Kirk Christiansen, began to make wooden toys in his little workshop. The production of wooden bricks ceased at the beginning of the 1960s. The famous plastic bricks were introduced for the first time in 1949.

Creating a global brand with a unique value

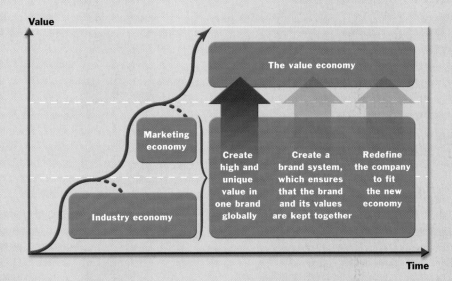

PART 1

CHAPTER 5

Growth via one high-value brand

In the value economy companies need to be economical in creating brands. A new brand should not be created just because the company has developed a new product; only if there is a new value proposition to communicate to customers.

Too many large international companies suffer from brand overload. In most cases, this multiplication of brands impedes international growth and market penetration.

The price of getting your message through to the market has increased because globalization is forcing companies to give each brand the same positioning and support in many markets.

In the old economy subsidiary companies would often grumble that market positioning suggested from head office would not work in their area. They would then take a product to market with an entirely different positioning from that of the parent company. This kind of confusion was dealt with in my book *Corporate Religion*. In the new value economy, it is disastrous. There is only one commandment in the value economy: cut through the noise – and do it globally with a clear and unique value.

What optimizes the value of a brand?

Companies that have built their business around one strong brand now have a unique value position. Moreover, this position has a long-established place in the minds of their customers. Think of:

Audi .... 'Vorsprung durch Technik'
Gillette .... 'The Best A Man Can Get'
Nike .... 'Just Do It'
LEGO .... 'Stimulating creative play'
Virgin .... 'Up Against Conventions'
Body Shop ... 'Cosmetics With a Conscience'

The washing powder Ariel from Procter & Gamble tries to conquer the position 'To wash the clothes clean with optimal effectiveness'.

What is it, then, that optimizes the value of a brand? The answer is to take the value position that consumers most want and identify with. If you can do that you will own a product or a customer category.

US consumer products giant Procter & Gamble (P&G) is exceptional at capturing product categories. When it enters a market with a washing powder, such as Ariel for example, it identifies the generic value position and builds up a brand that takes up that space. For Ariel, the winner position is to wash clean with optimal efficiency. This position is reflected in the product development, where ongoing improvements in washing efficiency strengthen the brand and its position. P&G's straightforward method appears so banal that, to me, it is a puzzle why more corporations do not work with a similar focus on capturing brand positions.

What devalues a brand?

Too many companies let themselves be ruled by product innovations that have nothing to do with their brand position or by competitors' new ideas, which equally are not rooted in their brand mindset.

A unique technical product makes little sense in the new value economy. Philips in the Netherlands, for example, has big problems trying to get the full value potential from its innovations because too many ordinary low-price household products water down its brand. Philips does not build the value into its brand that its persistent and well-considered innovations entitle it to. Philips needs to reassess its brand

Figure 5.1 Brands arise in a certain product category

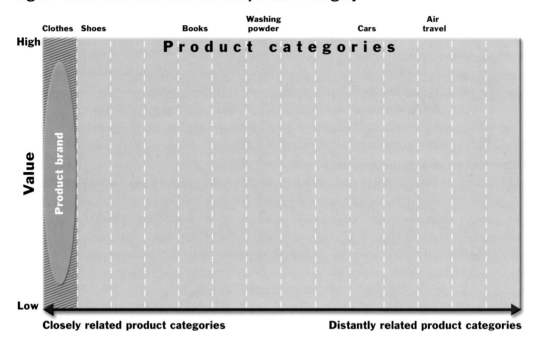

One way brands come about is through a product in a particular category achieving a distinct value position in the market – for example, premium, value for money, or discount. But they all start off in a certain product category and acquire their value as a brand by delivering a certain position. The traditional view of the market within the old economy is that your position is derived from the product category, such as the market for shoes, bank services, cars or air travel.

and product development strategy. Value focus is what separates large international brands. They have articulated their company through their brands and deliver unique value to their customers by offering a different proposition to the market. It's worth noting, though, that this might have happened in many different ways – not necessarily by having a mission and a structured mindset.

The broad positions

As shown in Figure 5.1, a company usually starts off in a product category and, if it becomes successful, perhaps ends up owning the category. In the old product-oriented econo-

Figure 5.2 A brand with a clear value position and direction

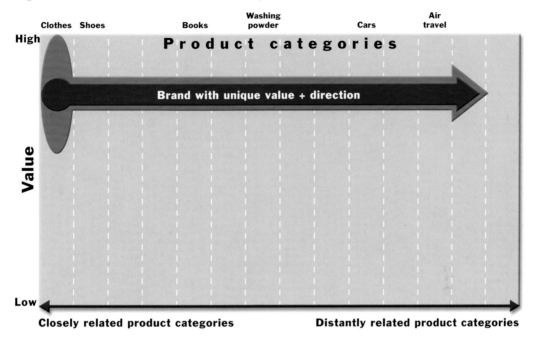

A prerequisite for expanding successfully into other product categories is an accumulation of high value and direction in the brand.

my the main focus was on developing a product to sell. The objective was to become big within your product category. As shown in figure 5.1, the market was perceived as a series of sub-markets, illustrated by the vertical lines. Each company usually ended up positioning itself in the market in a different way – on the value axis of Figure 5.1 – either as a premium, value-for-money or discount product. This was how companies developed a brand with a brand position.

The point about Figure 5.1 is that the usual way for a brand to develop is by capturing a product category and then gaining as high a value for the brand as possible.

The interesting thing about the development of brands and companies is whether management are capable of thinking ahead so that at an early stage they have already defined a brand position from which to expand.

Figure 5.3 The strong value position and direction of LEGO carry the brand across product categories

LEGO *has built up a narrow value position – stimulating children's creativity – within the product category of toys. LEGO can then use the brand value 'stimulating creative play' to expand into other product categories and, most importantly, it can use this same value when product catagories are being updated.*

A brand that owns a generic product category position will usually find it difficult expanding across product categories. If a brand becomes equal to a product category it will be difficult to move it into other product categories because the brand value equals the product value. There is no other value or direction it can transfer into other categories.

The opposite situation is likely to be the case for a brand with a narrower brand position within a product category but with a high value in its value position, as illustrated in Figure 5.2. By keeping to its brand position, such a company can expand into several product categories. Take LEGO, for instance. Today it sells clothes, computer products and entertainment for children as well as its famous bricks. In Figure 5.3 LEGO has been fitted into the model. It started off in the toy category and soon attributed a direction to the brand, which made it more attractive to customers. All its products have been developed in relation to a fixed set of values about creative play, which again has contributed to the strengthening of the brand position. Today, LEGO has one of the strongest brands in the world and is able to do almost anything with it, as long as it keeps to its value position of stimulating creative play.

Mercedes has expanded its brand to include bicycles.

Mercedes-Benz is in the same happy situation. Its exclusive value position can easily host other product areas such as bicycles.

The unique value

So, strong brands can move into closely related product areas. If you want your brand to possess the high value to make this possible you must give it direction, sharpness and clarity in the market. This means, though, that you must also limit your freedom of action within each product category. The emphasis must be on making something unique for the few rather than something quite good for the many.

This is illustrated in figure 5.3 which it shows how LEGO brand's freedom of action is limited by a very sharp direction. LEGO is also a prime example of a company that, based on a single product (plastic bricks), creates a whole new product category of toys. LEGO's desire for growth could have taken it into all sorts of other types of toys, as the international toy groups Hasbro and Mattel have done. But, instead, the family-owned business determined its own direction for product development and market positioning. The reward has been an incredibly strong brand that not only has its own high value but also adds a unique value to LEGO. This value is what allows it to expand into other product areas not necessarily closely related to the original product category.

With a high value and a sharp direction, Virgin has expanded the brand into 150 widely different product categories.

The important lesson taught by Virgin

Richard Branson's Virgin – an airline company, mobile phone company, megastore, financial company and lots more – started off as a mail-order business selling record albums through Branson's student magazine. Today Virgin is a prime example of a company that has built both value and direction into the brand.

When Branson sold the Virgin record business to EMI, he could afford to venture into air transport with Virgin Atlantic Airways. Everyone told Branson to stay well away from the airline business since there was little money in it. But Branson was convinced that if you could change a product area for the better, there would always be money in it.

It was especially the challenge to the established airline companies – particularly British Airways – that gave Virgin airlines its strong direction. British Airways made a number of attempts to harass Virgin out of the market. The British press found out, and what should have grounded Virgin Atlantic Airways became a media event, which the nation followed for years through the different stages of the court process. Branson won the case.

Value for money

The value that Branson built into his brand was the concept that everything the company did would give customers value for money. Virgin products should be sold at much lower prices than everyone else's – but still be of the same quality.

Using this value position, Virgin can enter any conceivable business and deliver the 'value for money, quality at low prices' message. So far the business consists of air transport, mobile phones, cola, rail travel, fashion, entertainment of all kinds via Virgin Mega Stores, insurance, pensions and bridal wear – in all, more than 150 companies. Everything

Figure 5.4 Virgin's value positioning goes across product categories

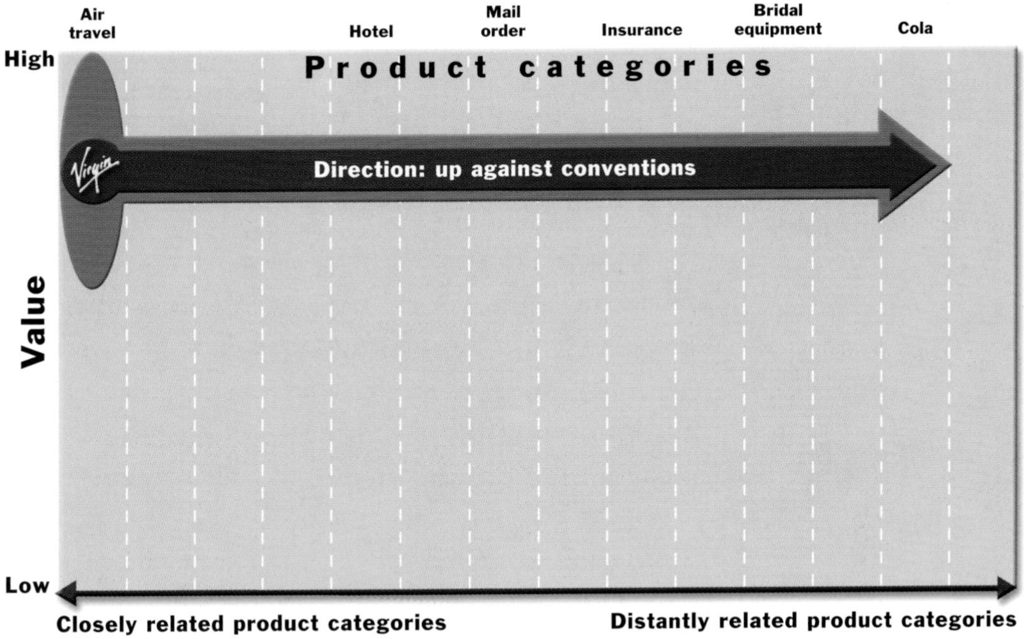

Virgin has won the value position – up against conventions – which it can use to enter different product categories – air travel, bridal wear, bank services and many others. Virgin has created a value market with its own brand and its own value position of 'up against conventions'.

Virgin does is driven by 'up against conventions', which is an obvious and widely sympathetic value. What links bridal equipment, insurance, train and air transport, clothes, cola and mobile phones is this strong brand position and direction (Figure 5.4).

Interestingly, I am convinced that if Branson had not been able to communicate his aggressive anti-establishment value with a little 'help' from British Airways, he could not have expanded his brand to cover so many different product categories. Branson got his lucky break by challenging a monopoly. More, he took up (and eventually won) a fight that would have seen most people running away with their tail between their legs. The most important lesson to be learned from the Virgin case is that Branson based his efforts on an attitude and a set of values. Those values and attitudes were not articulated to begin with – though no doubt they are now. But their effect has been that new business opportunities for the Virgin brand can be created within other product categories.

The brand must be self-aware

When LEGO was still a young company, the management were not thinking about brand and positions. They created a brand by imagining those attitudes and values that could give direction to the development of their products and determine their properties.

Any company that wants to take this route must move from merely creating products to building a brand around its products and establishing a high value for customers.

Whether this value represents the very cheapest product every time, a premium product, or something like Apple's 'think different' doesn't matter. The point is that the customer must get the unique value experience. The brand must 'understand' itself – be self-aware – and maintain a particular set of values, whatever they may be. Otherwise customers will become confused and the brand will lose clarity and credibility.

Companies that carry unique value in their brand suitcases can wander around the production landscape like nomads.

Now a question: why is it so important to work on your brand in such a focused way? The answer is simple. Companies that carry unique value in their brand suitcases can wander around the production landscape like nomads. Wherever they might feel like settling down, their unique value and brand focus will make them welcome. As a consequence, what were previously predictable patterns of competition will crack.

The Internet has given us a first inclination of this. It has revealed considerable fault lines between various areas of business and the breakdown of established structures of competition. What this means for business is that while once you may have been able to keep an eye on your competitors because they were doing the same things as you, the competition of the future will appear from anywhere. And the way they will force an entry into your market will be through brands and value positions.

Virgin benefits from this. When it moves into new product segments it picks up those customers who think they like to give a one-finger salute to conventions and who buy into the idea of value for money.

In an abundant society, where there is more than enough of everything, customers want unequalled value attached to an attractive product. Value makes it easier to attract the customers' attention. Value makes it simpler to sell yourself to those customers who recognize themselves in your value position. Not all markets are equally sensitive to brand values. But brand-proof markets are becoming fewer in number as the global village takes over.

My point is that companies must make an effort to get familiar with this new value dimension. With a high awareness of value construction it is easier to guide your company and your brand safely into the future.

While once you may have been able to keep an eye on your competitors because they were doing the same things as you, the competition of the future will appear from anywhere.

Defining brand position

When a product begins to falter, often the knee-jerk reaction is to pour money into unfocused marketing campaigns. These may raise customer awareness in the short term, but they can actually damage the long-term brand position.

When a product ceases to differentiate itself in the market, many chief executive officers (CEOs) and managing directors conclude that only a strong brand can provide direction and meaning. Many companies are tempted to throw money at the issue. Clever marketing campaigns, they reason, will boost customer awareness. That may be true, but awareness is not worth much if a company merely spends a fortune on marketing campaigns run by advertising agencies that have been given too much freedom to play with creative ideas.

Of course this will attract attention to your brand, but it will change direction every time marketing people and creatives have new ideas. A consistent building of your brand is much more preferable.

Transient marketing plans are not the fault of advertising companies alone. An erratic course is usually the outcome of marketing being too inspired by the product-focused mindset. The company must define itself in relation to the position it wishes to capture in the market. Only then can it begin to describe the values and attitudes that must pervade it to enable it to reach its goals.

The company must define itself in relation to the position it wishes to capture in the market.

There must be unity and coherence between the internal organization and the external market because customers buy brand personalities (this is explained in *Corporate Religion*).

Figure 6.1 Brand religion model

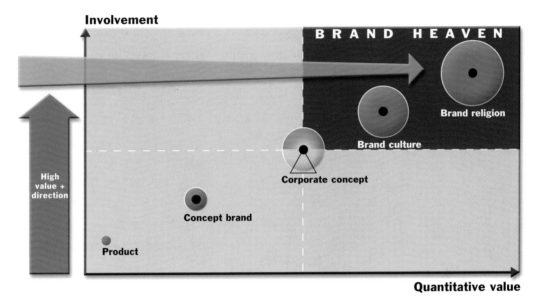

Strong brands are made when value is attributed to a product and consumers become involved with it. The generic product is constant (marked as a black core in the figure). It is the surrounding area that differentiates brands. It takes a consistent corporate concept to unify the company so that it can reach high involvement levels. The different brand positions can be summarized as follows:

• *Product: products without any kind of value added to the generic element.*
• *Concept brand: brands driven by emotional values rather than product properties.*
• *Corporate concept brand: brands that merge consistently with the company.*
• *Brand culture: brands that are so strong that to consumers they become synonymous with the function they perform.*
• *Brand religion: the ultimate brand position, held by brands that have become a must, a belief system, to consumers.*

Express yourself very clearly

Figure 6.1, which is one of this book's central models, shows how a mixture of quantitative values along the x-axis and qualitative values along the y-axis form a brand position. The quantitative values could be the technological proper-ties of the product, a high awareness, preference or good distribution. But what really involves customers in the strength and character of a brand is revealed along the y-axis.

There are brands that possess both high awareness and a high preference. In traditional terms, these brands ought to have a strong market position. But they don't. They lack the value content that makes them relevant to a well-defined customer group. In our abundant society, the sparsest resource is mind space in the heads of consumers. If you want to be memorable you must be very precise in articulating the brand position you want to adopt.

Figure 6.1 is a model that describes relative values between different brands and their positions in the market. Obviously a brand wants to move as high as possible up the y-axis, symbolized by the circle getting as large as possible. The ultimate level is 'brand religion'.

It may be no surprise to you that a 'corporate religion' is the ideal way of transforming a company that wants to be guided by values and attitudes. For people who haven't read *Corporate Religion*, there is a description of the internal and external relations in a company and its market in Chapter 7.

Focus the resources

As Figure 6.1 shows, companies need to define a brand position as high on the involvement axis as is possible for the customer group they want to own. Once that definition is in place, the company can focus its resources. From now on, product development must be geared to fulfilling the promise that the brand makes to customers. And the brand must give new products a direction. The definition also contributes to the optimizing of both the organization and its marketing so that the company can smoothly communicate the promise of its brand position.

Figure 6.2 shows how different companies have defined the brand position they seek. Some have already consoli-

Figure 6.2 Strong brand positions with a clear direction

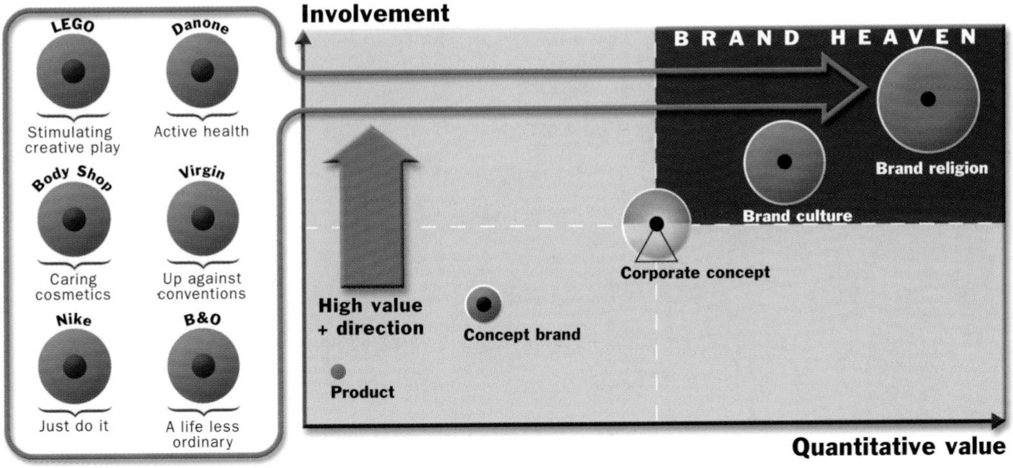

LEGO	**Danone**
Stimulating creative play	Active health
Body Shop	**Virgin**
Caring cosmetics	Up against conventions
Nike	**B&O**
Just do it	A life less ordinary

Involvement

BRAND HEAVEN

Brand religion

Brand culture

Corporate concept

High value + direction

Concept brand

Product

Quantitative value

It is important, both for customers and employees, that a company can clearly define the value position it wants to capture. Today's strongest brands have understood and achieved this.

dated it, while for others it is a target they are working towards. Common to all companies is that their management can articulate the value positions that they have either won or aim to capture. Consequently, they are ready for success in the value economy because they are aware of their focus.

The speed of change is high in the value economy and companies constantly face new challenges. Product innovations may be altering the market or new competitors may be emerging. Companies equipped to succeed in the value economy know exactly what it is that they should take into this new era. Consumers know what the company stands for, which is why they buy its products, and they expect to be able to acquire the same values in new areas. This is how values and attitudes are accumulated in a value position and why they are now the most important asset for companies.

This is why all companies should begin a self-awareness project. Senior managers should ask some simple questions:

- Who are we?
- Who do our customers think we are?
- Who would we like to be?
- How do we become that?

The company must specify the direction and the values. This cannot be left to the customers to dictate. Customers will not come up with innovations.

One company that has defined the value position it wishes to capture is Danone.

Danone – combining branding with a clear value position

The French Danone Group's dairy brand, Danone, is a prime example of combining a branding strategy with a very precise value position. This clear value position is the basis for the marketing of the dairy brand and it also ensures a constant check on its sub-brands.

Figure 6.3 Danone's value position

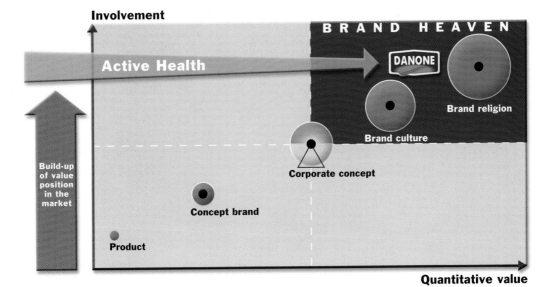

Danone's aim is to capture the value position 'Active Health'.

The Danone Group has carefully defined the dairy brand. It has made it easily understandable and Danone has succeeded in capturing the value position 'Active Health' (Figure 6.3). As its aim is so clear, it is also possible for the Danone Group to control the dairy brand and its sub-brands, even though Danone is a very decentralized organization.

Branding strategy

Danone markets each individual sub-brand so that they deliver value back to the corporate brand. On each market, key drivers ('A' sub-brands) are defined, which through efficient marketing

Figure 6.4 Danone's value accumulation and spreading of 'Active Health'

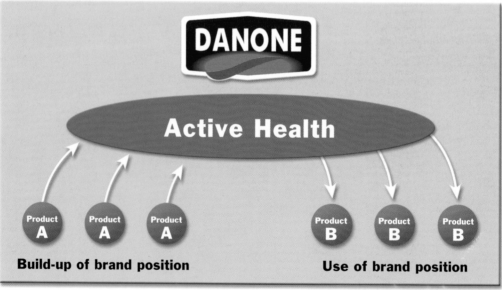

Before entering new markets Danone estimates which product areas would be best for it. Within each specific product area, Danone uses different 'A' sub-brands, which it actively markets. Since each sub-brand delivers the central position 'Active Health' as well as its own sub-brand position, the brand value can be used for the passive marketing of 'B' sub-brands. This means the company achieves a value synergy.

provide value to the dairy brand and the 'Active Health' position. 'B' sub-brands, which are not marketed so intensely, benefit from the overall position (Figure 6.4).

The system is flexible and control of sub-branding is decentralized. Each market chooses for itself which segments it wants to put its efforts into and which sub-brands to market. This turns Danone's sub-brands into value generators for the corporate brand. In order to keep a check on its sub-brands, Danone measures whether they live up to their own sub-brand

Figure 6.5 Danone's combined branding system

Corporate brand	Corporate brand with graduation	Corporate brand with denomination	Corporate brand with differentiation	Combined brand	Endorsing brand	One-product, one-brand

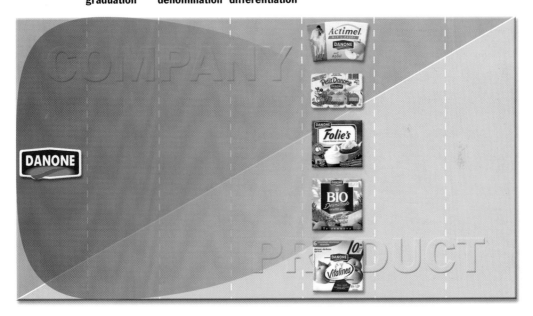

Danone deploys a combined branding strategy, in which sub-brands for the different product categories work as drivers for the Danone brand. The reason for the successful building up of brand value in the corporate brand is that the corporate brand and the sub-brand are clearly combined on the package, as stated in the well-planned brand strategy. This way, value is transferred from the corporate brand to the sub-brand – and vice versa.

value and to its 'Active Health' position. They must always generate 'Active Health' value as well as their own sub-brand value (Figure 6.5).

More than a yogurt

By taking a closer look at the packaging of one of Danone's products, Danette, you can get a good idea of the group's branding strategy. On the original pack, to the right in Figure 6.6, the Danone logo was not particularly striking and the sub-brand became too dominant. As a result it did not live up to the 'Active Health' value rule. Danone changed the packaging to make the provenance clearer – see left in the figure.

Figure 6.6 Danette's stronger main branding – from endorsing to combined brand

Corporate brand	Corporate brand with graduation	Corporate brand with denomination	Corporate brand with differentiation	Combined brand	Endorsing brand	One-product, one-brand

The way Danette packaging was changed is a good example of how Danone's corporate branding delivers the position 'Active Health'. It has been done in the new design by adding more white and making the Danone logo much clearer.

Facts

In 1919, Spaniard Isaac Carasso, fascinated by the health-giving properties of yogurt, founded the Danone brand. He named the company after his son – in Spanish Danon is the diminutive of Daniel. From the Carasso basement in Barcelona, the Danone Group has grown to employ 80,000 people around the world. The Danone Group has a research centre that supports development and quality control of products and helps ensure the value position 'Active Health'.

Spaniard Isaac Carasso founded Danone in 1919.

The Body Shop's 'cosmetics with a conscience' raises controversial issues, such as 'never again testing on animals', 'save the rainforests' and 'support developing countries'.

The corporation as a brand

Figure 4.1 illustrates the three important prerequisites for ascending the involvement axis of the corporate religion model in Figure 6.1. Management must define the company itself as a consistent brand. Customers have an expectation that your company, just like your brand, has a philosophy that is in accordance with their own standards. If not, you will not be able to convince them to buy your brand.

Procter & Gamble, Unilever and Mars, for example, will undoubtedly have problems in the future because their brands are little but shiny facades in the shape of logos and nice packaging.

Are you prepared?

Those customers who are deeply involved with a brand will look behind the fronts companies erect. Any company that has been selling an illusion to its customers will not be prepared for this attention. So the higher a brand makes it up the involvement axis of Figure 6.1, the more there is to live up to and the steeper the fall for the company that doesn't.

The Body Shop has a concept that it calls 'cosmetics with a conscience'. This is based on its products not being tested on animals and that raw materials are bought in developing countries at fair prices. So The Body Shop has a great deal to live up to. It could not withstand, for example, journalists digging up a story proving the opposite. The Body Shop must demonstrate that it takes 'cosmetics with a conscience' seriously. It does this by constantly raising controversial issues, such as 'never again testing on animals', 'save the rainforests' and 'support developing countries'.

An example of how The Body Shop instills its 'cosmetics with a conscience' with true value is its product line of traditional Indian health products based on ancient ayurveda principles. The company has even started up ayurveda production in India run by local people.

Figure 6.7 Mission-controlled corporate concept

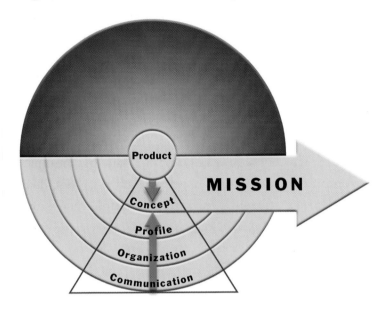

To create the necessary credibility in different brands, they must be linked with a corporate concept, which is a clearly defined and consistent unity between mission, product, concept profile, organization and communication.

It is an inescapable requirement of the value economy that the company offers unique value. If it doesn't it will be invisible and unheard in the crowd. Unique value calls for high credibility and consistency in the corporate brand. The company as a brand is depicted in Figure 6.7 (also from *Corporate Religion*). The model shows how you must have a mission that guides your company.

But shouldn't management run the company by its brand? Well, the mission is an articulation of what you want to do – in other words, a promise the brand makes to consumers. You should choose the words carefully to make sure that the mission really provides you with a direction and articulates who the company is and wants to be. If you cannot put words to the very lifeblood of the company, how can you develop products and services and market them? And how can you employ the right people and manage them?

The manager is the glue

The mission is the most essential issue in the life of a company and the most important task for any manager. Unfortunately, there are only a few managers who can communicate the core of a company so that everyone shares a clear conception of it both internally and externally. In the past, a good managing director would articulate the product and its innovative qualities and the company would be directed by product, logistics, and sales systems. Within the value economy the definition of a good manager is that he or she has high value, can read the future, and can acquire a good sense of customers and the business.

Only a few managers can communicate the core of a company so that everyone shares a clear conception of it both internally and externally.

The manager is the glue between the company and its customers. It is a demanding job and only a few can handle it. As there is only room for unique brands within the value economy, likewise there is only room for unique leaders who are conscious of the significance of the values that can articulate their companies and direct them into new areas created by a constantly changing market.

Figure 6.7 shows how the mission guides the articulation of the value and the direction of the company brand. Only later is a creative concept developed. Above all the brand must have a profile that yields a completely trustworthy image of the desired value position.

Express the soul

Steer your company well clear of the traditional design agencies.

A word of advice: steer your company well clear of the traditional design agencies. They think that graphics are the answer to all problems. This is nonsense. Management must co-ordinate all of the company's potential contact with the public so that they ensure a consistent profile. The same goes for a lot of the so-called brand bureaus. They perform countless analyses and turn up with a mission and a written concept for a new logo. After that, it is up to the company. But the real solution for the company is to be found in the consistency of the whole, as shown in Figure 6.7. All elements have to be thought through in context.

Communication with employees – telling them what you want to do, where you want to go and how to do it – is also vital. Employees want to understand the company that employs them. And if they do so and grasp the direction, they will do their best. They like to be part of something big. What matters is setting clear targets that they can strive to reach.

Employees like to be part of something big. What matters is setting some clear targets that they can strive to reach.

This kind of internal communication about who the company is and where it is headed did not get a high priority in the old product-fixated industry society. Now it should – and leadership is a priority. This kind of attention is the basis of an intense, mutual, result-orientated work effort. Scrap all the organization theory rubbish; it is useless in a constantly changing world.

When the company needs to be able to make quick decisions, it needs strong communication systems, not hierarchical management procedures. Clear speech is one of the most important management tools of the value economy.

Clear speech is one of the most important management tools of the value economy.

Knowledge will be another central commodity in the value economy. But knowledge must have a direction in order to be at the service of the company brand. That is why the human factor is crucial when the company is delivering a unique brand position to the market. Human beings are back in the centre again – that is the good news of the value economy. So the final brick in Figure 6.7 is communication with the surrounding world.

More for the few

Communication is actually an enormous challenge for companies in the value economy because we are up against an old rule that says that communication must entertain and make as many people as possible remember it.

In the value economy, all we want is to win a unique value position – even if it is only for the few.

What we want to achieve in the value economy is exactly the opposite. All we want is to win a unique value position – even if it is only for the few. Unfortunately, it is hard for companies to move in this direction. Advertising and other agencies work with brands in a far too traditional way. They think that it is a matter of creating awareness. And in order to get a message across in this communication-dominated society, they opt for entertainment.

'It is the only way if you want everybody in' the agencies misinform companies. The agencies' only way of testing for success is the level of enjoyment, which they rate as equivalent to involvement in a specific brand and position. This traditional advertising line misses the point of the value economy. We want to aim for something special rather than being a clown entertaining the masses.

But it isn't easy. Several of the corporations included in this book as case studies have done completely the right thing by building up a unique value. But many have had great trouble analyzing their brand and producing the right kind of advertising communication.

Communicating a brand is a long-term task. Part 3 deals with communication, which usually potters about somewhere in the middle of the organizational pyramid and has often, quite wrongly, been delegated to subsidiary companies in different countries.

This mess is the reason why so many companies have communicated so badly that they are no longer globally consistent and are therefore unable to keep up with the pace of the value economy.

CHAPTER 7

Brand = corporate personality

Companies are like people. They are about three basic things: How do we perceive ourselves? How does the surrounding world perceive us? And how would we like others to perceive us? The more harmony and coherence between the three perceptions, the stronger the personality.

Alfred Adler – one of the founders of modern psychology – is behind the idea of the harmonious personality. Adapted to the world of business, the idea appears in Figure 7.1. Begin at the far left and watch the movement from management to customers at the far right of the figure. The numbers are indicators of a total description of the company. (See Chapter 4 in *Corporate Religion* for an elaboration of the model.)

This outlines the company's position in the market: how do customers perceive us; who are they; and what do they want the company to be?

After that, you can turn to the internal culture: who are we and how are we going to explain it?

Only a few companies can do this. The straightforward explanation of who we are can be too closely related to the products a company currently produces. But since products rapidly become out of date, it is important to make clear the attitudes and the culture within the company. Attitudes and culture are the essence of the qualitative values that contribute to developing new products.

Attitudes and culture are the essence of the qualitative values that contribute to developing new products.

Figure 7.1 The company personality – a total description of the internal and external company

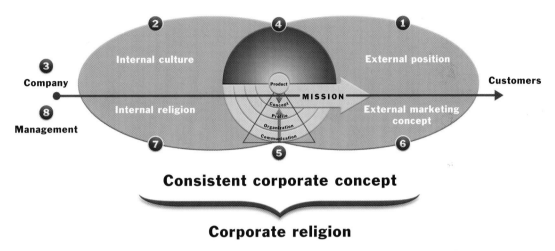

Consistent corporate concept

Corporate religion

A series of steps must be taken before a company can appear internally and externally consistent.

1. *How does the world perceive the company? An analysis of the external positioning of the company.*
2. *How does the company perceive itself? A description of the internal culture, primarily the history of the company and the values that have made it what it is today.*
3. *How would the company like to perceive itself in the future? An analysis and an articulation of management's ideas of where the company should be going.*
4. *Based on the above descriptions, a 'corporate concept' is articulated. A corporate concept is a clearly defined and consistent relationship between product, concept, profile, organization and communication. For further explanation, see Chapter 6.*
5. *The validity of the corporate concept must be tested internally and externally. Importantly, management must feel they have expressed the personality of the company. It is management who must stand up and be the main communicators of the new company. A 'concept bible' should be produced that accurately describes the corporate concept (not to be mistaken for a design manual).*
6. *Based on the corporate concept, a marketing concept is developed that can communicate it and lead to capturing the desired market position.*
7. *The internal religion is developed. The aim is a company direction that allows it to deliver consistent, branded goods to the market.*
8. *The management of the company must act as leaders and communicate the new message clearly.*

Words that everybody has been waiting for

The next step is to make clear where management are headed. Most managers would claim that already happens via strategic planning. Possibly. But often very few people in the company get the message. Too often, communication with employees is a neglected discipline, even though employees show a lot of interest in the company, its personality and where it is going. After all, they are expected to spend a great deal of time and energy at work. Even in cases where management have done some thinking about the aims of the company, no one really understands how to communicate it. The only motivation ever spoken about is result-oriented information, which deals solely with the past.

Too often, communication with employees is a neglected discipline.

I have undertaken a number of corporate religion projects for international companies. In my experience, there is a great sense of relief for everyone when the essence of what the company is about is finally put into words. With companies listed on the stock markets, it also makes the lives of financial analysts a lot easier when they have a simple statement of what the company is really about.

Spiritual intelligence

Using the corporate concept we can produce an overall description of the company as a brand, as shown in the middle of Figure 7.1.

It is possible to draw on other behavioural or psychological/medical research in a similar way. For example, everyone is familiar with IQ as an indicator of how fast we can interpret symbols, draw logical conclusions and solve problems. In recent years, the concept of emotional intelligence (EQ) has aroused a great deal of interest in business. Emotional intelligence describes our ability to read a social landscape – crisis, conflicts, love and joy. Emotional intelligence is based on properties such as self-awareness, self-control, persistence, diligence, motivation, empathy and tact.

These ideas are elaborated in the book *Emotional Intelligence* (Bloomsbury, London, 1996) by Daniel Goleman. It is vital reading for anyone who would like to better understand how to improve at a personal level. But equally, many of these theories can be useful for improving your company.

Recent research into the human brain in the US has introduced the term SQ, which is the concept of spiritual intelligence, as a link between IQ and EQ. The rational intelligence, IQ, is used in solving logical and strategic problems. The 'irrational' intelligence, EQ, is used in reacting to the feelings of others and yourself. SQ is what you use for making sense of and ascribing meaning to actions and experiences. We use SQ when we need to find our place in a larger context and to understand how we function there. Likewise with companies. It is important to be constantly aware of the larger context the company is part of and what position it will take in the future.

It is important to be constantly aware of the larger context the company is part of and what position it will take in the future.

Brands are illogical

These reflections may seem abstract and not terribly well documented but they make sense in reaching an understanding of the complexity of human beings. Humans are so much more than just the tangible things we can say about them. The same is true for companies. In future, all corporate value will be bound up in something you cannot see, let alone put in your pocket.

The movement away from a physical product to value positions in the minds of consumers calls for an interest in the workings of the mind. It is important to examine brands in holistic contexts.

Brands consist partly of something physical that we can see and understand. But the most valuable parts of a brand

A brand's empathic qualities are decisive for whether we take to it or turn our backs and find something else.

are its qualitative values. If we can talk about empathy in the context of emotional intelligence, then we can equally well talk about a brand's ability to enter into our spirit as consumers. A brand's empathic qualities are decisive for whether we take to it or turn our backs and find something else.

A brand's power of penetration is determined by the value it represents to me as a consumer. Branding is essentially about creating understanding and sympathy. Those feelings do not come out of the blue, either externally in the market or internally in the organization. The concepts of emotional and spiritual intelligence may help us discover how we can build a strong brand culture.

Entering into the spirit of the company

The theory of spiritual intelligence has a lot of relevance in making sense of actions and experiences within a company. All company managers should be aware of the need to describe their company. What are we good at? What are we not so good at? What does our new product mean to us? How does it relate to the old one? The most important management task is to gather information and interpret it so that everybody in the organization is constantly aware of what is going on and understands what it is doing in the market.

In Figure 7.1 IQ stands for everything tangible in the company while EQ is the company culture. SQ is the basis for a total description of the company where management, the internal culture and the external position are in harmony with each other. Not until a description of the company's personality has been put together can work begin on a marketing concept that will ultimately capture the value position you want.

Simultaneously, management should develop a 'corporate religion'. This guides the internal culture so that the company is able to deliver its brand values consistently.

Communication and flexibility

Mechanical management cannot keep up with the speed of the value economy. It would only just be getting systems in place before some unexpected change happened and the systems had to be changed all over again.

Mechanical management cannot keep up with the speed of the value economy.

So what is the managerial style of the future? It will be a matter of knowledge and intuition – far removed from systems and dogmatic precepts. You must manage through communication and flexibility, which brings us back to Figure 7.1 and the ability to explain the content, direction, meaning and values of the company. It also brings us back to the questions. In fact, you might as well pin these up on a notice board – you will have to answer them again and again in the future.

- What are the aims of the company?
- Which customers do we wish to own?
- Which value position do we want?
- Which culture shall we aim at to capture our external position?
- What kind of management and what kind of external and internal communication?

Customers demand brands with unique value. That type of brand is hard to deliver via the typical company organization. But if you let the brand control the development of your company, market success will follow.

Even proponents of the old school, who would rather think new products and product improvements, will be forced into the new way of thinking by the merciless acceleration of the value centrifuge (see Chapter 3). If you do not redefine your product business to suit the value economy, the market will forget you.

Three powerful values

In 1997, B&O managing director Anders Knutsen and a group of managers defined the essence of B&O in three words – excellence, synthesis and poetry – as part of an exercise (in which I was involved) to improve brand perception.

Excellence because the products must always have an expressive, inherent quality. Creating something expensive and exclusive for its own sake is not enough.

Synthesis because it reflects the way the company works. A thesis and an anti-thesis lead to improvement via synthesis. This means that everyone is encouraged to fight internally in order to get better all the time. You cannot develop unique products without explosions.

Poetry because it is the extra dimension that customers want. By adopting poetry as an objective, B&O shows it understands this.

Invisible attitude

The process started by Knutsen stimulated a lot of thinking in a company that, until then, had been extremely product oriented. After a preliminary self-awareness process, a new realization followed at B&O – 'we only communicate our physical products to customers and never show them who we are.'

An analysis indicated that the B&O brand stood for only one thing in customers' minds – design. This was reinforced by B&O ads and catalogues – clean, white pages with sharply rendered

BeoVision
– one of B&O's TV models.

Figure 7.2 An internal and an external analysis led to 'A life less ordinary'

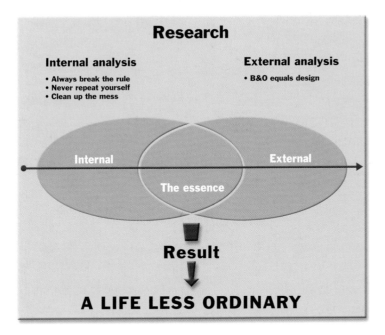

B&O has a particularly strong and clear internal culture expressed as 'never repeat yourself, always break the rule and clean up the mess'. However, an external analysis showed that to most people, B&O equals design.

products and text. The interesting point was that deep inside the company there was a rather aggressive attitude to product development. This was synthesis operating within the company culture. And it showed that the people involved in product development had a quite different mindset to what external marketing implied.

Let out your distinctive character

It is rare to find a company like B&O with such a clear identity that is not just based on the physical product. B&O has system-

B&O's products express excellence, synthesis and poetry – above, BeoSound 9000.

atized concept development and has taken an incredibly aggressive approach to the task. Some of the attitudes behind this approach are:

• Never repeat yourself.
• Always break the rule.
• Clean up the mess.

These are values that B&O needed to build into its brand position in the market. Buying B&O implies the courage to stand out and be different. This is a much more powerful value position because it says so much about who B&O is.

As a result B&O developed a marketing concept that articulated the value position that the company actually delivers – you have chosen to be different. The external communication concept was phrased as 'A life less ordinary'.

Profundity and value

At first B&O could not understand why it could not just present its unique products. But how else could it dramatize the extra dimension – which is the brand – and stand out, be different, provoke?

In the context of the value centrifuge, B&O products and product concepts are unique, so what really matters is to

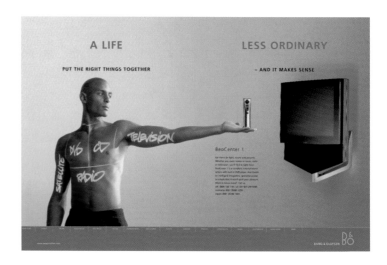

An example of the B&O concept 'A life less ordinary'.

further this position. By incorporating the internal attitudes that go into product development in the marketing concept, consumers acquire even more value. This is exactly the involvement and differentiation that customers desire. They want to see and understand who B&O is before they buy the brand.

During the internal process of redefining the brand, the company vision was altered from 'the unique combination of technological excellence and emotional appeal' to 'courage to constantly challenge the ordinary in search of surprising, long-lasting experiences'. This new phrase switches the focus from the product to the brand.

Facts

On November 17, 1925, Peter Bang and Svend Andreas Grøn Olufsen formed B&O Ltd in Quistrup in West Jutland. The company had early success with a mains receiver – a radio – that didn't need batteries or an accumulator. From the beginning, the company targeted the wealthier part of the market. For example, B&O's first radio gramophone cost more than an average annual income at the time. With that, the value position was established – excellent products of high quality for a narrow target group, a value position that for B&O covers radios, hi-fis, TVs, videos and telephones.

Create a brand system ensuring that the brand values are controlled

PART 2

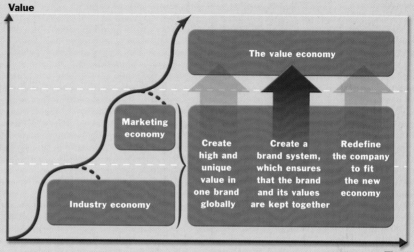

CHAPTER 8

Aligning the brand and the values

Managing growth in the value economy presents new challenges. By harnessing the value centrifuge a company can enjoy rapid penetration of new markets. This requires alignment between brand and values.

When a company grows in size and moves into new product categories, it faces a dilemma. The traditional response is to choose between two evils. Either it can make a brand so wide that it becomes diluted or it can start from scratch by creating a new brand. Neither is the best course. But a middle way does exist that combines sub-brands with a superbrand.

Plenty of room for differentiation

Figure 8.1 fits the brand system into a model. To the far left is the branding point of departure in a corporate brand – Heinz is an example of how this is done.

At the right-hand side of the figure is one-product, one-brand, the classic way of thinking where the brand equals the product category. Companies such as Procter & Gamble have perfected this strategy.

Between the corporate brand and the one-product, one-brand strategies come sub-branding and differentiation – that is, forms of branding that draw on the value of the corporate brand and offer various forms of payback in return.

What is new about this model is the inclusion of sub-brands that relate as closely as possible with the corporate brand. There are many examples of how to differentiate your branding to make it consistently increase the value of a superbrand. Primarily it involves creating a logical sub-

Figure 8.1 The value-oriented brand system

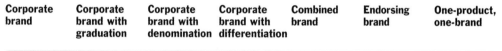

Corporate brand	Corporate brand with graduation	Corporate brand with denomination	Corporate brand with differentiation	Combined brand	Endorsing brand	One-product, one-brand

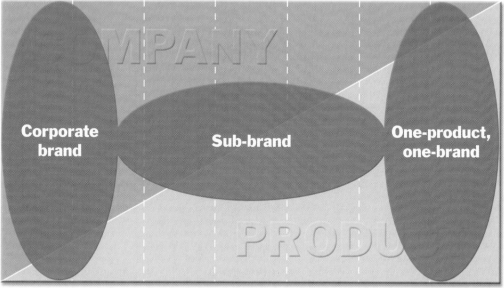

The common areas for branding are corporate branding at one end of the scale and one-product, one-brand at the other. In between there are various forms of sub-branding. Companies can achieve high value by developing sub-brands, which steadily build up value in a superbrand.

branding system or family of sub-brands which fit together to strengthen the superbrand. I call this graduation. At one end of the scale you can operate with small graduations of a corporate brand and at the other you can have sub-brands with individual names and identities, all taking their starting point in a strong corporate brand.

The starting point is the value position

The further away from the corporate brand at the far left of the model, the more the sub-brand gets differentiated. When the rubber band connecting the sub-brand and the corporate brand cannot be stretched any further, you create a new, independent brand. In the future branding will be a much more radical and extensive discipline for companies than it has been. Corporate management will have to consider much more important questions than graphic identity, or whether the packaging should be blue, yellow or red, or whether the advertising is effective.

In the value economy, customers expect intelligent branding. They can easily understand a brand differentiation that encompasses new segments and product categories, as long as the differentiation is based on the company's value position. Within the value economy, the logo is not necessarily equivalent to the brand and its identity.

Be valuable to the few

Figure 8.2 shows the development of branding philosophy from the product economy through the marketing economy to the value economy.

In the product economy, the product and its packaging led the way in branding. Later, the marketing economy took over and made the logo and graphic identity direct the brand. As long as everyone stuck to the design manual, everything would be fine.

Within the value economy, the key is in the brand and its strong value position. In this context, the graphic identity is little more than a hollow shell. In the value economy content is everything. No one wants fancy packaging that has no aim or focus.

In the value economy content is everything. No one wants fancy packaging that has no aim or focus.

A key issue of the value economy is to avoid becoming everything for everyone when you can deliver a high-value content for a very particular target group. That is why it has become so essential to work with a dynamic brand system.

The perfect example

Giorgio Armani and the sub-brand Emporio Armani is a wonderful example of how easy it is to do away with old-

Figure 8.2 Developments in the ways of viewing branding

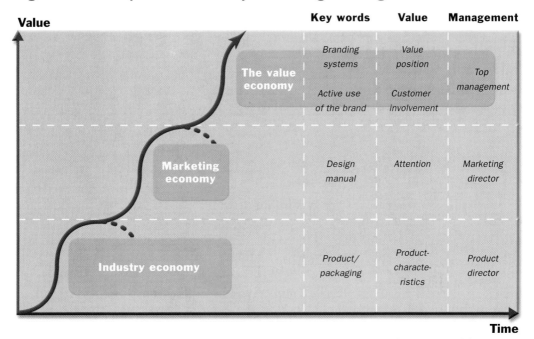

The development from industry economy to value economy calls for a corresponding change of focus. Manoeuvring within the value economy is the primary task of top management.

school thinking about branding and replace it with differentiated branding. All Armani has done is to use its strong corporate brand and add a sub-brand that targets a particular group (see the case study in Chapter 12).

In other words, do not spend resources on an entirely new brand. The sub-brand will fit into a brand system with all the value gathered into one superbrand. Needless to say, this is a job for top management. Such brand systems cannot be left to a product manager. The brand system is depicted in Figure 8.3 and is elaborated in Chapters 9–15.

Brand heaven's above

The first differentiation after the corporate brand is the corporate brand with graduation. Major brands have succeeded in keeping to a very tight brand system and only use letters and numbers for the variations in the brand. This form of adjustment has the huge advantage of concentrating the value in a corporate brand. Audi, with its simple A3, A4 and A6 branding for various models, is a good example.

The next class of branding is the corporate brand with denomination, where the corporate brand has a denominating name added to it i.e. Virgin bride. It will never turn into an independent brand and the brand value is preserved in the corporate brand.

When the need arises for differentiating the sub-brand from the corporate brand by more than mere denomination and you don't want to create an independent brand, you can use a very progressive form of sub-branding – differentiation. With this form of branding you ignore the graphics laws and add new name combinations to the existing brand name. The best example of this, as mentioned above, is the sub-brand Emporio Armani within the corporate brand Giorgio Armani.

When the aim is to develop a new independent brand that also carries some of the market power of the corporate brand, this is called a corporate brand with combined brand. However, you will not achieve a combined brand by printing your corporate brand in ten-point characters at the bottom of the packaging. It must be very clearly connected with the new brand, for example in the way that Kellogg's has done with Special K.

Some companies reach a point in their growth when they have to develop a new independent brand. They can give the newborn brand a good start with an endorsed corporate brand. The case study in Chapter 14 describes Skoda and Volkswagen as an example of the power of endorsing.

Now we are up to the one-product, one-brand class. P&G does it brilliantly. If you can afford it, it is definitely

Figure 8.3 The value-oriented brand system

Corporate brand	Corporate brand with graduation	Corporate brand with denomination	Corporate brand with differentiation	Combined brand	Endorsing brand	One-product, one-brand

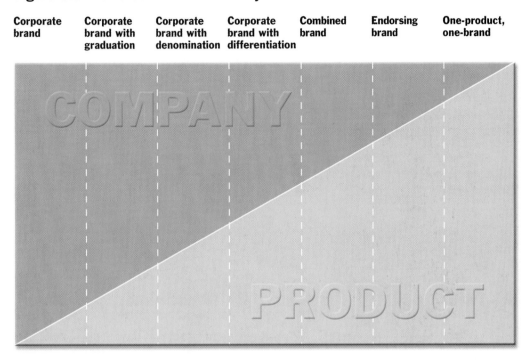

It is necessary to exploit high brand value with a well-defined brand system. Then you can create controlled growth without watering down the brand value.

a possibility. But who can? Not Unilever, which is reducing more than 1000 brands to just 250.

Companies are, belatedly, realizing how important it is to unify the brand. Customers look for clarity and where they fail to find it they will reject the brand. In the coming chapters we will look at some of the world's best brand strategies.

CHAPTER 9

Creating a corporate brand

The desire to achieve more market penetration is one of the main reasons to turn a company into a brand. A single coherent brand allows it to focus resources and punch its way through the noise.

No longer can companies possess many different brands and spend huge amounts of resources in an attempt to win strong market positions for each. The market trend is towards fewer, stronger and more reliable brands that can justify consumers' faith in them.

The issue, however, is how to avoid stagnating as a narrow corporate brand, as a company that merely projects a traditional one-product, one-brand mindset to the marketing of one valuable brand.

Heinz, Heinz and Heinz again

As the case study on the following pages shows, the purest form of corporate branding, placed to the far left in the brand system, is that of the foods giant Heinz.

Heinz product names are generic and span tomato ketchup, baked beans and soups. Whenever marketing people talk about the company as a brand, Heinz is inevitably mentioned. Heinz has chosen to stay at the far left of the brand system as a pure corporate brand. There is no thought of branding with graduation, differentiation or combined branding. Heinz creates growth in new areas via other brands to avoid watering down the value of the Heinz brand. Consequently, Heinz has many different brands selling more than 5,700 different products. Only a few of its products are sold under the Heinz brand.

Heinz broke with the one-product, one-brand strategy. It had tomato ketchup and chicken soup under the same corporate brand and the products were labelled in exactly the same way. Though it actually uses it for more than one product, Heinz keeps its brand narrow.

Major international brands such as Nike, Sony, LEGO, Virgin, Mercedes, Audi, Giorgio Armani, Kellogg's and Bang & Olufsen use the company extensively as a brand and they have, like Heinz, had large growth within new product areas and customer segments. But they have managed to build the new segments closely to the corporate brand with intelligent branding methods, as we shall see shortly.

In broad outline, many of the above-mentioned brands are corporate brands because they keep the branding in-house rather than let it drift off into independent sub-brands. To stress it one more time: there is only one way to a successful company – create one powerful international brand.

There is only one way to a successful company – create one powerful international brand.

In the value economy, every effort has to go into cutting through our noisy, affluent society to reach consumers. And all your effort and vigour must go into one brand that has a clear and sharp direction that is easily communicated to consumers. It is no good becoming a wide-reaching brand like Philips and Nestlé. Nor should you be a brand that is too narrow, otherwise it will be diluted and end up as too many independent brands. Each company must try to become a superbrand itself and then marry that with an effective and appropriate brand system. Superbrands fit the times; they cut through the noise of the value economy.

In future, brands will become so important that every company will have to learn to relate to consumers, investors, employees, and society at large in an intelligent, reliable and illuminating way. Dull mediocrity will be ignored in the value economy, where only the unique will survive. So start nurturing your uniqueness, make it consistent, and make sure that it gets out to your customers. Branding has become a serious matter. It entails far more than a logo or a nice graphic identity.

Dull mediocrity will be ignored in the value economy, where only the unique will survive.

When ketchup is a corporate brand

'If it isn't Heinz, it isn't ketchup...' say the Americans.

If Heinz isn't synonymous with ketchup to you, then you

must be over 130 years old. Heinz itself says that it sets

the standards of quality, convenience and good taste.

Today, Heinz is primarily known for its tomato ketchup. Strange, because it all actually started 130 years ago with horseradish. That makes Heinz one of the first corporations ever to use corporate branding.

Heinz produces many traditionally American products. Its corporate brand strategy ensures that the consumer is never in any doubt that Heinz is behind the products (Figure 9.1).

Figure 9.1 Heinz is behind all its generic products

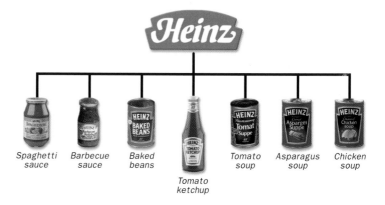

Heinz is behind a wide range of different products, all featuring Heinz as a clear Corporate Brand.

By using Heinz above all the generic names, it ensures that we not only buy ketchup, soup and sauces, what we get is Heinz ketchup, Heinz soup, and Heinz sauces.

The corporate brand strategy

This corporate brand strategy also has the advantage that Heinz can transfer the positive attitude of one product to all other food products. Of course, the reverse situation could also arise, where the profile of the whole corporation is damaged by, for example, bad press received by one product. The management issues also concern how far a brand can be stretched without causing any damage to Heinz, and how Heinz can differentiate into new product areas and customer

Figure 9.2 Heinz Company also covers independent brands

Corporate brand	Corporate brand with graduation	Corporate brand with denomination	Corporate brand with differentiation	Combined brand	Endorsing brand	One-product, one-brand

H.J. Heinz Company

Apart from the Heinz brand, the H.J. Heinz Company covers a number of independent brands.

Ketchup is the value driver for the Heinz brand.

segments while still appearing reliable. Heinz management has understood that the brand can only encompass a certain variety of products. The Heinz brand is largely reserved for foods. Meanwhile, most of the other 5,700 products H.J. Heinz Company produces are independent brands (see Figure 9.2). Could Heinz produce different products, such as canned dog food? It tried, though only in the UK. The question is whether Heinz's strong value position can cover both people and people's best friend. As old Heinz used to say: 'Quality is to a product what character is to a man.'

Facts

In 1869, Henry J. Heinz and his neighbour, L. Clarence Noble formed Heinz & Noble to make food products. The family residence in Pittsburgh served as a factory and the first product line was the family's home-grown horseradish. Heinz placed great importance on the quality of the products and used glass jars so that people could see that the purity and quality of the product were up to standard. In 1876 he added the commodity today synonymous with Heinz to his product portfolio, ketchup. Heinz's nose for business and for marketing soon made the new company successful. He invented the trademark with the pickle and the slogan '57 varieties', still the Heinz trademark.

An aggressive corporate brand system

If you have built a powerful corporate brand value, you try to maximize the total value of your company by using the brand as a relevant endorsement for other companies you acquire.

This means that even if you no longer use the brand directly you can still use its value indirectly – especially if there is a high value that can be transferred onto a less attractive acquisition. The Spanish carmaker Seat and the Czech Skoda, which have been provided with a high endorsement value by Germany's Volkswagen, are good examples.

The name of the game is building a valuable corporate brand and then deploying an aggressive corporate brand system to optimize its value.

Can consumers remember your brand?

Many companies think they have a corporate brand strategy because they promote a product name and put their own at the bottom of the packaging. All this means is that the product name will be what customers remember. Soon this sub-brand will become an independent brand, probably as a complete surprise to the organization. Yet this may cost the company in the long run, simply because everyone in the company works as if the sub-brand is the corporate brand. But as the product inevitably declines and disappears, unless some of its brand value has been moved into the corporate brand, the company risks losing it along with the dying product.

Branding can take another direction if the product name evolves into a brand and builds up an independent position in the market. It then becomes possible to place other product launches under this new brand position. This works well if you plan to extend your company by letting product names win brand status. However, it will only work if several brands share marketing investment

Spain's Seat and the Czech Skoda have both been provided with high endorsement value by Germany's Volkswagen.

and the sales and distribution system. In the early days of a company's life cycle, when it is concerned only with its home market, this is not a major challenge. It doesn't become critical until the company starts to be involved with the international market. Many sizeable international companies run into trouble because what they perceive as a corporate brand neither makes sense nor has value to present or potential customers.

As they grow they turn several product names into brands without realizing it. This poses a problem as the competition parameter moves from a product focus to a brand focus. The physical product plays a less and less prominent part in the process of consumer choice. The competition is about brands and their positions in the market. So every brand must have a lot of value accumulated in it. This makes it harder to support a number of brands. Consequently, the company is left with a muddle of a corporate brand and several smaller brands.

The situation becomes even more difficult when competitors gets their branding under control and suddenly appear as reliable and serious producers.

At some point, a company in this situation must make a choice. Should it invest in all its brands or should it group them under one powerful corporate brand? The simplest solution is to deploy a progressive branding system. This means thinking in terms of a corporate brand with graduation, differentiation, perhaps even combined branding. But most crucially, the company must be aware of which positions it owns, in which brands, and how.

The issue of the corporate brand must be debated at top management level.

The issue of the corporate brand must be debated at top management level. Senior management must be aware of the signals the company gives out. As a minimum, they must ensure consumers are in no doubt about what the corporate brand stands for. Too many companies do not realize they have been building one, two or three different brands without deploying anything even resembling a strategy. Top management have to get involved in the detail, such as the size of the logos in ads and on the packaging. Logo sizes and their positions are not insignificant. Most organizations have mid-level managers who are not beyond building their own little brands to satisfy their egos. Management must put an end to such sub-optimization.

Corporate branding – a strategic choice

In most major companies the product is the most valuable asset. A product will have given them their raison d'être. With time, the product becomes a brand and the brand holds together those values that turn into a position, in other words what the company owns in the minds of consumers. That's the best-case scenario. But companies will often aim for growth within a product mindset and overlook the possibilities of developing the brand – and the company – on the basis of the value and the position that the brand owns with consumers. Meanwhile, the market slips, not in the sense that the product has not kept up but that the market offers the same product wrapped in a different and more attractive market position.

TINE – corporate brands and their names

The names used by major international corporations are important. Yet they may not help achieve the brands and position desired. A 40-year-old company name should not be sacred, even if it is loaded with high value and high awareness. Change the name if that makes it more appropriate and clear.

As the case study on TINE shows, it is possible to change a whole company. TINE began by selling generic dairy products under the name Norwegian Dairies, which appeared on the packaging more or less as an endorser, rather far to the right in the brand system. By developing the

Norwegian Dairies has united the name TINE with the corporate brand and thereby moved the knowledge from the old brand. Norwegian Dairies has gone from being an anonymous dealer to representing a clear corporate brand.

ARLA FOODS

Arla uses the desired position as a company name. Arla means 'early morning' in Swedish.

TINE brand as a corporate brand the Norwegians managed to transform a relatively anonymous company into a dynamic food corporation named TINE – a clear corporate brand. At the same time, the brand was systematized. Core product areas such as milk and yogurt would carry the corporate brand. TINE's sub-brands, such as Jarlsberg cheese, would be maintained as independent brands but joined to the corporate brand TINE in endorsed branding.

The most important market position for milk to own is the word 'morning', as this is when most of it is consumed. The Swedish dairy Arla, which used to be called 'The Dairy Central', knew this and acted accordingly. The word Arla comes from 'arla morgon', Swedish for 'early morning'.Using the word Arla is a good way of achieving a stance close to the main position. It is also important that the name suits the tonality of the product group, that the food names 'taste good'.

While Arla used the position it wanted to own as a name, another way is to find a neutral brand name that you then load with the values, positions and products you want. However this sounds a lot easier than it actually is. In reality, most names affect consumers in some way, depending on their cultural and geographic background. As soon as you begin to incorporate colours and symbols, it becomes even more complicated to develop the ideal brand name and logo. The point is that it should appeal to consumers wherever it is used and should contribute to capturing a market position.

TINE – a successful corporate brand

TINE is Norway's largest dairy, equivalent to the Swedish-Danish Arla, producing a wide range of brands. In 1992 the company's name was changed from Norwegian Dairies.

A lack of clear and visible identity was the problem Norwegian Dairies hoped to overcome when it established TINE as the corporate brand for all its products and introduced a unifying logo. Later, in 1997, the company changed its name by incorporating TINE to become TINE Norwegian Dairies. The change has contributed to a powerful and clear communication of the company and has given it an obvious position. The company has moved from making generic products under a more or less anonymous name to a strong brand – TINE has become one of Norway's strongest brands and tops most polls of profile and brand power.

Historical roots and natural renewal

The change was to a great extent the outcome of new thinking about the company. Until then, many products had been carrying generic denominations; now focus was placed on branding. TINE was to be established as a corporate brand.

In Norwegian, 'tine' is a traditional food storage box, which for generations has also been used for dairies. By adopting this word, the company stresses its historical roots. Mated with nostalgia and authenticity in the brand name and logo, it corresponds well to the pure and natural quality of dairy products.

The development from 'Norske Meierier' to the brand TINE.

Figure 9.3 From Norske Meierier to TINE

Corporate brand	Corporate brand with graduation	Corporate brand with denomination	Corporate brand with differentiation	Combined brand	Endorsing brand	One-product, one-brand

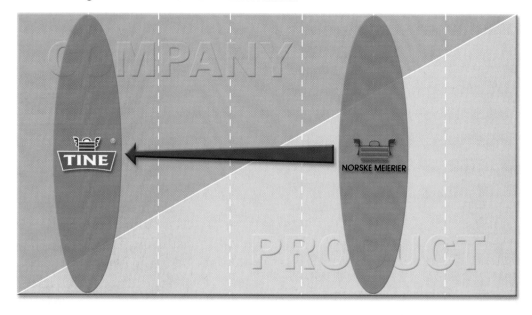

In 1992, Norske Meierier established a corporate brand, TINE, for all its products. It became one of Norway's most powerful brands.

There is even something feminine about the brand, since TINE is also a girl's name. The name was selected from several that scored just as well on values. TINE won because it is easy to pronounce internationally. It is short and can be put in quite big print on packaging – considerably larger than was possible with 'Norske Meierier' (Figure 9.3).

The change from Norske Meierier to TINE had a great impact. The new logo, new designs for packaging and the company's transport and TV ads were all introduced at the same time.

TINE is always the brand

The new branding strategy gathers the products under one unifying, powerful corporate brand, TINE. More than 200 products with generic denominations are gathered under the brand as well as over 20 independent sub-brands endorsed by TINE (Figure 9.4). The product portfolio is controlled by a well-structured and well-defined set of values with a clear value position for TINE and for the individual sub-brands. On large bulk products with generic denominations the company aims for differentiation by incorporating TINE in the name – for example, TINE butter and TINE milk. On generic products, TINE is emphasized as a family name. The various sub-brands have their own conceptual value, which supplements the TINE set of values.

Figure 9.4 The TINE corporate brand covers different dairy products

Corporate brand	Corporate brand with graduation	Corporate brand with denomination	Corporate brand with differentiation	Combined brand	Endorsing brand	One-product, one-brand

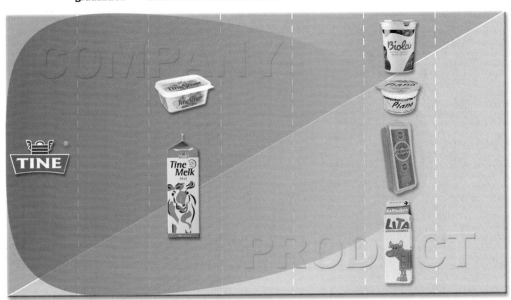

TINE has gathered most of its products under one powerful corporate brand, although a few strong, individual brands have maintained their own identity.

Jarlsberg cheese was launched at the beginning of the 1970s – a long time before TINE was established – and is consequently independently marketed in some export markets.

Independent Jarlsberg

TINE also possesses strong individual brands with a history, which it would be a mistake not to maintain. Jarlsberg cheese has, for example, been promoted as a powerful brand since the beginning of the 1970s – a long time before TINE was established – and is independently marketed in some export markets.

An example of the new strategy – on the left is generic milk with no branding (before 1992); in the middle is milk with a generic denomination and logo (as it was launched in 1992); to the right is the current Tine milk with a generic branding.

Facts

The basis of Norway's dairies was created during the 19th century by Swiss experts. As knowledge increased, new dairies were founded in larger farms and villages. In 1856 the first co-operative dairy owned by 40 farmers was established in Rausjødalen in Tolga. Apart from milk, their first products were Swiss and Edam cheese. However, the product portfolio was extended and technological developments towards the end of the century, such as cooling systems and extraction of cream, had a great impact on production.

The growth of dairies led to a demand for more co-operation and a number of local dairy associations were formed during the 1880s. The forerunner of Norske Meierier was established in 1928 as an attempt to boost exports of Norwegian dairy products. The company was called Norske Meieriers eksportforlag but changed its name in 1942 to Norske Meieriers salgscentral, and again, in 1984, to Norske Meierier. This lasted until 1992, when TINE was established as the corporate brand for all products. Later, in 1997, TINE was incorporated into the company name – TINE Norske Meierier.

Corporate branding increases both value and risk

Corporate branding is a very efficient form of branding. If you can integrate the external communication of the brand, you capture the value and position in one major, progressive force. This is not problem-free, however, because higher value and involvement in the brand by consumers means that they have more expectations of it. This is particularly true of the core brand values, where there will be an expectation of reliability and consistency. That is why corporate brands are more vulnerable; it is the entire brand and its value that comes under fire if it fails in any way.

The core values of The Body Shop are ethics and morals. But what happens if it cannot live up to them?

The core values of Mercedes are prestige, immaculate quality and safety. Rather unfortunate then, when the new Mercedes A-class fails a simple car test.

The core values of Mercedes are prestige, immaculate quality and safety. Rather unfortunate then, when the new Mercedes A-class fails a simple car test. Nike's core value is 'winning' – not very fortunate when the Brazilian national team keeps getting beaten or the Danish women's handball team fails to win the world championships.

LEGO's core value is educational toys – not very good if the press should suddenly find out that some of them present a health risk to children.

All these scenarios have, to a greater or lesser extent, happened to the companies mentioned. Hence the importance of knowing exactly what it takes to build and protect corporate values, realizing the risks you take by moving into a new product area with your brand, and understanding what the costs may be.

When Mercedes came down to earth

Mercedes ventured into unknown territory with the launch of a small luxury car. When the A-class car failed a test in Sweden, in November 1997, it became world news.

This is how vulnerable a brand can be when its core position values are hit. This is how strongly the world reacts if a brand religion, such as Mercedes, fails.

Mercedes never dreamed that a problem with the A-class car could cause such damage to its overall brand value. All of a sudden, Mercedes came down to earth. The accident raised doubts over general quality and safety in all its products. For some time yet, a little remnant of doubt will remain in consumers' minds. Whenever you see a Mercedes, your subconscious will remind you that one day you had a doubt.

One of the main reasons why it did not go totally wrong for Mercedes was that, after a fumbled beginning, the company handled the affair very professionally. It was quick to come up with a credible solution to the problem. Some would say that it came out of the whole affair stronger than before. Mercedes is a powerful brand that has built its value over many years. It has loyal customers and the company invests heavily in the expansion of the brand. These things came to its aid and were a positive strength in solving the problem.

Powerful brands have strong reserves. Rather than using risk as an excuse for creating several brands to diversify it, you should try to identify those areas where things could go wrong – and those areas where they must not go wrong. In other words, be aware of what is most crucial for the credibility of the brand and how to ensure that you can always live up to it.

Powerful brands have strong reserves.

Uncover the pitfalls

One of the main reasons why Mercedes overcame its problems was that it had used corporate branding to build up all the positive elements, products, values and experiences into a Mercedes superbrand. A lesser brand with no such history would have been crushed.

LEGO, just like Mercedes, ran into problems with one of its products. In the same way as Mercedes, LEGO had the strength to combat the problem. An infant's rattle had a loose part that could come off and present a danger to children, who could swallow it and suffocate. LEGO reacted immediately and pulled the product from the market. The cost was enormous, but by minimizing the negative press LEGO saved its corporate brand from irreparable damage.

One day, the winning brand – Nike – could wake up to discover that all its stars are no longer winning. It can only safeguard against this by having contracts with as many of the sports people who stand chances of winning as possible.

Common to all these examples is that they illustrate the importance of uncovering the pitfalls of the core value positions of the brand.

The best defence is to strengthen the brand by building as much content and credibility into it as possible.

The best defence is to strengthen the brand by building as much content and credibility into it as possible. When trouble arises, the company must react straight away. All powerful brands should always be on red alert.

One day you use the media to build your brand; the next day the media could present a major threat to it. Powerful brands are under constant surveillance by the press. Success is a good story, failure even better.

CHAPTER 10

Corporate brand with graduation

Once you have established a powerful corporate brand, how do you communicate different products, their target customers and their price levels? Especially, how can you differentiate them without moving too far away from the corporate brand? The answer lies not with clever marketing campaigns but with enlightened management.

First, different products have to have different names. But you must get this right from the beginning. If a product name becomes too powerful it can easily take over the branding, leaving you with two brands sharing one market investment.

The advantage is that, providing you stick to the rules, all value goes into the corporate brand.

The answer is to use graduation under the same corporate brand. The advantage is that, providing you stick to the rules – the graduation must be as neutral as possible; never use independent names for the graduation – all value goes into the corporate brand. Car manufacturers frequently use graduation in their branding.

For example, the numbers in BMW's branding system indicate both the sizes of the cars and the difference in the segments. Within each model – the 300 series, for example – BMW has a graduation system expressed in the 316, 320 and 325 numbering, which indicates engine sizes. By adding a letter to the number, 'i', it is clear that the 320i is a two-litre electronic injection model in the 300 series. Assigning the 300 number to the series also indicates that these are smaller and cheaper cars than the 500 and 700 series.

Audi also deploys a graduation system. Interestingly, it went from a numbering system similar to BMW's to an even more flexible one. Audi's two main models used to be denominated Audi 80 and Audi 100. Today, a greater number of models are simply labelled Audi A2, Audi A3, Audi A4, Audi A6 and Audi A8. The number is an indication of the size of the car (and engine) and the letter says something about the model. This system allows Audi to enlarge or reduce its range very easily or even come up with an entirely new range or a completely new design, perhaps called B1, B2, and so on.

Corporate brand with graduation is an incredibly efficient form of branding. You do not have to invent new sub-brands that will split the brand in two. By using numbers and letters you achieve a clear graduation of sizes and segments and the entire brand value goes into building the corporate brand.

However, there is a limit to how far you can stretch your label. Your brand owns a value position. In the case of BMW, this is high-quality cars in the high-price range, and there will be a natural limit to how far it could shrink its cars and still stick a BMW logo on the bonnet.

Cars are subject to natural limits: small cars at cheap prices, middle range or top of the range at high prices. You do not cross these limits unpunished. A good example of a brand that thought it could do so is Toyota. The Japanese wanted to challenge Mercedes and BMW. But how can a brand that stands for value for money in family cars in the middle and low-price segments do so? To guard its 'sensible' brand value, Toyota created an entirely new brand – Lexus.

What would have happened if it had attempted to move upwards with the Toyota brand? Normally, this is considered to be almost impossible. It is always easier to move down from a top position than up from a low one. But that begs a question: what happens if you appear to be undermining your top-of-the-range position?

One car manufacturer that seemed to risk doing exactly that was Mercedes when it launched its A-class model into the small car segment.

Corporate brand with graduation is an incredibly efficient form of branding. You do not have to invent new sub-brands that will split the brand in two.

The prerequisite for making such a move was an overhaul of the Mercedes corporate brand system. This led to a restructuring that divided Mercedes cars into new classes. The larger cars were denominated S-class, followed by the class denominations E and C, with the new, smaller car becoming the A-class. In this way, Mercedes can continue its numbering system for engine sizes and so on.

In many companies, the new A-class would have been given an independent name and launched as a sub-brand, which, with time, would have ended up as a new brand. Mercedes chose to keep the value in the brand. However, in doing so it ran a great risk because, as described later in this chapter, things went wrong.

But Mercedes wants to go further and expand its brand even more. It has launched a very high-price pedal bicycle that lives up to its value position. This extended graduation helps maintain the value of the Mercedes brand.

Typically, corporate brand with graduation is suitable for high-price consumer durables such as cars. It also works well in business-to-business companies where customers mainly 'buy' the company and what it stands for.

One of the great brands of the 1980s, Levi's, used corporate brand with graduation as its dominant form of branding and won a strong market position within a narrow market segment. Towards the end of the 20th century, this narrow focus became a major problem for Levi's. If it was to keep up with market developments, it had to expand. But this posed a real dilemma. Every time it moved away from its corporate brand it would weaken it.

The challenge for Levi's lay in developing a progressive branding system. Without that it could not differentiate itself as strongly as the market demanded. Yet it still had to hang on to its fundamental values. Now, as described in Chapter 2 and Figure 2.8, Levi's is attempting to develop sub-brands linked to its main brand.

Branding with numbers and letters

A car with four rings on the grill is credited with special values. Audi has built up these values over a century and they are expressed in the slogan 'Vorsprung durch Technik'.

Audi's branding strategy is a graduation strategy where each model class is signified by a letter and a number. The number indicates the model size and the letter the model type (Figure 10.1). So far, only an A has been used as a model denomination but the system opens up the possibility of introducing new designs. In addition, the system gives the opportunity for further

Figure 10.1 Audi's branding strategy has given it access to more segments

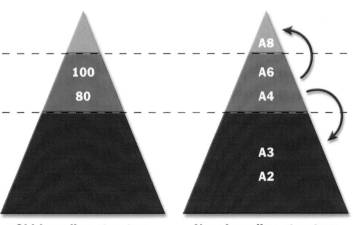

Old branding structure   New branding structure

The Audi 80 and 100 models were part of the old branding structure. In the new branding system, Audi has opened up the possibility of expanding into other segments and model classes yet retained control of the value of the corporate brand.

Figure 10.2 Audi's graduated car model programme

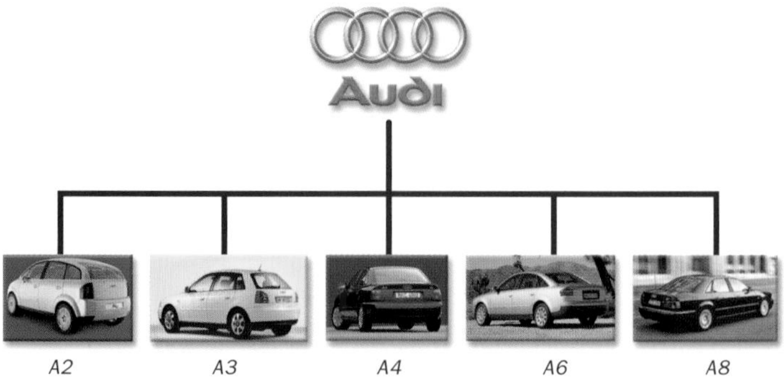

Audi's car models cover different product lines with graduation.

graduation according to engine size and specification for each class (Figure 10.2). This form of branding concentrates the value in the Audi corporate brand (Figure 10.3). The company does not have to invest resources unnecessarily in building independent brands. Of course, Audi's branding strategy calls

Figure 10.3 Audi in the brand system

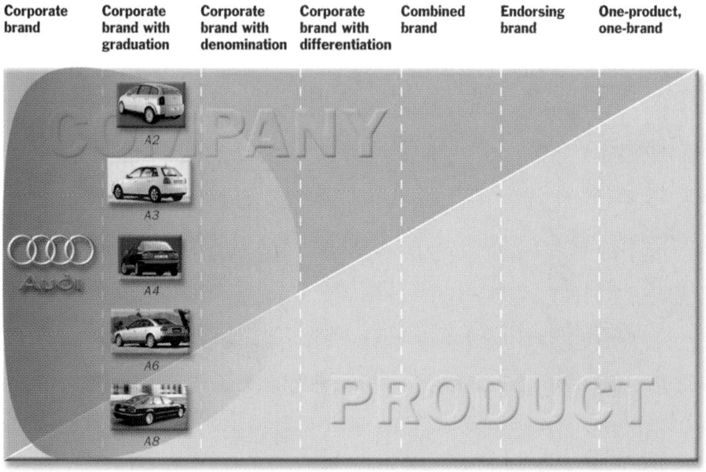

Audi deploys a corporate brand with graduation strategy, maintaining the value in the corporate brand.

for a marked and clear accumulation of value in its corporate brand that can be dispersed into all the model classes.

Until 1995 the Audi 80 and the Audi 100 were the company's only models. They were replaced by the A4 and the A6. Now the A3 has been introduced as a compact car, the A2 as a small car, and the A8 as a luxury limousine.

Audi is capable of moving up and down in segments with ease thanks to its clear value position. Inside Audi the belief is that whether you get into an A8 or an A2, the positive ambience must be the same. Audi's sharp value position makes this possible.

The Audi A4 replaced the classic Audi 80 above.

The Audi 100 above was replaced by the Audi A6.

Facts

August Horch registered Audi Automobilwerke GmbH Zwickau as a company in 1910. However, the four rings did not turn up as a symbol until later – June 29, 1932 – when Audi merged with Horch, DKW and Wanderer to form Auto Union AG. From the very start technology was the foundation of the company. As Horch said back in 1908: 'Technology should enrich the lives of individuals.' Since the beginning, Audi has offered both private cars and racing cars. In 1969, after having merged NSU into the corporation, it added luxury cars. This was when 'Vorsprung durch Technik' was first articulated.

The Mercedes value position – a study in stardom

Mercedes-Benz

To most people, a Mercedes is an unattainable object. But since the introduction of the A-class, the dream has come a little closer to reality. The A-class is the latest addition to a branding strategy begun in 1993.

Mercedes has a graduation strategy that divides its model classes according to a letter system. This ended a previous graduation where models were denominated according to an impenetrable number system. For example, the C-class used to be the series 202 and the E-class the series 124.

The new model classes range from the A-class, a small car, through the slightly larger C-class, the even larger E-class, to the S-class, which is the largest and most expensive car (Figure 10.4). In addition, off-road cars are gathered in the M-class and in the classic G-class. There is also a V-class (vans) as well as a number of special cars, such as the Mercedes SLK.

The old series, W123 above, was replaced by the E-class.

Using this branding strategy, Mercedes can transfer the value accumulated in the main brand to each of the model classes. Using a letter system means there is no danger of, for example, the E-class turning into an independent brand. You do not buy an E-class, you buy a Mercedes.

While the value is maintained in the main brand, Mercedes can still use the strategy for expansion, because it has built up a clear position. Finally, as with Audi, this strategy allows

The 190 above was replaced by the C-class.

Figure 10.4 A selection of Mercedes car models

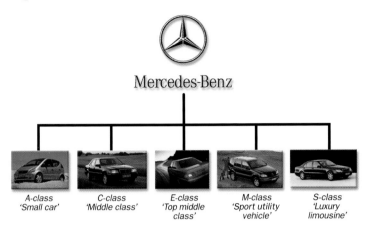

| A-class
'Small car' | C-class
'Middle class' | E-class
'Top middle
class' | M-class
'Sport utility
vehicle' | S-class
'Luxury
limousine' |

Mercedes covers a number of model classes, all with denominations that don't drain value out of the corporate brand.

further graduation according to engine size and specification within each class.

This branding strategy is the outcome of a new perception of the market by Mercedes. Previously, it divided the market hierarchically and limited itself to serving the absolute top segment. Today, it sees the market as consisting of a series of smaller sub-markets, each representing a particular demand – 'off-road' cars, for example. Mercedes' strategy is to offer a car in the top range of each of these sub-markets (Figure 10.5).

This strategy divides Mercedes models along market segments and makes it easier to maintain values in each class. In doing so Mercedes has expanded its brand so that even its absolute top-of-the-range model may provoke some interest in other sub-segments.

Of course, such a branding strategy requires that there is value in the main brand and Mercedes has accumulated this value over more than 100 years. Mercedes' value position always has been, and still is, luxurious, exclusive and innovative vehicles of high quality. And since this position has been

Figure 10.5 Mercedes in the brand system

Mercedes deploys a corporate brand with graduation strategy.

Mercedes' silver arrow has been a great value accumulator, just like Formula 1 is today.

consistent, it possesses credibility. Building this value has been supported by Mercedes' involvement in motor sport, which since the beginning of the 20th century (with only a few exceptions) has run alongside the production of exclusive quality cars. In motor sport, Mercedes is best known for the 'silver arrows' racing cars of the 1930s and the silver colour has since become synonymous with Mercedes. In fact it was a coincidence. At the first weigh-in, the Mercedes car was too heavy and in an attempt to reduce weight, the paint was stripped off, revealing the pure metal. Silver has since moved into other products and today around 35 per cent of all Mercedes passenger cars are silver coloured.

When luck runs out

The Mercedes A-class was introduced in 1997 as the ultimate small car aimed at the top of the small car segment. However, it was a risk for Mercedes since it had always been synonymous with large cars, high prices, top quality, comfort and so on. Of course, Mercedes was aware of this problem, and the A-class was not introduced until it could live up to the standard of the other models in terms of quality.

Unfortunately for Mercedes, the car turned over during a test drive in Sweden with a journalist on board. It is debatable whether the car was being pressed into situations that a normal user would never get into, but still, the formerly invincible and unsurpassed Mercedes had failed. The accident caused damage to the entire Mercedes corporate brand and the general quality of all models was called into question.

It took a while for the company to realize the extent of the damage to its reputation. At first it was considered a minor problem that would soon be over. This didn't happen and when Mercedes recognized that it reacted quickly and openly. Less than a week after the accident, it presented a credible solution to the problem at a press conference.

It is impossible to say how much damage this incident caused to Mercedes. It could be argued that the company came out of the whole affair stronger than before. However, the brand

Figure 10.6 The expansion of the Mercedes brand

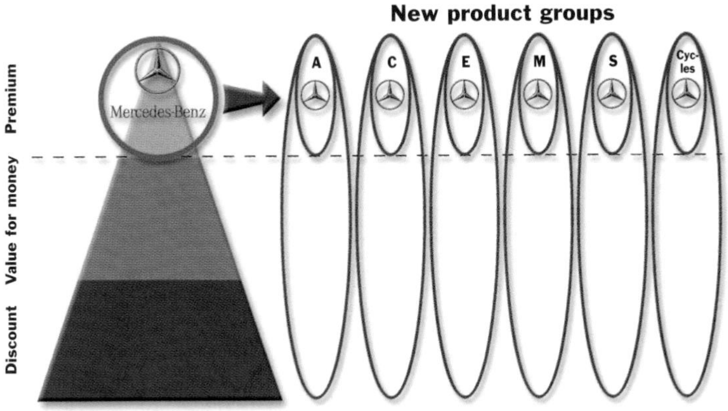

The Mercedes branding system enables the company to expand into many customer segments with a series of different model classes. Recently, the corporation has begun producing bicycles.

has undoubtedly suffered a little, though not irreparably – because of the value built into the Mercedes brand over the long term it could absorb the accident (See Figure 10.6).

Inside Mercedes there was talk that the episode, which demonstrated that the company wasn't infallible, actually benefited the brand. First of all because sales of the A-class had been going as expected and, also, because a reputation for infallibility is both unrealistic and possibly even damaging. By showing a bit of human fallibility, some prejudice is overcome and the general attitude to the brand improved.

Facts

Mercedes is the German division of DaimlerChrysler. In 1883, Karl Benz founded Benz & Co in Mannheim, Germany. The same year, Gottlieb Daimler patented two inventions that formed the basis of the first combustion engine. The two corporations merged in 1926 and formed Daimler-Benz AG. Since then, the corporation has produced millions of Mercedes cars, trucks and buses.

Blue jeans USA

Levi-Strauss Company produces the only piece of
clothing invented during the 19th century that is still
used today – denim jeans. Levi's 501 jeans have been
pronounced the most important fashion accessory of
the 20th century by Time magazine.

From products to segments

Levi's, which is part of the Levi-Strauss Company, uses a branding strategy with denomination, where the models are given generic names according to product line. Under each model line, each product is also given a number.

The number system is derived from the way jeans are produced – a hangover from old times. Years of value accumulation have made the brand global and protected Levi's jeans from competitors. But even a 130-year-old success story doesn't go on for ever and at the beginning of the new millennium Levi's had to differentiate its brand into sub-segments with sub-brands linked to the corporate brand.

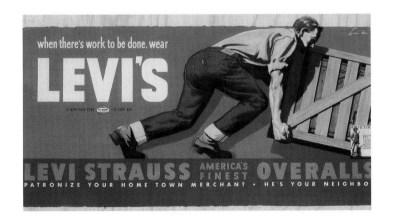

From the beginning, Levi's has provided the original work clothes.

Figure 10.7 Levi's branding system

In its new branding system, Levi's has defined its sub-brands very carefully. Sub-brands borrow their value from Levi's and in return make Levi's appear as a dynamic, fashion brand.

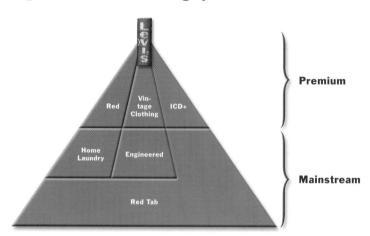

This was a shift from the traditional product view to a brand-oriented organization. The product areas into which this strategy has carried Levi's are set out in Figure 10.7. As this shows, the product lines Red and Vintage Clothing also appear in versions with broader appeal called Home Laundry and Engineered. Red is an attempt to create a fashion denim sub-brand.

Each Levi's product is given a number – 501, 507, etc – which has become a sort of Levi's trademark (Figure 10.8). But the number system, which is effectively a 100-year-old graduation

Figure 10.8 An example of the old number system

Levi's old branding system with numbers covered several series.

Figure 10.9 The redefinition of the Levi's brand

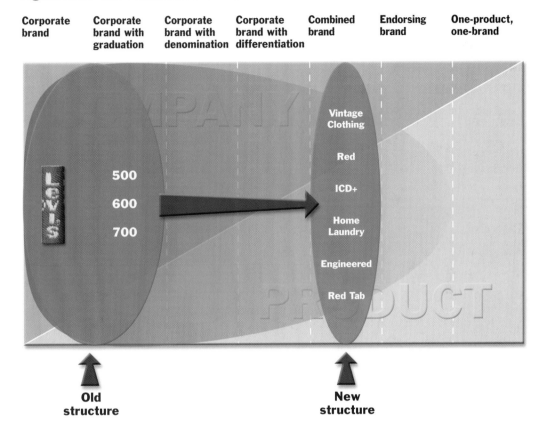

Corporate brand	Corporate brand with graduation	Corporate brand with denomination	Corporate brand with differentiation	Combined brand	Endorsing brand	One-product, one-brand

Apart from the traditional number series, Levi's covers a number of brands that have grown up following the changes to its branding strategy. But new sub-brands are still linked to the corporate brand.

strategy, has now been changed to branding by product lines linked to the Levi's corporate brand (Figure 10.9).

Using a denomination within the combined brand strategy, Levi's can name the products without interfering with its corporate brand. And when the sub-brands have generic names, their value is accumulated in the corporate brand. This differentiated sub-brand strategy, which is effectively combined branding, ensures Levi's will not stagnate in its old 'original cowboy jeans' situation. The combined sub-brand strategy makes it easier for Levi's to operate within many different and fast-moving segments and to maintain the Levi's brand dynamism and vitality.

The classic waist label

from Levi's.

Facts

In 1847, German-born Levi Strauss sailed to New York along with his mother and two sisters to join his two half-brothers in their manufacturing business.

He went on to San Francisco and started his own business in 1853. However, jeans were not part of the business until 20 years later when Jacob Davis, a tailor, noticed how quickly gold-diggers' trousers became worn out. Davis came up with the idea of riveted trousers – the first jeans – and asked Levi to join him in their production.

The two men began to produce trousers made of brown cotton canvas and the strong French cloth, denime, though Levi's denim came from an American mill. Denim can be made in any colour but Levi and Jacob chose a blue indigo dye since blue denim was the traditional fabric for work clothes. Today, it is still the signature colour of jeans. At first the jeans were produced for gold-diggers but they were soon taken up by other working people and, later on, the population generally. During the middle of the 20th century jeans became a fashion item, especially among young people, and today almost everyone owns at least one pair of jeans.

CHAPTER 11

Corporate brand with generic names

Product ranges can also be differentiated using generic names. An alternative to the graduation model in Chapter 10, this form of branding is an adaptation that uses different names for sub-brands.

Corporate branding with names is a good and efficient form of branding but it is not universally applicable. When talking of using different names, the big question is how far your brand can be stretched.

The airline group SAS's sub-branding of SAS Cargo is a good example of corporate branding with names. Its corporate brand is SAS and its business is air transport. But apart from passenger traffic, SAS also carries cargo. By adding the word 'Cargo', SAS has provided this subsidiary with a clear description of its business. Cargo does not interfere with the corporate brand or with travellers. Cargo is a generic denomination for freight and SAS does not have to create a sub-brand for its cargo operations and can spend the money building its corporate brand.

No waste – only strength

SAS can use the strength of its corporate brand – SAS – to support its cargo business and also channel the value from SAS Cargo into the SAS brand. There is no confusion or waste but there is an increase in strength.

A prerequisite for corporate branding using different names is that you find a generic name for the area you wish to brand separately. The better the name explains the generic nature of the business, the less chance there is that an independent sub-brand will build up around the name.

SAS has used branding with names widely – SAS Euroclass, SAS Cargo, SAS Eurobonus and SAS Pleasure.

A prerequisite for corporate branding using different names is that you find a generic name for the area you wish to brand separately. The reason that SAS uses such a tight branding system, which places the different sub-brands close to the corporate brand, is that at one time it did have a strong sub-brand that ran off with almost all SAS's brand value.

The sub-brand was Jackpot, a discounted ticket operation. Through intense marketing efforts, the Jackpot sub-brand became so powerful in itself that it hollowed out the SAS corporate brand, making SAS equivalent to cheap travel despite the airline's dependence on full-price business travel. In a 1998 restructuring, SAS abandoned Jackpot and began to use different brand names to keep the corporate brand together.

B&O avoids sub-brands

Bang & Olufsen is an even purer example of using names. More than any other international corporation, it has constructed all its brand value around the corporate brand. B&O has avoided creating sub-brands by using graduation and names to describe its product areas (see Figure 11.1).

Televisions are named BeoVision, hi-fis are called BeoSound followed by either numbers – BeoSound 9000 – or words – BeoSound Overture, while hi-fi speakers are called BeoLab 1, BeoLab 4000, BeoLab 6000 and BeoLab 8000. Under BeoCom B&O has moved into telephones; An answerphone has been named BeoTalk. The latest addition is a software product to link a hi-fi to a computer called BeoLink Office. B&O uses numbers to gradate the products according to their sizes, though these are not quite as descriptive as most car numbering systems.

Branding must be controlled

B&O is a prime example of how using names can build up a long-lasting branding system that can span electronics products ranging from TVs to phones. This is possible only if you control the value in your brand very tightly and if all product areas can live up to that value. However, from a branding point of view, problems can arise if there is no central control over the brand. For example, telephones must concentrate on design as much as on function since the main value in B&O is design. Launching new phones that do not fit in with the overall brand values could cause damage to the corporate brand.

Interestingly, B&O moved a part of telephone development and design into its main concept development department, using the people who normally create the external corporate brand. As a result, design wise the phones live up to the company's core brand values. They also fit perfectly with the overall communication concept 'a life less ordinary'.

Figure 11.1 Bang & Olufsen's branding structure using names

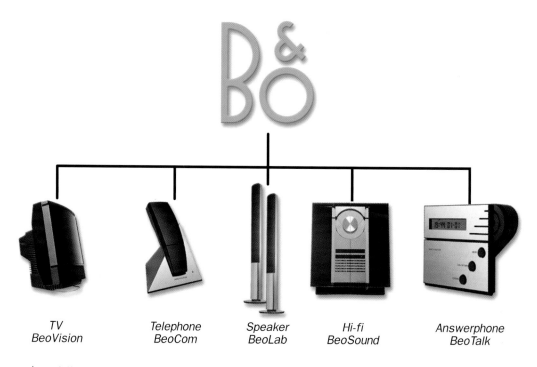

| TV | Telephone | Speaker | Hi-fi | Answerphone |
| BeoVision | BeoCom | BeoLab | BeoSound | BeoTalk |

B&O's different product lines all have names in combination with the corporate name.

Be warned, though, that it is difficult to carry through such a tight branding with names as B&O has done – the larger and more differentiated a company becomes, the more each organization will want to stand out.

In a company such as B&O, producing exciting and innovative products, product developers and designers occasionally believe that the new product they have created is so revolutionary that it deserves its own special sub-brand. At B&O, it is said that former managing director Anders Knutsen often had to intervene personally to prevent such attempts to create sub-brands.

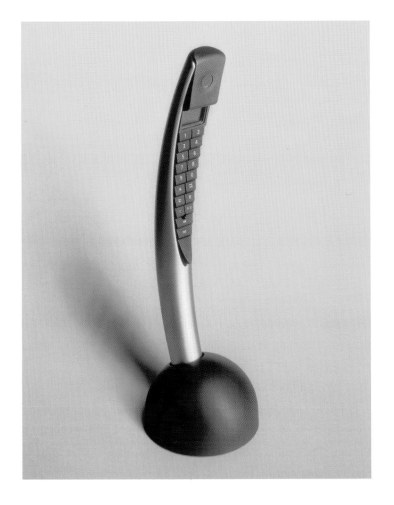

B&O moved a part of telephone development and design into its main concept development department, using the people who normally create the external corporate brand. The phones fit perfectly with the communication concept, 'a life less ordinary'.

SAS regains control over its brand

There was a time when SAS had a very positive image with travellers. During the 1980s the airline's image was so strong that the company was often perceived to be doing better than it actually was.

However, this situation reversed during the 1990s and in an effort to regain its lost image, SAS began attempting to add more value to its brand. It abandoned its earlier branding strategy and replaced it with a branding strategy using names.

Should the sub-brands be in charge?

SAS was involved in a number of services and business areas, each of which was branded independently. The effect was that sub-brands were swamping the corporate brand, moving SAS to the right of the brand system (Figure 11.2).

No doubt that is why SAS Jackpot no longer exists, even though customers still try to book Jackpot tickets. This pulled the corporate brand value down to its level – low-price tickets. This had a negative impact on the corporate brand position as a quality, high-status company.

The marketing of the Jackpot sub-brand was very efficient, and for a while dominated SAS's marketing effort. Because SAS itself was not clear which brand position it wanted, moving from being 'The businessman's airline' to Jackpot in just a few years made the corporate brand very vulnerable.

SAS Jackpot

SAS's now-abandoned sub-brand Jackpot became so strong it took over the entire brand and drained it.

Figure 11.2 SAS's old branding system

Corporate brand	Corporate brand with graduation	Corporate brand with denomination	Corporate brand with differentiation	Combined brand	Endorsing brand	One-product, one-brand

SAS used to be the relatively anonymous owner of various sub-brands, of which Jackpot in particular had a strong independent identity.

Something had to be done – but what?

At that time, SAS was conscious that its position as a market leader in Scandinavia would have to be maintained and reinforced.

In 1998 it decided to concentrate the branding and make the corporate brand communicate the trademark – SAS – and those values that SAS wanted to be known for. It is easier and cheaper to 'speak with one voice' and to market just one brand. SAS can be the owner and operator of everything and the value can be transferred to the individual sub-brands without spending money on building up independent brands.

Figure 11.3 SAS's new branding system

Corporate brand	Corporate brand with graduation	Corporate brand with denomination	Corporate brand with differentiation	Combined brand	Endorsing brand	One-product, one-brand

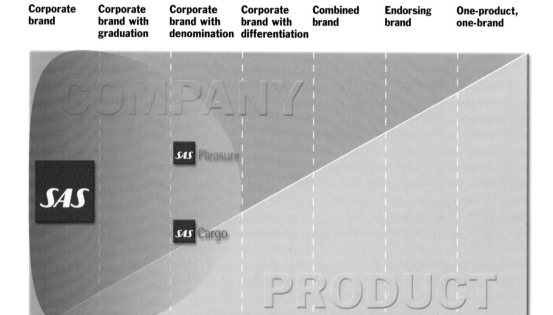

SAS's new branding system has regained control over the brand and closed the sub-brand Jackpot. Now, SAS is the clear consignor of the sub-brands, which have been given denominations to avoid them stealing value from the corporate brand.

By ending the threat of sub-brands once again diluting the corporate brand, SAS has moved towards the left in the brand system (Figure 11.3). It now uses names that describe the individual business areas. However, two names – SAS Cargo and SAS Pleasure – stand out and are branded with a higher degree of freedom because they are independent business areas (Figure 11.4). Cargo is SAS's freight company and Pleasure is aimed at holidaymakers, replacing Jackpot. As long as these names remain generic, they won't turn into independent brands and neither will they steal value from the corporate brand.

Figure 11.4 The SAS business areas with names

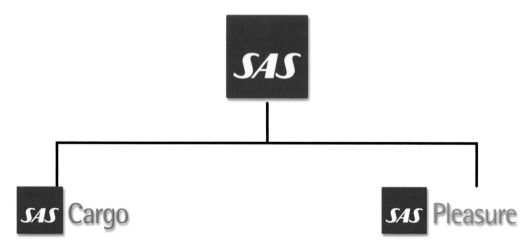

SAS is the clear and visible owner and operator of the freight and holiday divisions.

Hence the new branding strategy positions SAS as the corporate brand and as the owner and operator of the generic denominators. With control of the brand regained, there should be no more risk of another Jackpot-like episode.

Facts

SAS can be traced back to 1940 when a delegation from four Scandinavian airlines – Danish DDL, Swedish ABA, Norwegian DNL and Aero Oy from Finland – met in the US. These four agreed with US airline PanAm to begin flights between the US and Bergen in Norway. However, the German invasion of Denmark and Norway in April of the same year put the plans on hold.

Negotiatons for the creation of a Scandinavian airline resumed after the war and in 1946 SAS was formed as a consortium between the national airlines – apart from Finland. The national companies in the consortium are SAS Denmark Ltd, SAS Norway ASA and SAS Sweden AB. The first two own 29 per cent of the consortium each and SAS Sweden AB owns 42 per cent.

In 1981, SAS launched 'The businessman's airline' concept as part of a strategy focusing on the business traveller. The concept lost some of its force during the early 1990s when business travel ceased to be the sole preserve of senior business executives. Today, everyone travels this way and any feeling of exclusivity or status has disappeared.

SAS had to find a new value and in 1998, 'It's Scandinavian' was launched as part of a radical programme of change called '2000+'. The programme is designed to increase profits and competitive power and lead to a new identity, new design and new planes. The campaign is an attempt to build the new SAS identity around Scandinavian values such as quality, design and environment. The new profile is also close to the SAS vision of making Scandinavians proud of their airline.

Virgin uses sub-branding with names

Virgin is another example of a corporation using names for its sub-branding, although contrary to B&O, where headquarters runs most activities, Virgin's subsidiaries are largely run by their own managements and are frequently joint ventures.

Richard Branson created the Virgin brand initially with Virgin Records (since sold to EMI Thorn) and later numerous companies that, in reality, are synonymous with the personality of Branson himself. Virgin's corporate brand value is 'up against conventions' and, in a way, echoes David's fight against Goliath.

Branson knows that he owns a position in the minds of his customers that is worth a lot of money. So he outsources his brand to other companies, which can use Virgin as a value position in the market. Branson benefits from this outsourcing by having the overall value of the Virgin brand increased.

Branson is engaged in a spellbinding experiment and it will be very exciting to see whether he succeeds in creating a superbrand. It seems likely.

Richard Branson's many companies

It takes a lot of discipline for a number of different sub-brand companies to keep to the basic values of the Virgin brand. Each of them could spoil it for the others if they were to step out of line and not live up to the value position of Virgin. Branson is very much aware that he must channel the value from Virgin Atlantic Airways, Virgin Express, Virgin Clothing, Virgin Radio, Virgin Cola, Virgin Brides, Virgin Megastores, Virgin Holidays/Virgin Sun, Virgin Train, Virgin Direct and Virgin Mobile back into the Virgin corporate brand. This is why he uses names.

This is new thinking. But it is also quite risky. One of Branson's sub-brands, Virgin Train, has had great difficulty living up to the rebellious, anti-conventional attitude of the corporate brand. Too many failures serve the corporate brand cause badly. But corporate branding with names is an excellent way of unifying a brand while a corporation is growing and differentiating into new product areas and customer segments.

Corporate branding with names is an excellent way of unifying a brand while the corporation is growing and differentiating into new product areas and customer segments.

However, many companies pull back from this approach, particularly if they are independent companies carrying their own brand name. They cannot see the benefits of being owned by a larger international corporation with a more powerful brand name, perhaps feeling they would be swallowed up by the larger company. Yet such operations can easily continue to function as an entirely independent company – the challenge is in controlling the brand. If the brand position is carefully described and if the sub-brand fits into it, then brand building can be mutually beneficial.

In future, one of the greatest challenges for companies will be building superbrands with a tight brand system.

In future, one of the greatest challenges for companies will be building superbrands with a tight brand system. This must be focused on a particular brand position even though there may be a very flexible company structure underneath with independent companies working on optimizing different product areas.

Virgin – against the conventions

Who would ever dare take up a fight with soft drinks and airline giants – at the same time? Richard Branson would.

If ever a person has become synonymous with rebellion against the establishment, it is Richard Branson. Through his company, Virgin, and its approximately 150 subsidiary companies, he represents the little man's fight against the big guys in many different fields.

Spread your value position

Virgin deploys a branding strategy with names. Branson outsources his Virgin brand to companies that can benefit from his 'up against conventions' positioning. All products and services are supplied with the Virgin value and so become sub-brands. All sub-brands label their areas with generic names – Virgin Mobile, Virgin Cola, Virgin Train, Virgin Clothes, Virgin Brides, Virgin Radio, Virgin Megastore, Virgin Atlantic, Virgin Express, Virgin Direct, Virgin BizNet, and so on (Figure 11.5).

In this way, the value position Virgin has captured in the minds of customers is spread across many different business areas. By using generic names, the sub-brands can never turn into independent brands that might take value from the corporate brand. On the contrary, they all play a part in building even more value for Virgin.

Since the value position is a broad attitude, 'up against conventions', it can be shared over many different fields, such as trains, bridal equipment, flight journeys, cola, vodka,

Richard Branson and Virgin are synonymous with the little man's fight against the big guys.

Figure 11.5 Virgin's brands with names

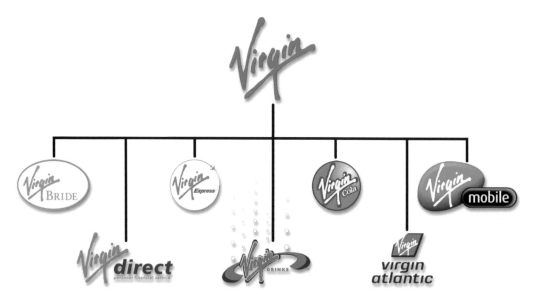

Virgin is the owner of a corporate brand with more than 150 companies.

Virgin has also started competing with the Cola giants.

and financial affairs. This is a conscious strategy with the credibility of the brand as the crucial driver. As long as it is intact, there is no field Virgin could not enter.

Spell out your value position

Today, Virgin is a brand that represents change, quality, value, renewal and fun. The brand challenges established companies by giving its customers more value for money.

One of the main reasons why Virgin is capable of expanding into so many different fields is that the value has been built up in a credible way (Figure 11.6). 'up against conventions' is not just something that Branson says, it is also something he does. Virgin Records was the first Virgin company and from the beginning was associated with rebellious recording artists.

Figure 11.6 Virgin's brand religion – 'up against conventions'

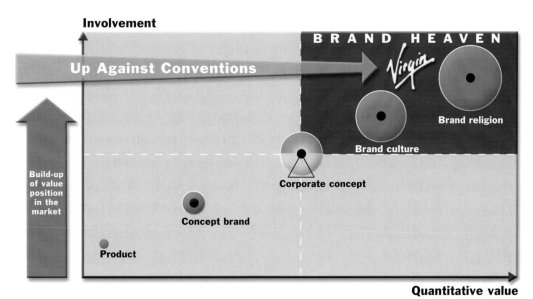

Virgin is a strong brand religion that has captured the value position 'up against conventions'.
Everything that Virgin does, regardless of the business, is imbued with this value position.

This created the basis for the position. But the real stimulus came with Virgin Atlantic Airways' battle with British Airways. British Airways never succeeded in crushing Branson and in fact only managed to strengthen Virgin even more. Personally, Branson has contributed to building this unique value via his balloon trips across the Pacific and the Atlantic.

Branson knows that he owns a value position in the minds of customers and that he can profit from this. It still does not seem as if he has met any limits to how far he can take the brand.

Facts

'The best reason to go into business? Because you feel strongly that you can change things'. Richard Branson put it as simply as that in the magazine Fast Company when explaining his motivation for running his business.

The Virgin era began in 1969 when Branson, a magazine publisher who was still at school, chose the name Virgin Records (rather than Slipped Disc Records) for the mail order record business he launched through the magazine. The magazine itself displayed some of Branson's remarkable persuasive powers. Aged only 17, he managed to get celebrities such as the writer James Baldwin, philosopher Jean-Paul Sartre and actress Vanessa Redgrave to either write for the magazine or to give interviews.

The original logo was right for the long-haired hippies of the 1970s but later, when the punk wave, and the Virgin band Sex Pistols, broke over the UK, something more personal was required. It was then that the signature-like logo we know today was developed. It took three years to achieve a patent on the name Virgin, which some people thought blasphemous – perhaps not so strange a notion given that the Virgin Mary is one of the most effective 'logos' of the Catholic Church. Now the name has become synonymous with a sharp, unique and absolutely clear attitude: Virgin – 'up against conventions'.

CHAPTER 12

Corporate brand with differentiation

The two forms of branding outlined in Chapters 10 and 11 have both in their different ways been closely related to the corporate brand.

Both have been centred on a corporate brand and both have been variations of that brand. The companies profiled have not meddled with their corporate brand; they have merely added a sub-category.

Traditionally, the key issues involved in this area have been the logo and the design manual, both of which have been treated with huge reverence. Consistency was regarded as paramount since designers are interested in only one thing: that everyone sticks to their graphic ideas.

Corporate brand with differentiation does away with this way of thinking. Any company that wants to work with modern brand ideas should begin by firing their design agency.

Any company that wants to work with modern brand ideas should begin by firing their design agency.

Don't be afraid of the logo

In the past, brands have stuck slavishly to graphical designs and logos. Consistency of design was seen as all important. The brand was subjugated to the logo. But to get the maximum benefit from a corporate brand, you have to elevate it above its graphical representation.

Why? Because in future, awareness of the brand itself will rule out the dominance of graphic creativity.

In Figure 8.2, we find ourselves at brand level number 3, with the customer group you own and the value position you have. Companies that are operating at this level are typically attempting to create more value and already have a strong brand with a strong value position.

But problems arise when a company wants to grow and expand. The original brand sets clear limits for what can be done at product and price levels. You are probably also operating in a particular market segment that may not accept too many alterations. This high level of involvement means that everything to do with the brand must have consistency and credibility. If companies want to develop such brands further, they need to be able to differentiate more than is possible using just graduation or generic names. Again, the first hurdle is the traditional perception of the untouchable logo.

A key fact to remember: the logo is very positive in relation to the group that the brand currently owns but it may have negative connotations for new market segments.

The normal solution to this problem is to develop a new brand. The drawback is that you then have to invest in two brands. More value can be generated if some of the original brand's value position can be transferred to another target group. If you are to succeed in transferring the values of the main brand's position and brand quality, forget the designers and try something new.

Giorgio Armani understands this problem. He has moved into new product areas and customer segments with sub-brands for women and perfumes. Giorgio Armani's children's clothes are in the sub-brand Giorgio Junior and you can also acquire a pair of Giorgio Jeans. Sometimes Giorgio Armani uses corporate branding with generic names, at others times the company works with corporate branding with differentiation. The case study on the following pages shows how Armani has moved across new product categories and customer segments. For a premium brand, this is normally an impossible strategy to follow without watering down its value.

But everything seems to work for Giorgio Armani. When it created the sub-brand Emporio Armani, which addresses a younger market segment, for example, it changed the main logo radically, combining it with a Roman eagle because the younger segment wants powerful, visible symbols.

This is effectively a differentiation of the logo itself and this is part of the reason for its success. The older, wealthier market for the Giorgio Armani brand is not affected by the young brand – the difference between the corporate brand and the sub-brand is clear enough. This is a sensible strategy. Anyone who has spent thousands of dollars for a Giorgio Armani suit will have no problem with the young buying Emporio Armani suits for a few hundred – the difference is visible. Similarly, the young get a sub-brand specially developed for them, not a cheap line of a corporate brand.

Strong brand development in the clothes market

The advantage of corporate branding with differentiation is that the branding can be directed towards a particular target group without losing the connection with the corporate brand. It gives the corporation high flexibility in developing a market, particularly the clothing sector where trends are constantly changing.

Giorgio Armani
– when a fashion
brand expands

Giorgio Armani has been very successful with a differentiated branding strategy that expands a well-defined brand to a much larger target group.

GIORGIO ARMANI

Giorgio Armani's differentiated branding strategy includes the sub-brand Emporio Armani. Giorgio Armani is a brand aimed at the modern, quality-conscious and prosperous man, or woman. So how could Armani extend brand value further and take in other segments without building new brands – and without harming the existing brand?

Armani has spread itself to other product segments of the same quality and price level, for example with a women's brand, Armani Collezioni, and the perfume series Aqua di Gio. In other words it has expanded laterally.

It also wants to develop itself and build further on the strong value position that Giorgio Armani represents.

Giorgio Armani could have solved the problem by using graduation or a generic naming strategy, which is what it has done with Armani Jeans and Armani Junior. This carries some risk, however. For example, the top market segment that Armani serves may perceive such differentiation as a watering down of the Giorgio Armani label.

This type of branding development can lead to a situation where it is necessary to use a new brand to enter a new product area or customer segment. However, rather than building a whole

Figure 12.1 The expansion of the Armani brand

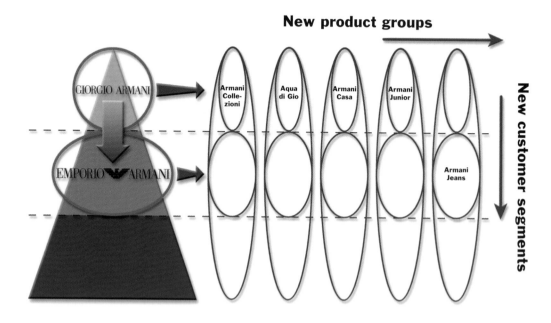

Giorgio Armani has expanded into other product categories and customer segments in a way that has not caused any damage to the corporate brand. By deploying corporate brand with differentiation, the sub-brand Emporio Armani has expanded successfully without watering down the premium position of the corporate brand.

new brand it makes more financial sense to combine the new brand with a corporate brand. This is traditionally called a sub-brand, where though there is a new name it is combined with the corporate brand. In this way, some of the core value of the corporate brand is transferred to the sub-brand.

Giorgio Armani solved the problem by launching Emporio Armani for the less prosperous segment, which wants quality and style. By using only one name, Armani, the new brand is attributed with the same values built up in the Giorgio Armani brand but by differentiating it by dropping the first name you address a new segment without losing the original credibility (Figure 12.1 and 12.2).

By giving the new sub-brand its own name and profile, the

Figure 12.2 Giorgio Armani's brand system

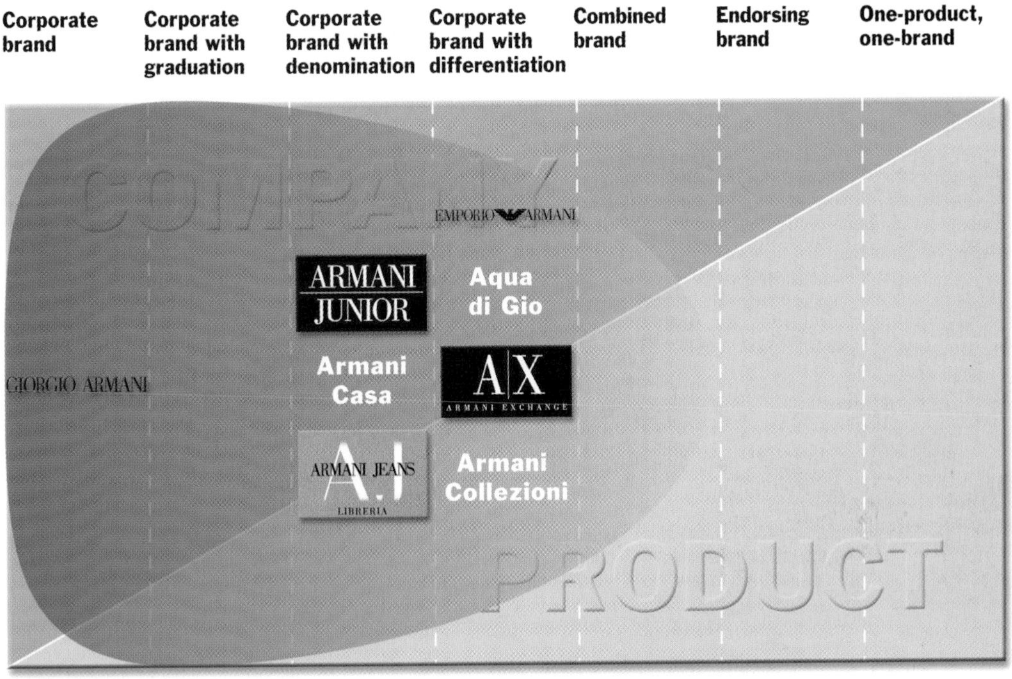

Corporate brand	Corporate brand with graduation	Corporate brand with denomination	Corporate brand with differentiation	Combined brand	Endorsing brand	One-product, one-brand

All of Giorgio Armani's sub-brands are within the borders of the corporate brand.

younger market segment received a higher-value experience that also added new vitality to the corporate brand. Thanks to Emporio Armani, the company can sell clothes of a younger cut at a cheaper price and the young won't feel that they are buying an old man's label. Neither is there a danger that the Giorgio Armani core customers will experience being squeezed into a 'young brand'.

All labels benefit from the value position

Being clearly owned by Giorgio Armani, Emporio Armani benefits from the value position built up in the corporate brand (Figure 12.3). This value accumulation happens via regular fashion shows and TV programmes, magazines and newspapers,

Figure 12.3 The Giorgio Armani brand portfolio

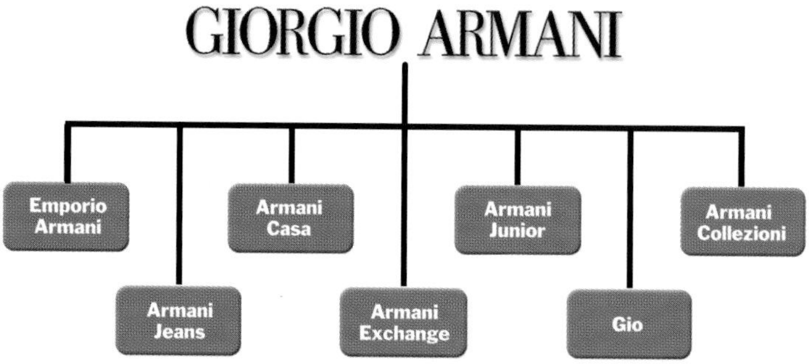

GIORGIO ARMANI

Giorgio Armani includes sub-brands that are all closely linked with the corporate brand.

and through the 2,000 – plus shops across the world selling Armani clothes. Giorgio Armani's different labels are also sold in its own exclusive shops, which count for a significant part of the value accumulation.

The sacred logo was changed

Giorgio Armani has not been afraid to meddle with the company logo. Of course he ran the risk of damaging the original Giorgio Armani brand. But by using an aggressive branding strategy, Armani has successfully expanded a narrow, expensive brand to include children's clothes, sportswear, accessories, perfumes and interior design.

As Figure 12.2 shows, Armani deploys different forms of branding from corporate brand with generic names closely related to the corporate brand, such as Armani Junior, Armani Jeans and so on to corporate branding with differentiation, such as Emporio Armani, A/X, Aqua di Gio and Armani Collezioni. An interesting detail is that he is using corporate branding with denomination for Armani Jeans, but placed in the Emporio Armani shops addressing the youth segment, this sub-brand is positioned in the mid price range, as shown in figure 12.1.

Facts

Giorgio Armani was born on July 11, 1934 in Piacenza in North Italy. In 1961, after a few years as a medical student and a job as a window dresser, he joined Nino Cerruti as a designer. He worked there until 1970, when he became a freelance designer. In 1975, he founded Giorgio Armani along with his close friend Sergio Galeotti. Only nine years later, in 1984, he launched Emporio Armani.

Over the years, Giorgio Armani has received a long series of sought-after fashion and design awards. The company has reached an annual turnover of $850 million in its 2,000 shops around the world.

Customers are intelligent people and they need to be able to recognize a brand. We take an active interest in brands and we can become very involved with them. That is why companies can employ far more intelligent forms of branding than simply relying on the same old logo.

Consumers can become increasingly confused if there are too many different things under one logo just for the sake of uniformity.

Consumers can become increasingly confused if there are too many different things under one logo just for the sake of uniformity. Consumers react very positively to differentiated forms of branding because they understand right away how the different sub-brands address different segments. The branding actually helps them form an overview. For example, in a stylish shop Donna Karan clothes cost a lot of money. In a DKNY shop stocking the hard-hitting, sporty brand, prices are much lower.

The fashion brand Donna Karan soon followed in the footsteps of the Giorgio Armani brand system to allow DKNY to exploit its high brand value in the wider youth segment. It shows a corporate brand with very precise differentiation (Figure 12.4). Donna Karan manages to both

Figure 12.4 The Donna Karan brand system

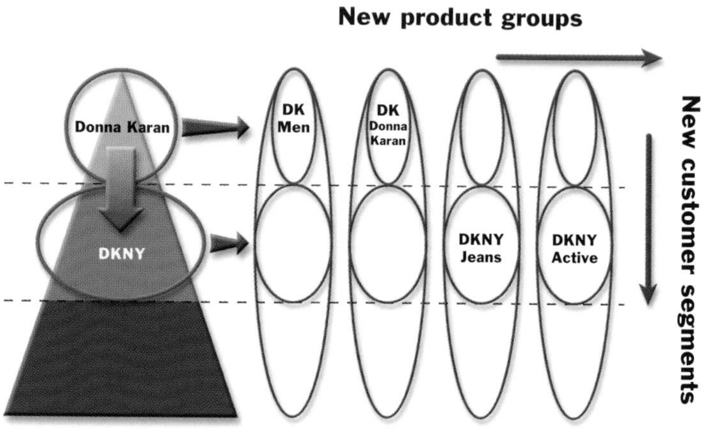

Donna Karan uses a progressive branding with differentiation. The sub-brand DKNY makes it possible to reach the very young customer segment.

sell expensive clothes to a woman aged over 50 and to dress her daughter in DKNY products. Both women are equally happy. Donna Karan is probably even happier – these two different customers contribute to the accumulation of value in the powerful corporate brand.

Design agencies must redefine their view of branding

Most major, international corporations consult old-school design agencies, but they can impede new developments.

Many companies recognize the dilemma Armani solved so brilliantly by differentiating his corporate brand. But many companies that would like to address new segments dare not use their established brand in this way for fear of losing their core customers. These companies are looking for ways of building on their existing brand values while differentiating towards new segments.

The answer is simple. Look at Armani and Donna Karan. Learn from them and try projecting the ideas onto your own business.

The segment decides

But marketing people and their managers still find it difficult to see these possibilities in their brands. For example, it is not unlikely that B&O, like Armani, would one day want to venture into lower price and age segments.

A B&O core customer is above 40 – almost essential to be able to afford the high-priced products. If B&O did want to attract a younger audience, it could draw on the corporate brand rather than creating a new label that might appear to be a B&O cheap line. A good route would be to copy Armani with a new, aggressive, differentiated sub-brand.

CHAPTER 13

Corporate brand with sub-brands

There are situations which justify the creation of a brand. But new brands should be handled with care. They should not be allowed to develop without reference to the master brand. Wherever possible they should be combined with the corporate brand to enhance the positioning of both.

For combined branding to be successful the Corporate Brand must be strong and have a high value position.

Sometimes it is necessary to differentiate a new product area or a new customer segment with a new brand. In this situation you could create an entirely new brand, but it is often more effective to combine a new brand with your corporate brand. This is generally called a sub-brand.

A new name is created, but the corporate brand is used as a platform for combined branding. This allows some of the core value from the corporate brand to be transferred to the sub-brand. But the sub-brand must be placed in a proper context with the existing brand. There is always a danger that the sub-brand will become a new, independent brand.

To avoid that, it is important that the corporate brand is powerful and has a high value position. Second, the combination of the two brands must be properly managed. Finally, the sub-brand must be a derivative of the corporate brand.

Kellogg's has developed a branding system, in which the corporate brand is always placed on top with a second brand name underneath. An interesting aspect of this is that the square box framing the corporate brand and the combined second brand name has become a brand in itself. This means that you can combine many different sub-brands with the corporate brand, as long as they follow the strict logo system.

This is the opposite of corporate brand with differentiation described in Chapter 12. There it was important that the logo was used to indicate the difference between segments while making sure that the corporate brand name was present either in full or abbreviated, such as DKNY.

In a combined branding strategy, it is also important to combine the sub-brand names. It is, for example, a good idea to use some kind of denominator in the name of the sub-brand to ensure that the branding is maintained. But unlike the use of generic names (see Chapter 11), you must use a name, which, apart from describing the direction of the sub-brand, also functions as an independent brand name. The combined brand Kellogg's Chocos is a good example. While it is obviously something to do with chocolate, Chocos can stand alone as a brand name.

The advantage of a combined brand strategy is that you can establish new positions around your corporate brand and significantly expand your market area. What is difficult is predicting how far the brand chain can be stretched before it snaps and weakens the strength of the corporate brand.

Kellogg's has been able to do this. Each time it has launched a new sub-brand, the corporate brand has become more dynamic. However, Kellogg's has controlled the brand so strictly, via the use of logo and visuals, that there might almost be a fear that consumers could come to see Kellogg's products as being a bit boring.

The advantage of a combined brand strategy is that you can establish new positions around your corporate brand and so significantly expand your market area.

Kellogg's – A bowl full of brands

Every day, millions of families start the day with a Kellogg's product. This is the story of how Kellogg's combined branding has been a vital part of its 100-year success story.

More than 100 years ago, the Kellogg brothers founded a breakfast culture.

The Kellogg brothers' branding system

With a product portfolio ranging from traditional ready-to-eat cereals such as Kellogg's Corn Flakes, Kellogg's All Bran and Kellogg's Rice Krispies to convenience foods such as Kellogg's Egg Waffles and the Kellogg's Nutri-grain, Kellogg's has seven of the top ten brands in the breakfast foods sector. Indeed, the Kellogg's name has become synonymous with breakfast.

Strong brand positioning

Over a long period, Kellogg's has built up a very strong value position in breakfast food products. It owns the position 'healthy breakfast' and therefore has a corporate brand with a high value that all the sub-brands can be alongside. The mainstay for Kellogg's – and common to all its products – is the active use of the corporate brand. Kellogg's uses combined branding that allows the strong corporate brand to deliver value to the individual sub-brands while they in turn contribute to the corporate brand. The secret of this successful balancing act is never to allow the sub-brands to turn into drivers of the corporate brand, as happened with the Jackpot sub-brand in the SAS case study (Chapter 11).

Ever since the first packages, the Kellogg's name has been given the same characteristic position and design.

Branding injects new life into products

Kellogg's branding system is very active. The company works consistently to bring new life into the brand, for example by giving sub-brands their own life. You can see this strategy unfolding in children's products such as Frosties and Rice Krispies. Since the 1950s, Kellogg's has made these products synonymous with the characters Tony the Tiger and Snap, Crackle & Pop, who help keep these brands new and alive (Figure 13.1).

This branding strategy has also been used with Kellogg's Special K, which is aimed primarily at women who want a low-fat breakfast meal.

Figure 13.1 Examples of Kellogg's combined branding

Corporate brand	Corporate brand with graduation	Corporate brand with denomination	Corporate brand with differentiation	Combined brand	Endorsing brand	One-product, one-brand

Kellogg's breakfast products use a combined branding strategy that keeps sub-brands within the framework of the corporate brand.

How the packaging of Kellogg's Corn Flakes has changed.

Furthermore, Kellogg's has built its own theme park – Kellogg's city – where people can hear about the company's history, meet brand characters, taste new products, and so on.

Successful sub-brands

Kellogg's has managed to build up successful sub-brands that all draw on the corporate brand without stealing value from each other. How many other brands span such a wide target group? But achieving it is a difficult balancing act.

From crispy flakes to new segments

For years, Kellogg's has had a dominant position in the breakfast products market, but the company is now experiencing

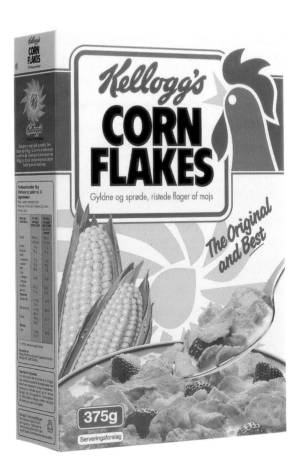

The most recent packaging for Kellogg's Corn Flakes.

increased competition. Since 1988, Kellogg's share of the US market has dropped from 40 per cent to 32 per cent.

Increased competition in the traditional breakfast foods market has forced Kellogg's to look for new product market areas where market share can be captured more easily. In the global market, for example, the company has increasingly focused on the 'convenience food business' with products such as Pop-Tarts and Rice Krispies Treats. In this way, Kellogg's keeps expanding the limits for how far its brand can be stretched.

A company must constantly make sure that its branding system stays dynamic and flexible. The system must be supportive, while giving new opportunities rather than setting limitations. But remember that every system has a built-in limit to how far it can be stretched. If you get too far away from your starting point, consumers can no longer understand the connection between brand/product and the company.

With this in mind, Kellogg's has established an independent brand platform, Ensemble, as a launching pad for breads, pasta, frozen breakfasts, and so on. It is also making New Country Inn Specialities, a product aimed at the top market segment. It is avoiding using Kellogg's as the Corporate Brand. The new brands must carry all the weight.

The first packet of Kellogg's Rice Krispies.

Emphasizing the special properties of Kellogg's products.

Facts – from sanatorium to shop

At a sanatorium for the wealthy in Battle Creek, brothers Dr John Harvey Kellogg and William Keith Kellogg developed a product that was very different from traditional foods. The idea behind it was just as radical as the ideas behind many of the technological breakthroughs of today. They were to change the eating habits of millions of people.

In 1906, the Battle Creek Toasted Corn Flake Company began production of what the world has come to know and love as Kellogg's Corn Flakes. However, the company was soon in competition with 42 other breakfast producers that crowded Battle Creek to join the bandwagon. Kellogg's could not succeed just by being the first or the best in the market. The road to success had to be through imaginative advertising, continuing launches of new products, and maintaining a quality offering. But it was the clear branding strategy in particular that won the battle to become America's preferred breakfast brand.

Think carefully when combining

Combined branding can turn into simple endorsing if you are not careful. If the corporate brand does not appear clearly on packaging, it won't work as planned. You will end up building a new brand that is endorsed by the corporate brand. In this situation, no further value is accumulated in the corporate brand.

Combined branding can turn into simple endorsing if you are not careful.

The Body Shop has built a very powerful corporate brand with an incredibly strong value position. Like so many other major international corporations using a corporate brand, it has had to expand its product range to differentiate new products for particular segments. It has done this by developing sub-brands that it tries to fit into the framework of the corporate brand. Doing this achieves a combined branding effect where the new sub-brand has both a separate position and contributes to the reinforcement of the corporate brand. One of these sub-brands is Hemp. As the case study on the following pages shows, the Hemp logo itself has such a central position that it could easily develop into an entirely new brand. In recent years, new sub-brands such as Africa and Ayurveda, a health product based on old Indian methods, have also appeared.

If a company wants to focus on a particular segment, it will have to move towards the right in the brand system. Whether it chooses graduation, differentiation or, as in this case, combination is a management decision.

Though there are many ways of implementing a combined strategy, often a strategy seems more like an accident. Many major international corporations have gained a strategy after making an acquisition. Often this means that value is neither accumulated in the sub-brand nor in the corporate brand. Instead, everything gets weaker. Nestle is an example. It uses all sorts of branding, including combined branding, but appears to lack any overall system.

Though there are many ways of implementing a combined strategy, often a strategy seems more like an accident.

Other food concerns have created a successful combined

brand strategy without being quite as strict with their logo policy. Danone makes sure that its logo has a central position on products, which range from natural yogurt to a children's dessert. Danone focuses on fresh dairy products – see the case study in Chapter 6 – and has a very well-defined brand system.

Figure 13.2 shows some Danone products. You can see how Danone uses each product packaging to optimize the entire range and create a combined branding effect. It can do this because the logo has a central position and the sub-brand delivers the value 'Active Health'.

Some combined brandings do not work as well as they should because the relationship between the corporate brand and the combined brand is not balanced.

However, some combined brandings do not work as well as they should because the relationship between the corporate brand and the sub-brand is not balanced. Placing two logos next to each other on a package will, as a rule, create confusion. Which is the brand, what is the central value, and what is it that differentiates the sub-brand from the central value?

LEGO (see the case study in Chapter 4) has re-structured its branding system and is trying to place as much as possible under its Corporate Brand. At the same time, it has developed a combined brand strategy for sub-brands such as MINDSTORMS and LEGO BELVILLE. There is also a LEGO logo on the LEGOLAND logo, so now this is also a combined brand. The whole thing hangs well together because the LEGO brand has a clear value position in wanting to 'stimulate creative play'. All sub-brands live up to this value and, in return, get their value from it.

Any messy branding system must be tidied up – the sooner the better. First, a strong value position must be established. Then, the labelling of products, marketing and everything else must be adjusted in accordance with a balanced branding. In most cases, there will be some internal resistance against change even if the current situation causes confusion among customers.

Figure 13.2 Danone's combined branding is used for all product categories

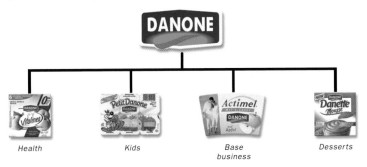

| Health | Kids | Base business | Desserts |

Danone covers four different product categories.

Confused branding systems usually arise from compromises between different internal factions in a company. These compromises then become the customers' problem – a grotesque situation. When you understand the power of market penetration of a strong and comprehensible brand, you realize why some corporations are more successful than others.

As top managers begin to understand the brand system way of thinking, more major corporations will begin this tidying process. There is a lot of difference between messy double branding and combined branding with a clear direction for the corporate brand and an equally clear differentiation for the combined brand.

The Body Shop

The Body Shop has built a powerful corporate brand with clear messages and values. It has used a combined branding strategy to develop and exploit that value.

Branding strategy

Consumers have never had any doubts as to the values on which Body Shop products are based – cosmetics with a conscience (Figure 13.3). These values pervade everything that The Body Shop does and they form the basis of a very clear value position built up in the minds of consumers.

Figure 13.3 The Body Shop – a clear value position

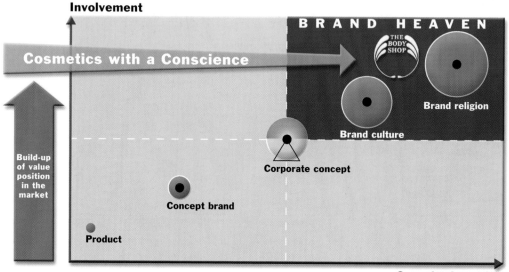

By capturing the position, cosmetics with a conscience, The Body Shop has created a powerful brand religion.

Necessary sub-brands

However, with more than 100 new products every year, there are natural limits to the extension of The Body Shop brand. Consequently, The Body Shop has developed various sub-brands that are placed within the corporate brand framework to achieve a combined branding effect.

At first, Colourings was marketed outside the corporate brand but it failed. It was then placed closer to the corporate brand via a combined strategy.

The Colourings range was launched almost as an independent brand but is now marketed as a combined brand (Figure 13.4). It was originally independently branded because the product – nail varnish and nail varnish remover – was seen as too remote from The Body Shop core.

Figure 13.4 The Body Shop has regained the control of Colourings

After having been launched almost as an independent brand, The Body Shop has regained control of the sub-brand Colourings, which is now marketed as a combined brand. At first, it was independently branded, because the products – nail varnish and nail varnish remover – were slightly apart from The Body Shop core.

Products are mostly divided into various lines, each of which carries an independent name and visual identity along with The Body Shop logo. This achieves a combined branding effect where the corporate brand – The Body Shop – supplies each sub-brand with value (Figure 13.5). Products gain the value that is characteristic of The Body Shop as a whole but also accumulate their own value via the combined branding. Having built a powerful brand The Body Shop is now using that value actively by renewing itself. The sub-brands contribute to the expansion and vitalization of The Body Shop brand without diluting it.

Figure 13.5 The combined branding of The Body Shop

Corporate brand	Corporate brand with graduation	Corporate brand with denomination	Corporate brand with differentiation	Combined brand	Endorsing brand	One-product, one-brand

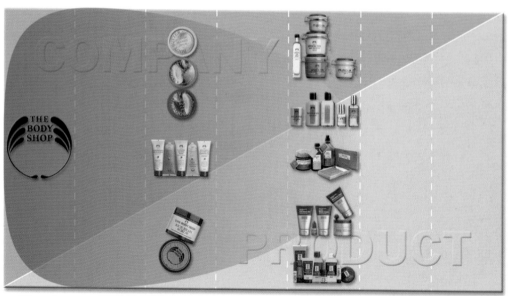

Step 1   **Step 2**

The Body Shop primarily uses its corporate brand in a combined branding strategy, but it also offers 'independent' products. At first, it built the brand using a tight corporate brand using denominating product names. More recently, dynamics and value have been accumulated in the brand via the introduction of new sub-brands as combined brandings.

Hemp

Hemp is one of The Body Shop's sub-brands, the outcome of founder Anita Roddick's ideas of offering counter cosmetics in competition with established cosmetics producers. On the packaging, the Hemp name is emphasized and it carries its own visual identity (the hemp leaf) while The Body Shop logo is toned down.

This form of sub-branding has credibility, not least because Hemp has a story to tell. The use of hemp seed, the main ingredient in the products, goes back 2000 years and it has long been recognized for its moisturizing effect. Consumers buy the story of the seed and not just a smart name and a nice design. It is precisely this story and the fact that Hemp is a special product that allows The Body Shop to sell Hemp in different packaging to its regular products.

On the packaging, the Hemp name is emphasized and it carries its own visual identity (the hemp leaf).

Well thought – through branding

However, The Body Shop has realized that even if a sub-brand is powerful, it cannot stand alone. The company thought at first that it could launch the Colourings make-up series without the Body Shop logo. But sales were slack until the logo was added. Launching Colourings without The Body Shop logo was

The Body Shop series, Ayurveda, an old natural Indian treatment, is one of the latest additions to the value accumulation in the brand.

essentially the same as moving into the one-product, one-brand system. But the company regained control over the sub-brand by adding the corporate brand and the whole brand line moved further towards the left in the branding system.

In a similar way, it was believed that a male product line, Skin Mechanics, would not sell if it featured Body Shop on the package. The logo was toned down and The Body Shop became more of an endorser, or a quality stamp, for the product. But in this case, too, that approach failed. Men did not buy the range because the product was not perceived as 'The Body Shop', either in content, design or value.

The future

The Body Shop's combined branding strategy seems sensible. The good thing about such a strategy is that there is an exchange of value taking place between the corporate brand and the sub-brand and they support each other. But The Body Shop must still be careful that its sub-brands don't grow too fast and into new independent brands. It is important to con-

Skin Mechanics did not sell at first because The Body Shop logo was toned down and the product was not perceived as 'The Body Shop'.

trol the process – whether a combined or a differentiated branding strategy is used.

The example of Colourings shows that you must be extremely conscious of which strategy you choose. A corporate brand such as The Body Shop, characterized by product innovations, quickly reaches the limit of how many generic products can be placed under the corporate brand. When moving towards the right in the branding system, structured thinking is essential.

On the other hand, the sub-brand strategy contributes to an ongoing revitalization of the corporate brand. The brand and the chain appear more dynamic and more and more value accumulates in the value position – cosmetics with a conscience – because each sub-brand participates in building that position.

A religion is born

The first Body Shop store opened in 1976 in Brighton in the UK, with the first international franchiser – a kiosk in Brussels – opening two years later. Since then, things have developed quickly. Due to its very clear values, The Body Shop enjoys a special status with many consumers as a company directed by altruistic attitudes and a strong corporate religion.

The Body Shop, has consistently promoted world peace, improved conditions for the poor, children, the environment, and human and animal rights. Official recognition came in 1997 when Anita Roddick was nominated by UNIQUE as one of the 25 female leaders in the world who had made a major contribution to the maintenance and care of the environment. Because of this reliable and powerful corporate religion, the products have become about more than just personal care – they have actually become a brand religion.

CHAPTER 14

Corporate brand with endorsing

Endorsing is a way of transferring some of the positive value accumulated in a corporate brand to another brand. It can be used as both an aggressive and a defensive strategy.

Brand endorsement can be a powerful tool. It is a way of leveraging the strength of an existing brand to enhance another. An aggressive use of endorsing is employing it to profit from an already established value without expanding the original brand.

A good example is Volkswagen, which bought Seat and Skoda. Both these brands were weak, characterized by low quality and low prestige. But by marketing them under the VW name, their value went up as they gained from the high value position accumulated in the VW brand, though in fact endorsement was never a conscious VW strategy.

The difference between endorsing and ordinary branding

Endorsing differs from combined branding because the endorsing brand plays a subordinate role to the brand that is endorsed. Typically, the endorser brand features in small print at the bottom of packaging or advertising or, as Volkswagen has done, by using a plain typeface for Volkswagen Group. This gives the signal that the context is not the corporate brand or a sub-brand derived from it. To the ordinary consumer the Seat and Skoda brands appear far removed from the values of VW. Endorsing Spanish and Czech cars with a German quality name was a major decision.

The risk in endorsing is that it may end up backing a brand that fails. Any negative response can easily rub off

Endorsing differs from combined branding because the endorsing brand plays a subordinate role to the brand that is endorsed.

on the corporate brand. Endorsing works best when the endorser succeeds in communicating to consumers that there is a powerful brand behind a less powerful one. It works best of all when the strong and the weak brands join forces in a way that is useful to consumers.

Volkswagen does it aggressively

VW has succeeded in convincing consumers that it co-operates with Seat in the development and production of Seat cars, raising Seat from its position as a low-quality, low-price car to a new position as a mid-range car at a cheap price. VW's strong brand position raises the Seat brand. Later, VW achieved the same trick with the Czech Skoda band, probably even more successfully.

Before the fall of the Berlin Wall, Skoda was an Eastern bloc car with a low reputation surpassed only by Trabant. It has probably been an easier task for Volkswagen to raise Skoda from an absolute low than it was with Seat, even though Spain has long had a poor quality image for large consumer durables such as cars. Skoda existed before the communist takeover in 1948 and this is a strong point in its favour, as is the Czech Republic's current integration into Western Europe. The more the Czech Republic is perceived as just another European country, the easier it is for Skoda to gain the maximum benefit from VW's endorsement.

Endorsing Skoda and Seat has been a great success for VW, possibly even a surprising success given that it was never actually a formal strategy. Apart from being part of the VW Group, each brand is independent, with its own set of values. In the future, it will be these values, rather than ownership, that will have to be communicated.

But VW has undoubtedly benefited. Buying Skoda and Seat has given it access to customer segments that it could not reach with its own brand. By understanding branding and using it effectively, VW has promoted both

Seat and Skoda from low-quality, discount options to a dominant position in the value-for-money sector. VW has maximized the value in the group as a whole by using a very aggressive brand system strategy.

VW – success via strong brands

The VW Group has a portfolio of nine strong brands, each of them presented with an individual personality within a multi-brand strategy.

This approach – and the precise positioning of the individual brands – is the basis of a global marketing strategy that supports a broad product programme in all markets and segments.

Brand strategy

Even though individual brands possess their own image, each brand also profits from being part of the VW Group. Mainly this comes from technical and financial strength, but also, to an extent, from the image of the VW Group. For brands that are aimed at larger-volume markets, this means that so-called 'knock-out' factors can be eliminated. Knock-out factors – such as reliability, safety, fuel consumption, social obligations, accessibility, and so on – are factors that, if not present, can impede the acceptance of a brand in the market.

Furthermore, each brand must develop its own personality and attraction by emphasizing certain features based on its particular potentials, such as heritage, image and competence, that positively differentiate the brand from competitors. This type of strategy – a marketing business strategy – has been implemented for Skoda and Seat. When VW bought the companies, both of them had a poor reputation. Skoda, apart from being an Eastern bloc brand, was also perceived as one of the poorest car producers in the world. But both brands had

The VW Group eliminated the 'knock-out' factors of Seat and Skoda.

One of the brands that the VW Group has bought is Lamborghini.

potential, which VW, thanks to its technical and financial power, has been capable of exploiting. Yet at the same time both needed to build a brand personality based on brand-specific differentiators. For Seat these are an emphasis on design and sportiness, articulated as 'automotive happiness'. For Skoda it is 'top quality at attractive prices and a future based on tradition'.

The other brands in the VW Group – Audi, Lamborghini, Bugatti, Rolls-Royce and Bentley are also marketed in an individualistic way (Figure 14.1). The main reason for this is that they all have an individual, powerful brand story to tell.

Figure 14.1 Nine powerful brands

Corporate brand	Corporate brand with graduation	Corporate brand with denomination	Corporate brand with differentiation	Combined brand	Endorsing brand	One-product, one-brand

The VW Group is in charge of nine independent brands that all have their individual values and roles to play.

Why were these brands bought?

The main reason has been the necessity for a global player such as Volkswagen to be able to cover virtually all segments. Another reason, particularly relevant in the case of Bugatti, is for the VW Group to underline its automotive competence and obligation to protect and represent a unique European automobile culture.

Another crucial factor is the ability to communicate the brand values to a market where emotional values play a

Volkswagen Autostadt in Wolfsburg.

Seat pavilion in Autostadt.

Skoda pavilion in Autostadt.

The four generations of Golf.

significant part. Volkswagen is both innovative and active in marketing these value aspects of its brands. The new Autostadt museum in Wolfsburg, Germany, is a good example. Autostadt features past, present and future VW automobiles. Each brand pavilion and its thematic focus provides an emotional impression of the personality of the brand.

Facts

VW's history is inextricably tied to the first great success of the company – the original Volkswagen 'Beetle', which is still the most popular car model in the world with a total sale of 21 million.

Volkswagen's history goes back to 1934, when Professor Ferdinand Porsche introduced his 'design proposal for a German Volkswagen' to the ministry of transport. Today the VW Group is the world's fourth-largest producer of cars, including volume brands such as VW, Audi, Seat and Skoda, and luxury brands Lamborghini, Bugatti, Rolls-Royce and Bentley. Every ten seconds, a new car leaves one of the company's assembly lines somewhere in the world. To date, the VW Group has produced 78 million cars and the workforce comprises 306,000 people.

The original Volkswagen.

The VW case study demonstrates how to use branding as an organic way of expanding. The company uses an intelligent form of branding with endorsing to incorporate new brands that cover segments the corporate brand does not reach.

Nestlé endorses defensively

Unfortunately, endorsing is often little more than placing your own logo on a newly acquired brand to mark the new ownership. This is defensive branding – it is used neither properly nor actively. It may even be destructive for both the endorsing brand and the endorsed brand since both may end up being diluted.

One example is the Swiss food giant Nestlé, which owns ten global brands, about 120 regional brands, and more than 1,700 local strategic brands and 7,622 local non-strategic brands – and it is still acquiring more. In 1998, Nestlé proclaimed that it would try to limit its many brands to fewer stronger brands and would use its own brand, Nestlé, in a more appropriate manner. This move is all about quality. But it is difficult to give direction to this value position because the Nestlé brand is used for almost anything. You see it on baby food, ice cream, coffee, tea, chocolates and yogurt.

The different product categories cover many different positions and grades of branding. In some cases, the Nestlé brand is used as a corporate brand, in other cases as a corporate brand with differentiation, as with Nescafe, Nesquik or Nestea. Nestlé is also, to varying degrees, used as a combined brand.

And then there is After Eight

Finally, Nestlé is also used as an endorsing brand. One example is the takeover of the chocolate brand After Eight, which, after a while, was arrayed with an endorsing Nestlé logo.

But is this really endorsing? In other words, will After Eight benefit or lose from it? After Eight is synonymous with an English 'after dinner atmosphere'. It is 'the after dinner mint' and there is something original about the chocolates. Is this originality going to disappear with the addition of the Nestlé logo? Does anybody know what Nestlé really is? Is it an industry or a food corporation with a clear attitude and position? The brand spans a lot, but that does not have to matter at all. What matters is how customers perceive Nestlé.

Everybody knows Nestlé – but for what?

Given Nestlé's enormous distribution area, it is positioned as shown in the corporate religion model in Figure 14.2, at the bottom of the involvement axis yet to the far right on the quantity axis.

This means that there will be a huge number of consumers all over the world who know Nestlé as a food brand but who will find it very difficult to attribute a certain value position to the brand. This makes it difficult to enunciate a mission statement. Currently it is: 'The world food company dedicated to providing you with the best food throughout your life.'

This is a rather diffuse statement that contains an in-built promise that a Nestlé product is a quality stamp. But it is debatable whether the company is getting the maximum profit from the Nestlé brand. It should narrow the brand to give it a core that makes it more valuable and relevant for the customers.

One option would be for Nestlé to move further towards the left in the brand system so that the brand value goes to Nestlé. The company could develop a tight branding system, choose a core of products to drive the brand, and thereby build up a value position for the Nestlé brand. It might also decide on a corporate brand range that specifies the kind of product that can carry the name

Figure 14.2 Nestlé's value position

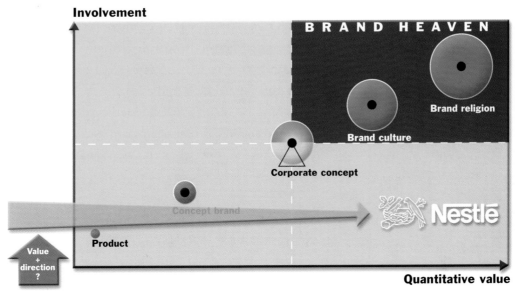

Nestlé's value position is characterized by a high quantitative level but slender involvement. Many people know of Nestlé but have difficulty trying to attribute a particular value position to it.

Nestlé. By identifying a core in the brand, it could build up a brand position. That would make it easier to get value from the brand and help it supply value to the other brands rather than being a mere quality stamp.

Use the corporate brand with care

As shown in Figure 14.2, you can choose between a quality orientation (the y-axis) or a quantity orientation (the x-axis) for the brand. So, it is not merely a matter of printing your brand name on every single brand you buy, as with After Eight.

A good example of the opposite case is the French mineral water, Perrier, which was taken over by Nestlé in 1992. There is no Nestlé brand name on the Perrier bottle, perhaps because the Swiss name would interfere with the idea of an original, French mineral water.

Perrier is one of Nestlé's independent brands.

There is a big difference between using your logo and writing your name. When using the logo, you signal corporate brand, whether it is actually the case or not. It is crucial to pay attention to the use of your corporate brand. The brand cannot be put into as many contexts as possible; you must consider what effect that may have on it. As shown in Figure 16.3, you could develop a logo that is different from the actual food logo – as Danone has done – to indicate which is the brand and which is the corporation.

On the other hand, too many companies go to the opposite extreme and use their corporate brand only within a very limited area. This is the reason that so many companies tend to develop far too many brands. We should be aware of the consequences and the price paid for this overabundance. You simply cannot support all the different brands and you fail to build up one strong brand position.

A corporate brand is no waste bin

In many larger corporations, the corporate brand often becomes a waste bin. If you cannot think of a good sub-brand, or it only needs to be something generic, you merely stick on your corporate brand because you cannot come up with anything better. This only leads to the watering down of the brand value, when the opposite should have been the case. You use your corporate brand as branding because it lives up to high ideals and quality demands. The brand and the products should be used in the service of building a high value position onto which you can later tie your sub-brands. It is important to do things in the right order and to concentrate on building one core in your corporate brand.

Everything under one hat

Nestlé is an example of a company that creates growth primarily through acquisitions.

This requires tight control and a clear branding strategy which, so far, has resulted in the printing of Nestlé's logo on most of the corporation's many sub-brands with various degrees of dominance.

Branding strategy

At Nestlé, branding strategy varies between using the name and the logo to play the main role and using them to provide a product with added value (Figure 14.3). Even though it does not seem as if the strategy is completely structured and well-defined, there is a pattern: within the product categories that are closest to the core – Nestlé started off with milk – the products are labelled with a high degree of corporate branding. This is a natural consequence of Nestlé's historical competence in this field. The Nestlé logo is therefore emphasized on confectionery products and also where the corporate brand has to play a strategic role. On products that are a bit further away from the core, the company uses endorsing or one-product, one-brand.

When using endorsed branding – check it out on a box of After Eight yourself – a small Nestlé logo is printed at the bottom of the packet as some kind of quality stamp. On the other hand, Perrier mineral water is marketed as an independent brand. A good example of a successful combined branding at Nestlé is Premier ice cream. When Nestlé bought the company,

After Eight is endorsed by Nestlé.

Figure 14.3 Nestlé's many different forms of branding

Corporate brand	Corporate brand with graduation	Corporate brand with denomination	Corporate brand with differentiation	Combined brand	Endorsing brand	One-product, one-brand

Nestlé is the consignor of a large number of brands, each of them carrying a different identity and degree of individuality.

it successfully incorporated its own brand into the Premier brand (Figure 14.4). The same happened with other acquisitions – see Figure 14.5. Of products that come under the corporate brand, then generally:

- the product is Nestlé's own invention;
- the product category is core business, or close;
- the acquisition took place a long time ago;
- at the time of the acquisition, it was a neutral type of brand.

In contrast, a higher degree of endorsing or product branding suggests:

- the product category is remote from the core business;
- the acquisition took place recently;
- at the time of the acquisition, it was a strong brand.

Regardless of which strategy is used, it is important to Nestlé that it is visible on the product packaging, whether as the primary owner of the brand with its logo on the front, or, if products have a greater customer contact potential, as a secondary owner with the logo on the back. The consumer must never be in any doubt as to the Nestlé origin of the product.

Figure 14.4 How Nestlé has incorporated other brands into its own system

| Corporate brand | Corporate brand with graduation | Corporate brand with denomination | Corporate brand with differentiation | Combined brand | Endorsing brand | One-product, one-brand |

Three examples of how Nestlé has acquired companies and incorporated them into its brand in the Nestlé brand system. When it acquired Quality Street, Nestlé merely replaced the Mackintosh logo with its own logo and maintained the original visual identity. When it took over Premier, Nestlé developed it as a combined brand by clearly stating Nestlé as the owner. When Nestlé bought Chambourcy, the name was completely incorporated.

Corporate branding cannot carry everything

Apart from using different degrees of sub-branding, Nestlé also brands on a corporate brand level. But the company believes overall corporate branding cannot be done in a way that would achieve a value position that could be transferred to all products. This would be possible only, if it operated within related categories. Nestlé believes that the brand covers too many different product categories for one universal value position to appear credible. This is the reason why the many brands and their individual value positions will survive in the future, even though it is expensive for the corporation to build and maintain them.

Figure 14.5 The hierarchical structure of the Nestlé brand system

Nestlé's many brands are structured according to a hierarchical system that illustrates how many levels they communicate at.

Brand hierarchy

As shown in Figure 14.5, the different Nestlé brands are structured according to a worldwide hierarchical system. This structure achieves a 'spill-over effect' that allows the global brands to transfer value to the other brands.

Facts

It was chemist Henri Nestlé's search for a healthy and economical alternative for mothers who were not able to breastfeed their children that laid the foundation of the Nestlé empire about 140 years ago.

The first product from Nestlé was Farine Lactée Nestlé, a breast milk substitute and after having saved the life of a 15-day-old boy, the product was marketed across most of Europe in only a few years. In 1905, Nestlé merged with The Anglo-Swiss Condensed Milk Company and formed The Nestlé Company. The company remained dedicated to food products until 1974 when it bought a major share in the French cosmetics giant L'Oreal. A few years later it acquired yet another non-food company, American Alcon Laboratories Inc, a maker of pharmaceutical and optical products.

Today, Nestlé is one of the market leaders in the food industry, with more than 225,000 employees in 500 factories in more than 70 countries. Nestlé products are sold in almost every country in the world.

CHAPTER 15

One-product, one-brand

One-product, one-brand is the most traditional and well-developed form of branding. It is also the safest way of building a strong and focused brand because it avoids confusing customers with a number of different signals.

Building and owning a strong position within a product area is a very efficient use of resources. But the cost of developing and maintaining a brand in a particular area unfortunately gets higher and higher. This forces traditional one-product, one-brand companies to expand their area of operation. Normally, they expand into related product areas that appear natural extensions. This is called 'line extension' and involves moving the range into different sizes and categories of the original product.

Progressive one-product, one-brand corporations

It becomes 'brand extension' when the brand itself is expanded into completely new product areas. Usually, line extension is preferred to brand extension, though this can depend on the particular brand situation since most brands possess not only a product position but also a value position. It is the value position that can be extended to cover new product areas and often, especially if you own a very high value position, it is just as easy as a normal line extension.

A good example of this is Virgin. Rather than developing the company via traditional line extensions it has built a strong value position and has had little difficulty launching differing products, each of which fits the value position of the brand.

Indeed, it is becoming increasingly difficult to point to traditional one-product, one-brand companies. In one way or another, most are moving into other areas, even turning into corporate brands. That is, they are moving from the right-hand side of the brand system to the left side, then moving back towards the right of the system to exploit the brand value. This requires many resources, high commitment and an understanding by top management of the importance of building a brand system.

P&G covers products from nappies…

Strong position and profile

Among the most successful one-product, one-brand corporations are Procter & Gamble and Mars Inc. P&G is the one-product, one-brand company par excellence and it owns many successful brands, all of which have built strong brand positions within their product areas. For example, P&G is firmly positioned in the washing powder market with the Ariel brand in the nappy market with Pampers in washing-up liquids with the Yes brand, and in the shampoo market with Head & Shoulders. The brand range stretches from Oil of Olay cosmetics to Vicks throat lozenges.

… to skin lotions.

Building such strong and independent positions in the international market requires enormous resources. But once you make it to that level, you have a strong hold on the market because each brand owns a clear, strong position and profile. However, each brand must be targeted precisely at the desired target group and must not adjust to fit a corporate brand.

Building such strong and independent positions in the international market requires enormous resources.

The price of a brand attack

One of the greatest threats to P&G is a particular brand getting into trouble and harming other P&G products. P&G, however, tends to build brands in separate product areas so that any damage can be limited to an individual brand.

Wash & Go had problems during the 1990s.

An example of this happened in Denmark at the beginning of the 1990s. A shampoo product, Wash & Go, had been successfully launched and captured significant market share. However, it came under attack in the press when it was alleged that using Wash & Go caused hair loss. This kind of attack can happen to any brand at any time. Sometimes the product is damaged, at others it is all soon forgotten. In this case, though, the brand was almost totally destroyed. It was difficult for P&G to restore confidence, even though all the allegations were repudiated. In the end P&G pulled the brand from the shelves and replaced it with a new product, Head & Shoulders.

If Wash & Go had been a corporate brand with sub-brands and products in other areas, the case could have caused much more damage. The troubles with the Mercedes A-class car, for example, left scars on the credibility of other Mercedes products and sub-brands. P&G was able to isolate the damage to one specific product area. The only loss was wasted accumulated brand value.

It could, of course, be argued that were Wash & Go a corporate brand, as with Mercedes, then its strong value position would have served as a much more effective protection. After all, P&G has demonstrated its reliability in many other areas. In the end, this is a question of brand strategies and overall corporate strategy. Both options can be successful if the branding is optimized and if the company, brand positions and values are built effectively.

The Mars company

Another major company that has chosen a product area strategy for its brand structure is Mars Inc. Mars owns many different brands – Mars Bars, Uncle Ben's Rice, and Pedigree pet food. It began in chocolates, using the corporate brand Mars, later adding Bounty, Snickers, M&Ms and Twix. Since then, it has expanded into other areas, such as rice and pet food. Like P&G, Mars owns very successful brands within different product categories.

Recently, it has attempted to spread its brands further to create a broader basis. For example, via brand extensions Mars now also retails as an ice cream and this move has been followed by other Mars chocolate brands. Like P&G, Mars allows each brand to appear as an independent company to consumers, even though they are all controlled from Mars offices around the world. And certainly it makes sense to keep some of the brands separate. Consumers might find it difficult to accept a link between chocolates and dog food, for example.

One-style, one-brand

Unilever is yet another major international company that has many brands in different product areas. It has also been very successful in building segment brands across categories. In particular, the brand Lätta – a low-calorie/low-fat brand – has done well and includes dressings, mayonnaise and even cheese. Another segment brand is Becel margarine, based on rapeseed oil, which is supposedly healthier than other edible oils.

Overall, thinking about traditional product boundaries is becoming increasingly relaxed as more and more brands move successfully across them. The low-fat category, in particular, has yielded great opportunities for brands to cross product boundaries.

As we have seen, fashion brands have easily crossed into new product areas. They are no longer merely a jeans brand, a shoe brand, a sports brand, a pullover brand or a suit brand. Successful fashion brands are a 'style'. But this inevitably means that value positions become increasingly decisive – much more decisive than the actual suits, shoes and jeans that the brand covers. Though focusing the name and the design of the brand means you should have much more freedom, certain product categories still demand certain symbols, colours and positions.

For example, at the very least a bank should appear reliable. This reliability must be emphasized and repeated in value positions, messages, name and even choice of colour. If these elements do not reflect this value then consumers will reject the brand because it does not live up to what is most important for the category – credibility. Likewise, all categories are defined by certain positions that are important to own. This is easier to do with a one-product, one-brand strategy.

If, like P&G, you want to own positions within the washing powder category, it is important that you capture the generic position; this is that your make of washing powder washes clothes cleaner and more efficiently. If you aim to own the most lucrative specific product area positions in the market, the one-product, one-brand strategy is the best, if not the only, brand strategy.

Procter & Gamble

Procter & Gamble is not as well known in Europe as in the US, where at any time of the day 95 per cent of the nation's households are using a P&G product, be it Pampers nappies Oil of Ulay beauty lotion, Vidal Sassoon shampoo or Ariel washing powder.

All these brands are the outcome of a one-product, one-brand strategy that markets every brand independently. There are no mutual relations and you will have to read the smallest print on the package to find out that Procter & Gamble is behind them.

Branding strategy

P&G is a master of this brand strategy. It does it so well that every one of its products is an independent brand characterized by clear, well-defined, individual values. Sub-brands are also marketed and handled independently. In many cases, products even have different names in different markets.

P&G's brand strategy aims at becoming the market leader in each product segment. Such a strategy is obviously very expensive. Each brand must develop and implement individual plans for building value and profile. There are no economies of scale and no P&G corporate brand owner of sub-brands. Since P&G's growth strategy is concentrated around research, product innovations and the continuing introduction of new brands, these economic factors become even more crucial. However, P&G's ownership can still be promoted as a brand to the retailer, where the corporate brand becomes equivalent to professional marketing (Figure 15.1).

Figure 15.1 P&G's brand system

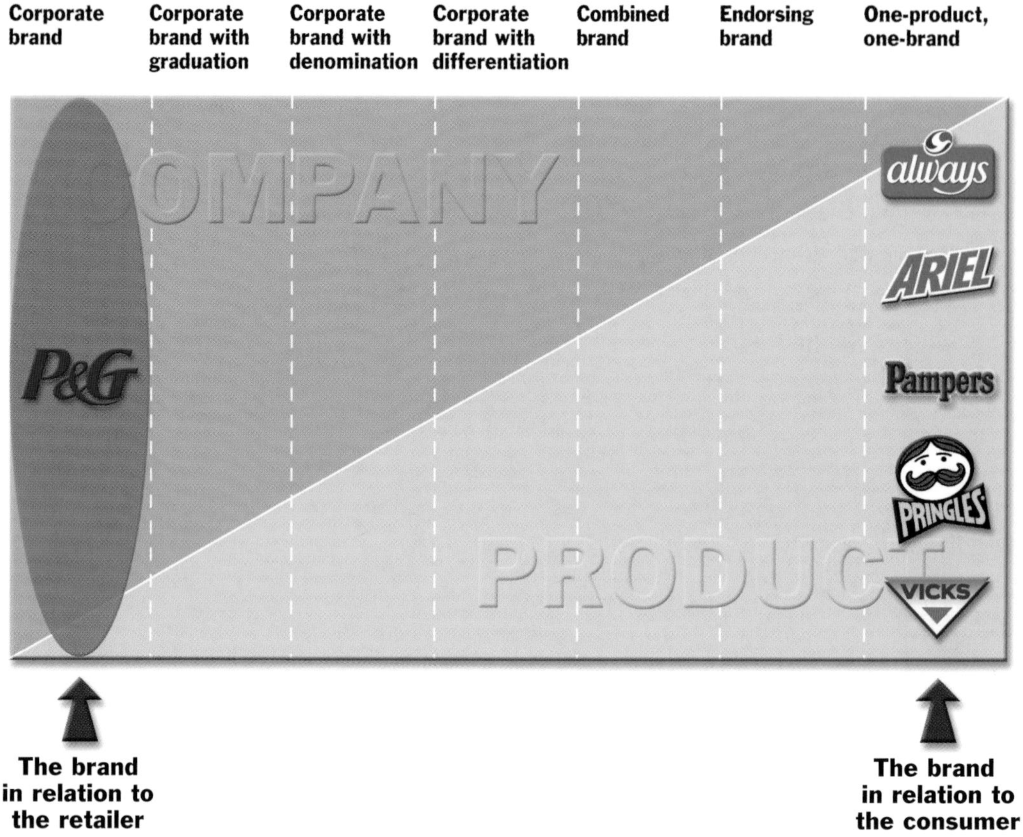
Corporate brand
Corporate brand with graduation
Corporate brand with denomination
Corporate brand with differentiation
Combined brand
Endorsing brand
One-product, one-brand
COMPANY
PRODUCT
P&G
always
ARIEL
Pampers
PRINGLES
VICKS
The brand in relation to the retailer
The brand in relation to the consumer

Procter & Gamble owns a number of independent brands, but P&G itself is promoted as a brand to the retailer.

Wash & Go

The strategy has obvious advantages. Should anything go wrong with one product, it will not affect the rest of the portfolio. It can easily be taken out of production and replaced with a new brand. In the early 1990s, Wash & Go shampoo was alleged to cause damage to the hair – perhaps unfoundedly – and the public soon rechristened it Wash & Gone. Sales slumped and soon Wash & Go disappeared. Shortly afterwards P&G launched a new shampoo under a new brand.

What is noteworthy about the Wash & Go case is that the negative press never spread to other P&G products. One shampoo brand suffered irretrievable damage, but the image of P&G was unharmed.

An expensive strategy

P&G is among the highest spenders on marketing in the world – otherwise it could not keep around 300 global brands going. It will be interesting to see if it can maintain such a resource-demanding strategy.

Pringles is one of P&G's
300 global brands.

Facts

The story began in the US in 1837 when William Procter, an Englishman who made candles, and the Irish soap factory owner James Gamble formed Procter & Gamble. From the beginning, P&G was in competition with 14 other soap manufacturers in Cincinnati, Ohio. On top of that, the US was, at that time, going through a period of financial panic causing several bank failures. But with product innovations and contracts with the Federal army during the American civil war, the company prospered. As early as 1890, P&G was marketing more than 30 varieties of soap.

P&Gs product innovations continued through the turn of the last century, all backed by research and accompanied by clever marketing campaigns. But as the product portfolio increased, the need for control and direction also grew. The P&G brand management system began to fall into place during the 1920s and in 1931 the company formed one of the first corporate marketing organizations in the world.

Since then, the company has grown and expanded into several product categories. P&G now owns around 300 brands globally and these are sold in more than 140 countries. A 1999 turnover of $38 billion makes P&G one of the market's real heavyweights.

CHAPTER 16

Structuring the company
with a brand system

This book was originally intended to be solely about corporate brand systems. But such systems only become fully apparent when they are viewed from a value economy perspective.

Chapter 3 outlined the value centrifuge – Figure 3.1 – and its impact on the speed at which everything is changing. It also emphasized the need to communicate unique values globally. A brand is not a neon sign invented to make you stand out in the market. A brand is a value economy focal point and an articulate voice in an ongoing conversation with consumers.

When a brand becomes as influential as the company, top management must be able to pass on that brand energy to its employees and create a supportive culture. They should ask themselves: are our messages clear? Do all interested parties get a consistent view of the corporation and what it is we want?

The brand is synonymous with the total description of a company (see Chapter 7 and *Corporate Religion*). This is the company as a brand – or corporate brand. In the future, values and attitudes will become the most important property companies own.

It has become fashionable to claim that the individual customer is king and that every company must bend itself to communicating directly with him or her. Of course, the customer is special. But this kind of thinking is really just a variation on customer service. Such an approach can never be the core of a brand.

Constantly trying to change a brand to suit everybody can be very harmful to it. Instead, a brand must be nurtured so that its strengths draw in those customers who are attracted by its position and value. Of course companies should try

A brand is not a neon sign invented to make you stand out in the market. A brand is a value economy focal point and an articulate voice in an ongoing conversation with consumers.

In the future, values and attitudes will become the most important property companies own.

to get closer to their customers, but it must be the values of the brand that serve as the core of customer communication.

The brand system demonstrates the advantages of moving in new directions and of helping consumers to understand why the move is being made. A traditional brand way of thinking is no longer enough. Managers should try to get as far to the left of the system as possible. After all, It has already worked well for Mercedes, Nike and LEGO.

Figure 16.1 is an attempt to illustrate an optimal branding process based on a corporate brand. To the left the brand is densely coloured and concentrated; as it moves further away from the corporate brand it becomes more diluted.

Figure 16.1 Organic growth via the use of brand and the brand system

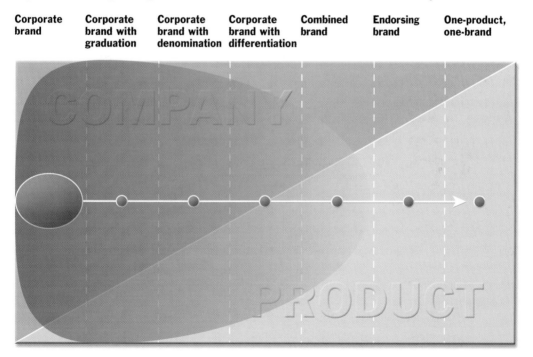

Corporate brand	Corporate brand with graduation	Corporate brand with denomination	Corporate brand with differentiation	Combined brand	Endorsing brand	One-product, one-brand

The optimal branding strategy within the new value economy is via organic growth based on the corporate brand and by using various sub-branding methods to keep the overall corporate brand universe together for as long as possible.

As shown in Figures 5.1 and 5.2 the aim is to establish a strong brand core where the brand is centred around a value position that provides a particular customer segment with high value (see Figure 6.1). As the brand grows, it should move carefully towards the right in Figure 16.1 using graduation and generic names, the two forms of branding that as well as being strong and clear also ensure the highest value accumulation in the corporate brand. Danone is placed well towards the right in the system, as is Kellogg's. Both corporations deploy a strong combined branding based on clear value positions. Danone's is 'Active Health' and Kellogg's is 'healthy breakfast'. Where the Danone corporate brand does not playing the lead role, it does not communicate as clearly and directly as with other brands.

The same thing goes for Giorgio Armani, which would be placed in the outer circle of Figure 16.1. Armani communicates less clearly than Mercedes and Virgin. Even if the consumer sees the connection between the sub-brand Emporio Armani and the corporate brand, the brand structure is less pure. However, this is counterbalanced by the sub-brands contributing to an intensive, ongoing value accumulation in the corporate brand.

Should Kellogg's, in its search for new growth opportunities, end up by diluting its value position with too many sub-brands unconnected to breakfast foods, it could find itself in the same situation as Nestlé. The brand will become an endorser for high-quality food products and be placed so far to the right in Figure 16.1 that it loses its value as a strong corporate brand.

We should look at the brand system as a very delicate mechanism, not unlike an orchestra where all the instruments must play together to produce music.

Figure 16.2 Incorporation of bought-up companies into the corporate brand

Corporate brand	Corporate brand with graduation	Corporate brand with denomination	Corporate brand with differentiation	Combined brand	Endorsing brand	One-product, one-brand

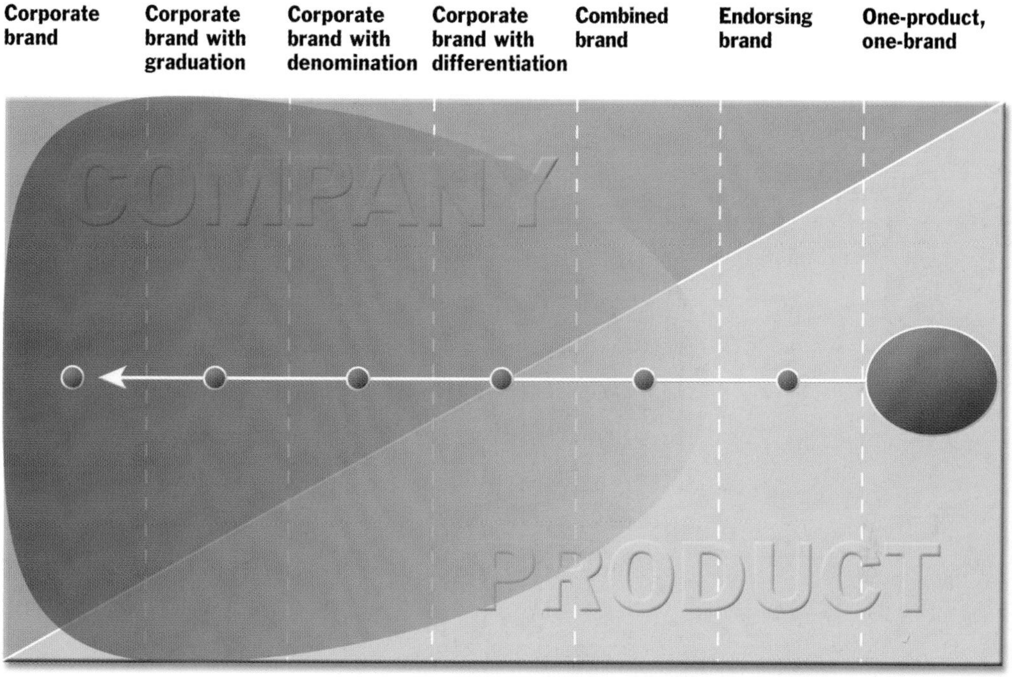

In acquisitions the process of incorporating the new company into the existing corporate brand must be carefully controlled. Should you endorse it or should it be an equal member of the corporate brand?

The brand system and buying up

Within the new value economy, growth will be partly organic and partly the result of mergers and acquisitions. This will place increased focus on branding.

The issue in a merger is not just creating a new culture but also optimizing the new market position via appropriate branding. A brand is a very powerful means of communication in a merger, both internally and externally. What is decisive for brand strategy in mergers and acquisitions is whether the new company already has a brand and whether or not it can be incorporated into the corporate brand.

Figure 16.2 illustrates how a new company or a new brand can be included in an already existing corporate brand and the resulting brand structure rationalized.

Acquisitions often involve the rationalization of duplicated functions. On the other hand, there is usually little interference with existing branding. This can be a great mistake and usually happens either because rationalizing branding is seen as too complex or the acquiring company has too much money – why else continue to run two brands?

What should happen is that managers try to merge the two companies in the brand sense as well as financially and operationally. This can save money both through the creation of an internal culture and via the external branding process.

As Figure 16.2 shows, you must evaluate whether to incorporate the acquired brand into the corporate brand and decide how far to the left you want to place it. Is it possible to annex the new company into the existing brand and place it to the left? Or should you settle for endorsement, as VW did with Skoda to inject its corporate brand value into the Czech car maker?

If the newly acquired company is incorporated into the corporate brand, it could be as a combined brand – see Nestlé's incorporation of Premier ice cream in Figure 14.4.

In other cases the acquired brand may be so weak that it is abolished and replaced by the corporate brand. Initially though, this may prove unprofitable because some consumers who have related to the brand in the past will be lost.

Another scenario is acquiring a brand within a new product area but one with a similar position to your own. This could be handled by starting with a combined brand strategy and later moving towards the left to let it become a descriptive corporate brand using a generic name. For example, Premier ice cream could be brought much closer to the Nestlé brand and after a few years renamed Nestlé Ice. However, because Nestlé lacks a strong corporate brand core, it is doubtful whether this would succeed.

In Figure 16.2, the further an acquired brand can be incorporated to the left of the brand system, the more favourable it will be for the future strengthening of the brand. The decisive factor is how value and positions fit together.

The move towards rationalization and fewer brands is undoubtedly the correct way forward in adjusting to new value economy conditions. The chairman of the board of Unilever, Antony Burgnam, realized this a few years ago.

Unilever owns 1,600 brands worldwide. Burgnam has said that over three to five years, this will be reduced to 400 and later even further to 250. Until the end of the 1990s, Unilever was one of the major, international food groups. It acted in a very similar way to Procter & Gamble: one-product, one-brand. The reason for a change to this strategy was the desire for a higher growth rate concentrated on fewer, stronger brands.

The battle for shelf space is getting tougher, not least because retailers want to promote their own-label products. Burgman has also pointed out that within several product categories Unilever owns up to five different brands competing with each other. This can sometimes be appropriate in monopoly markets but in general too many brands weaken the strong brands and provide openings for competitors.

A food industry producer without its own distribution system must own consumers. This can only be done through the development of powerful brands that retailers must stock because of consumer demand.

Unilever is not reducing its brand portfolio to save money. The 400 brands that remain will have their marketing budgets quadrupled, increasing their market penetration. In the future, Unilever will put its efforts into five main areas: culinary, frozen foods, ice cream, tea and yellow fats. It will be interesting to watch how Unilever implements this plan. It will obviously concentrate on those areas where it is already strong and on the brands that have built up the strongest markets and value positions. But even that can be difficult because many brands have different names, logos and positions in different countries.

The case study below is an example of how Unilever is trying to group its ice cream brands under one major brand. Unilever has expanded its ice cream business through acquisitions. Consequently, it has a jumble of names and logos, all of which are individually strong brands with powerful market positions in their individual countries. To create synergy, Unilever is marketing these independent products under the same name across borders. Magnum is probably the best-known example. But Unilever continues to use the name and the logo of the original company.

As the case study shows, Unilever has developed a heart-shaped logo that is used together with the local brand name. Once the heart logo has become visible and accepted, the next step for Unilever will probably be to use the same name everywhere. If it succeeds, it will be a neat way to rationalize a brand portfolio. A new major global brand would be born.

This case should inspire other major international corporations, whether they are a food company or in any other business. It is the technique that matters. In business-to-business sectors it is usually easier to do this because the costs of changing customer perception will be a lot less and the change can happen more quickly.

Unilever

Unilever one of the largest food concerns in the world, has changed its branding strategy. A desire to concentrate its marketing and reinforce selected brands has prompted the company to reduce its product portfolio to 400 brands. Unilever hopes to create larger and stronger brands as well as increase growth.

A new branding strategy

Unilever's rapid, acquisition-driven growth meant that by the end of 1999 it owned around 1,600 brands. Each of these was marketed independently as distinct product brands. Maintaining so many brands – and launching new ones – is a very expensive proposition.

Unilever has now dropped its strategy of achieving growth through brand acquisitions. Today's retail battle is about shelf space, and with 'only' 400 brands, Unilever can concentrate its efforts and achieve significantly greater penetration. Unilever's products will no longer fight with each other for shelf space. Resources can be concentrated on the battle with competitors. In order to exploit existing value positions, only the strongest brands within the same product category will survive.

The valuable ice cream heart

Unilever's branding is an example of this new strategy. Over the years, Unilever has acquired a large number of national producers of dairy products, each carrying their own brand names and visual identities.

In an attempt to rationalize these brands, Unilever has given each of them the same logo in the shape of an ice cream 'heart' but allowed them to retain their local names. By letting the ice cream brands share a logo, the mutual value accumulation is reinforced and the values from one brand can more easily be transferred to the others. The 'heart' then becomes both a value generator and a general quality stamp. With time, a single name can be used – a classic example of how to turn different brands within the same category into a new single global brand.

An example of one of Unilever's old ice cream logos and how the new uniform identity looks.

Facts

The Lever part of what was later to become Unilever was Lever Brothers, an English soap manufacturer formed in 1885 by William Hesketh Lever.

Lever Brothers produced soap worldwide and in 1917 also began to offer food products. In 1930, Unilever was formed from a merger of Lever Brothers and the Dutch margarine manufacturer Margarine Unie.

The Dutch company had grown via mergers with other margarine manufacturers during the 1920s. Since the merger, the Anglo-Dutch group has become one of the largest companies in the world with a turnover of more than £27 billion in 1999, divided between 300 companies in 80 countries.

Danone's organic brand system

Danone places a great deal of focus on the value of its brand. As shown in Figure 16.3, it has made a sharp division between the food brand Danone and the concern Danone. Approximately 26 per cent of the company's business is in the Danone brand, the rest being spread among various independent brands within several food categories.

The desire to become more international led to the French food group changing its name from BSN to Danone in 1994 (at that time Danone was one of BSN's brands). This inevitably created problems. Overnight one brand became the owner of all the other brands. At first sight, the fresh food brand does not seem to have much to do with LU biscuits, Kronenburg beer or Evian mineral water. So the company developed a corporate logo depicting a woman looking towards the stars, shown at the top of figure 16.3. This made it possible to separate fresh dairy produce such as Danone yogurt, Maille Dijon mustard and LU chocolate biscuits, while the attentive consumer can see that the items emanate from the same company, Danone Group.

The company achieved its aim. A giant international food corporation had achieved the visibility it desired. This is important. A survey reported in the *Financial Times* in the year 2000 shows that stock prices in the US are higher for companies whose brand is known to the public.

Figure 16.3 shows how Danone uses its brand thinking in companies it acquires, such as the Italian company Galbani, which produces mozzarella and gorgonzola. As the figure shows, Danone uses a progressive branding system and differentiated branding to achieve growth. Italian cheese and ham products have high value, so there is more growth in store for the Galbani brand if Danone maintains this approach with even more differentiated sub-brands.

Figure 16.3 Danone Group's total brand system

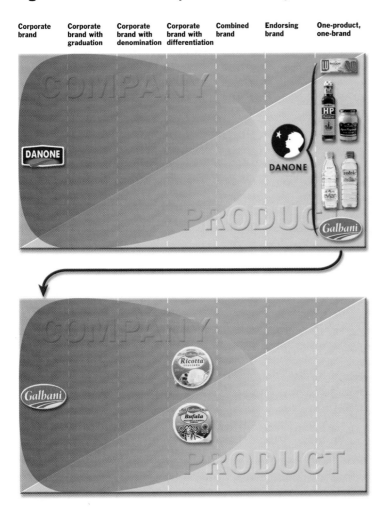

The Danone Group brand Galbani has been established as an independent brand and can now begin its own brand system. Danone has developed a Danone Group logo, used to signify ownership and endorsement of independent brands within the group.

Branding and mergers

Mergers create obvious cost advantages. But they can be extremely difficult to handle brand wise. Which of the brands will survive the merger? Mergers often involve many deals and compromises to make them happen. Branding and brand positions are forgotten and more damage is caused over names, logos, and so on. In many cases, and this is even more grotesque, merging companies frequently publicize the alliance as soon as possible without knowing anything about what their logo will be and which name they will use. Merging companies do not show much value economy sense by rushing out a logo in a couple of days. They might want to impress the media and investors, but the impact would be greater if the branding were in place. It is branding that will provide their profit, not the merger itself. The most valuable aspects of a merger are the two brands and their brand positions, yet these are often treated carelessly, even irresponsibly. The decision makers involved in a merger usually don't have the faintest idea about branding.

Managers should consider the signals they send to employees of merging companies when, more or less casually, they learn about the new name and logo. This is poor communication because it fails to acknowledge that the merged companies are living organisms that must work together successfully. Consumers can pose an even greater problem. They will assess the situation on the basis of the information they are given. If the messages are not complete, they will soon find another producer offering clearer values and attitudes.

The task should be viewed as shown in Figure 16.4. First, there must be a thorough analysis of both companies. Then you can work with different models to create a new and stronger merged company. It is the combination of the internal culture and the external position that makes a powerful company. Merging two companies means a new brand will arise that will have a relationship to the two companies' specific brand positions. This calls for a re-articulation of the corporate brand and an incorporation

> *Merging companies do not show much value economy sense by rushing out a logo in a couple of days. They might want to impress the media and investors, but the impact would be greater if the branding were in place.*

> *It is the combination of the internal culture and the external position that makes a powerful company.*

Figure 16.4 During a merger, the new company must be reformulated

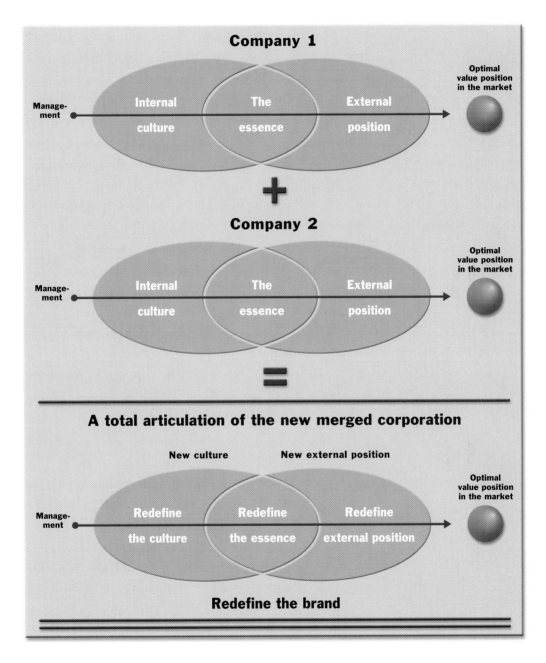

During a merger, a completely new corporate religion must be created for the newly merged company. It's not enough that the management agree to put the two companies together. You have to redefine a new common culture, essence and external positioning based on what the merged companies stand for.

of the aims of the new company and its business into a description of a new mutual culture.

Companies often say they cannot wait for that and that they must move fast, otherwise everything will come to a standstill. But it is difficult to move two company cultures and their customers to an understanding of what the merger means. In brief, if a merged company is to be dynamic and value generating from the beginning, it must have a total description of the new brand and the new brand culture.

Doing this helps to produce the ideal brand name and logo and optimize the external value position you want to capture. It all needs to be in harmony – remember that the best customers and employees are deeply involved in their company. If they can see the new direction, they will buy both the plan and the brand. If they cannot, everything will be uphill work.

The main reason that more than 50 per cent of mergers go wrong is that the management do not understand the concept of branding. What they are merging is a lot more than mere products; there are also people, attitudes and value positions wrapped up in the brands. It is not enough just to employ human resource consultants to make people get together and have a little chat about their future. That is patronizing and underestimates people's intelligence. What matters is whether you have a plan to create a new and exciting corporation employees would like to contribute to.

As company managers begin to understand the idea of the company as a brand, we will see more mergers being successful. It seems surprising that greater effort is not put into creating powerful brands when the idea of a merger in the first place is to achieve more market penetration.

If a merged company is to be dynamic and value generating from the beginning, it must have a total description of the new brand and the new brand culture.

The successful merger

An example of a successful merger is the one between business service groups Price Waterhouse and Coopers & Lybrand. Price Waterhouse had the higher value position in the market and the name was combined with Coopers to signal broadness: PricewaterhouseCoopers also deals with smaller clients. The merger is a good illustration of articulating a new brand capable of being sold both internally and externally.

PricewaterhouseCoopers

If you are a large corporation owning a dominant position in the market yet wish to grow even bigger, how do you do it?

One way is to take over another company or merge with it. But how do you combine different market and value positions in a new corporation with a new set of values?

This problem demands careful examination, not least out of consideration for employees, whose loyalty is the basis of a company's existence. Also, the value position must be clear and credible externally.

PricewaterhouseCoopers is the successful outcome of a merger between two major players, Price Waterhouse and Coopers & Lybrand, in the accountancy and consultancy sector. The result is a corporation employing more than 150,000 people working from 900 offices in 152 countries.

Two majors become one giant

Before the merger, Price Waterhouse and Coopers & Lybrand owned two different positions in the market. Even though they were both very large and, from the outside, seemed rather similar, there was quite a difference in their positions. Price Waterhouse had specialized in very large international companies – in many countries it would only take on the very biggest clients. Coopers & Lybrand, on the other hand, had both large and mid-sized customers and even smaller clients. This meant that no matter which of the two brand names they chose, the market could easily gain the impression that something had been lost.

As a brand, Price Waterhouse, no matter how much it would try to state the opposite, would send signals to smaller and mid-sized clients that the new merged company now wanted to focus only on large international customers. Prices would go up and the company would not spend time on smaller clients. If Coopers & Lybrand became the brand, large international companies would get the impression that the new corporation no longer focused 100 per cent on them.

Being able to handle major international companies means that you are probably among the very best. From this point of view, the higher value position in the market was in the brand name Price Waterhouse.

What a dilemma for a branding perfectionist. Whatever you do, you will get it wrong. Creating an entirely new brand name

Figure 16.5 The fusion between Price Waterhouse and Coopers & Lybrand

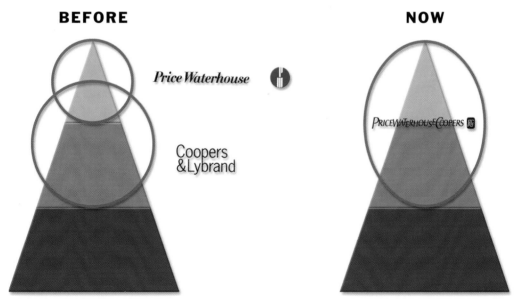

Price Waterhouse and Coopers & Lybrand occupied different value positions in the market before the merger. Together their position is shown after the merger.

Your worlds · Our people

The three elements in

PricewaterhouseCoopers'

new branding strategy are

people, knowledge and the

world – three elements

that are repeated in the

internal and external

communication. The vase

illustrates the coherence

and the interplay between

the elements.

would cost a lot of money and accountants are not in the habit of throwing their money about. The compromise became the solution: PricewaterhouseCoopers. Price Waterhouse has the high quality built into it while Coopers has the broadness Figure 16.5.

Is the new brand in danger of becoming too broad and thereby losing sharpness in the market? Perhaps. But intensive marketing can bring it into the superbrand class and provide it with some free brand value.

PricewaterhouseCoopers can become everything and nothing. It offers consultancy, customer relationship management, technology, general management, human resources, and so on. The company could develop a branding system to make its different business areas visible rather than building new brands. During the process of the merger, a lot of material that described the new brand and the new company was produced. It was very impressive and PricewaterhouseCoopers made an honest attempt at delivering clarity. By moving across the boundaries of the different working areas, PricewaterhouseCoopers has tried to articulate a new company culture. It makes the merger appear as an aggressive and progressive player in the market and draws a picture of a new and exciting company. This is how a merged brand communicates.

Though Price Waterhouse had a higher profile than Coopers & Lybrand, the new visual identity combines both the names and the market positions of the two companies. The cartoon-like typeface was a conscious provocation in a traditional and conservative field and symbolized a new and different company.

From the beginning, PricewaterhouseCoopers consciously chose not to have any sub-brands until the identity of the corporate brand was completely clear in clients' minds. Today, the Danish branding system consists of three sub-brands called service lines – accounting, business consultancy, and management consultancy and tax advice. The new branding strategy is based on a brand story containing three elements: people, knowledge and the world. They are the heart of the brand and they pervade all communication.

In the PricewaterhouseCoopers' printed material, faces are the symbol of the first factor. The people depicted are not famous models or actors, they are PricewaterhouseCoopers employees and are chosen for the message 'these are the people who deliver the job'. This is where the 'knowledge' aspect joins in. 'World' symbolizes the expansive coverage of the new company, yet globes are banned as a visual image because this symbol is overused by competitors. Instead, 'world' is illustrated by images of sights from around the globe which should arouse recognition in those who see them. Finally, PricewaterhouseCoopers uses a vase as a symbol of coherence and interplay between the three fundamental factors.

PricewaterhouseCoopers' staff appear in both the internal and external communications.

Facts

Like many other large accounting and consultancy businesses in London, Price Waterhouse and Coopers & Lybrand were formed when the UK was the centre of an empire. Samuel Lowell Price started his business in 1849 and five years later William Cooper founded his business, later named Coopers Brothers. In 1874, Price, Holyland and Waterhouse went into partnership and formed Price, Waterhouse & Co. In 1898, Lybrand, Ross Brothers and Montgomery was formed and a merger in 1957 created Coopers & Lybrand.
Price Waterhouse World Firm was established in 1982 and on July 1, 1998, the merger between Price Waterhouse and Coopers & Lybrand took place.

Redefining the company

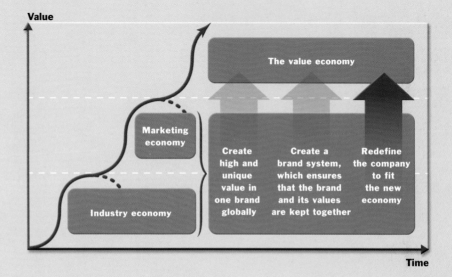

CHAPTER 17

Redefining the company

In the value economy, the strongest brands will rule the business world.

This has radical consequences for companies' strategic thinking and the way they operate. The value economy will belong to businesses that understand the brand is inseparable from the company.

The days of the product-oriented company are over. It is not good enough to go with the flow and simply make adjustments to product programmes. Nowadays, anyone can make anything. Anyone can make technologically advanced products, anyone can distribute them, anyone can set up good retail businesses, and everyone has learned how to market themselves.

Simply existing is just not enough. You have to make a choice. And a choice always entails eliminating some other option. You will have to believe in something, which you then become brilliant at. Unless you are a firm believer in what you are doing, you will never be successful in the new value economy. How else can you contribute something unique to the market?

A mere product is no longer enough. You have to add some value to the product via a high value brand that has a clear direction.

A mere product is no longer enough. You have to add some value to the product via a high value brand that has a clear direction. It is this value and direction that is most important for everyone, both for customers in the external market and for the internal culture. If you have nothing to offer to customers, you will have to leave the market. There will be no room for wishy-washy companies.

Believe or beat it

Of course, there will still be a few of that sort of company around, but they will have a hard time earning any money. They will also have a problem with their employees, who would rather work for companies that have something to offer the world that makes a difference.

An analogy might be a party, where there will always be some people who really make an effort to generate fun and where there are others who do not contribute. Within the new value economy, there will be a demand for active brands and corporations. Employees will insist that their company is exciting to work for and they will want something to believe in. The influence works both ways because the company can, in return, demand employees' full commitment. If they do not provide it, there is no place for them in the company, which must deliver ultimate value every day and therefore needs highly motivated and committed employees.

No company can survive by simply going with the flow and trying to make things just a little better than average. It takes something a lot more radical to participate in the value economy of the future.

> No company can survive by simply going with the flow and trying to make things just a little better than average. It takes something a lot more radical to participate in the value economy of the future.

To really optimize your organization and get ready for the future, you must create an internal revolution and question everything that you do.

A key exercise is to try to work out the essence of all parts of your company. As a company leader it could be interesting to step out for a while – perhaps for a month – and work your way through all of your company's processes. You could form between five and ten focus groups with customers and spend time alone with them. You and your company could benefit a lot from such an episode.

Most companies that have been successful and grown have almost inevitably allowed the corporate machinery to take over the power. A director may still be directing. However, if you take a look at how much of what is set in motion actually makes it out at the other end and how much does not even live up to the aims of the company, the result will probably be quite worrying. If those imbalances get out of hand, they will simply tear the company apart. It will be unable to deliver a brand with a high unique value, a brand with a clear and homogenous direction, a brand that is global within the new value economy.

Markets are changing fast and you must be able to act accordingly. The problem is that most of the values in companies are no longer the actual product, so a new way of tying the company together has to be found. We have returned to the need to develop a corporate religion to establish those values – and stick to them.

The difference between *Corporate Religion*, which pointed out the necessity of finding and articulating the essence of a company, and this book is that the message now is to use corporate religion to optimize the company. It is not enough just to create missions and define values for the company.

You need to optimize the company according to the brand and the values – not the product.

You need to define the value position, stand for it, and use it to manage the company. You must optimize the company according to the brand and the values – not the product. The product is changing all the time anyway. This kind of optimization has dramatic consequences, as described above, as you turn everything upside down and break down the old product inertia.

We are already witnessing this. Companies are buying CRM systems from any IT or consultancy company that can provide them with smart process descriptions. This is to absolutely no end because real CRM requires a complete change of mindset throughout the company.

The product-focused mindset must go, though most companies are not in a position to do so at a stroke. The point is that you cannot just forget the product – you still have to make outstanding goods. However, this should no longer be your main focus; the product alone cannot get through in the value economy.

Take stock and do something now

It is a matter of doing something outstanding and it must be done now if you don't want to be left behind. The things that need redefining for a move into the new value economy make up the remaining chapters of this book. Redefine means, in part, finding the essence of your company, what it is, and then, via its brand, bringing this essence into new product areas and new markets. And partly, it means that most companies will find themselves in a situation where their present earnings are coming from the old product-oriented economy. These companies must build themselves up to be competitive in the new value economy. Currently we have two economies running simultaneously and companies must keep a balance within both.

It is a matter of finding the essence of your company, what it is, and then, via its brand, bringing this essence into new product areas and new markets.

You could be fortunate enough to be a product-oriented company and earn a good living from a particular product market for many years, perhaps because you actually have a unique product. But you also run the risk that a strong brand will intervene and steal a major part of your market share, just as the mechanisms of the new value economy dictate. Calvin Klein Jeans and Armani Jeans did this to Levi's, and Virgin does it in all the product categories it ventures into.

This does not make running a company any easier. It requires that you concentrate both on products and now, as a new thing, on value positions. Only this will give you a realistic picture of where competition may appear from in the future. However, you could also use this insight to spot other directions in which your own company could move to build a strong brand.

Figure 17.1 lists some of the areas in which managers need to change their views. As already explained in Part 1, you must now think brand wherever you used to think product. While consultants might recommend an optimized product value chain, in future it will be much more interesting to optimize your brand value chain. (This is explained further in Chapter 18.) Only the companies that see themselves as a brand can hope to create the strong brand culture that is capable of capturing a valuable brand position – what we also call a value position.

Of course, you still have to sell products, but even in that area major changes are happening (see Chapters 19 and 22 about the company's way to the market and about where future competition may appear from). All these fluctuations require that companies redefine their perception of organization – the subject of Chapter 21.

Whatever changes the future holds, the major corporate challenge will be to focus on the value driver of the future – the company brand.

When top management wholeheartedly begins to think brand, it will seem obvious that organizations need to be more flat.

When top management wholeheartedly begin to think brand, it will become obvious that organizations need to be more flat. It will also be quite obvious why knowledge is the most important asset of a company and why constant change will be a day-to-day matter and not something you reluctantly face when it is unavoidable. In the future, the organization's ability to deliver current innovations will be crucial for its successful survival. Change does not happen unprompted. Someone must show the way. For top managers to manage this, they must really change their own behaviour. Managers must adopt a new role, from being the 'boss' to being the inspiring team builder. In other words, they must accustom their organizations to becoming good at renewing the company and the brand rather than being inflexibly oriented to products and systems. In the future, product innovations will be far down the agenda.

This is no job for a clever administrator. The era of the bookkeeper is over. A good manager must be a particularly competent communicator because it will be impossible to run a knowledge-based company without a more horizontally structured organization where several people contribute to managerial tasks.

Figure 17.1 Redefine your company in accordance with the new value economy

From the old economy → to the new value economy

1. Redefine the idea of company strategy (Chapter 18)

From optimizing the product value chain ⟶ to optimizing the brand value chain

2. Redefine your idea of value (Part 1)

From product ⟶ to value position in the market
From product brands ⟶ to the company as a brand
From logo and design ⟶ to brand systems

3. Redefine your idea of the company's way to the market (Chapter 19)

From long distribution chains ⟶ to short distribution chains
From physical distribution ⟶ to mental distribution
From customer relations ⟶ to brand relations

4. Redefine your idea of the company organization (Chapter 20)

From international and local domains ⟶ to global domains in specific segments
From product organization ⟶ to brand culture
From hierarchical organization ⟶ to a horizontal knowledge organization
From control and administration ⟶ to articulation and communication
From systems excellence ⟶ to innovation excellence
From titles ⟶ to actual knowledge and generating value

5. Redefine your idea of leadership (Chapter 21)

From product management ⟶ to brand management
From top-down ⟶ to team values
From management ⟶ to innovator
From administrator ⟶ to communicator
From tight management ⟶ to broad management
From rules and regulations ⟶ to the management of ideas, brand and culture

6. Redefine your idea of market boundaries (Chapter 22)

From local ⟶ to global
From product barrier ⟶ to brand barrier
From product value ⟶ to brand value

To be successful within the new value economy company, managers will have to redefine their company in a number of key areas and change focus from a product-oriented to a brand-oriented mindset.

CHAPTER 18

The brand value chain:
the new corporate strategy

As the value economy changes the rules of the game,
managers are experiencing a radical reordering
of priorities over the allocation of resources. In
the future, resources will have to be divided more
equally between the physical distributions system
and the mental distribution of the brand.

Most companies that operate on industry economy principles will be inefficient within the value economy. They over-invest in products, services, divisions and departments and are over-valued in relation to their actual market access.

One of the clearest symptoms of this malaise is products that are over-engineered by production departments. Huge sums of money are spent on developing products that lack relevance in the market. Anyone who believes that irrelevant products strengthen a market position, let alone a value position, is mistaken.

Anyone who believes
that irrelevant products
strengthen a market
position, let alone a value
position, is mistaken.

Innovation is not a solution

Last year alone, Sony launched more than 10,000 new products. Imagine how many resources it takes to pull all that through a corporate system. Take, for example, Sony's video cameras. It seems as though a new model appears every few months. Consumers can find this irritating, perhaps feeling they have bought the wrong camera. The differences between the camera they buy one month and next month's model are very small. So why does Sony do this? Why is it wasting vast amounts of resources on a product-fixated organization and consequently sacrificing its value position on the altar of the product range? This is an inefficient use of resources. Sony would probably defend itself by talking about a need to be innovative and ahead of the game. But tiny product improvements do not add up to innovation, particularly if you lack the resources to communicate them to the market.

Involvement, thanks!

Figures 18.1 and 18.2 illustrate how companies should balance the distribution of resources to prepare themselves for the future.

Figure 18.1 shows how a product fixation inflates a company in relation to the value of its external position. The company needs to be cut – indicated by the arrows pointing inwards in figure 18.2 – and the resources saved invested in a stronger external position. Within the value

Figure 18.1 The product-oriented company is out of balance

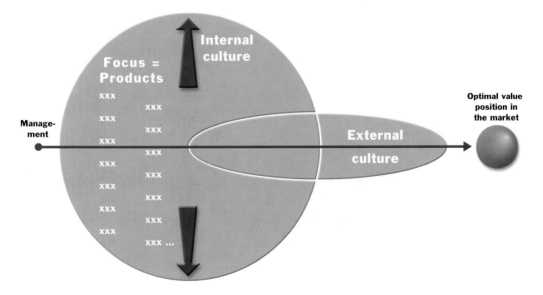

Product fixation imbalances many companies. The result is an unrealistic over-valuation of the company in relation to its access to the market.

Figure 18.2 Optimizing the resources within the value economy

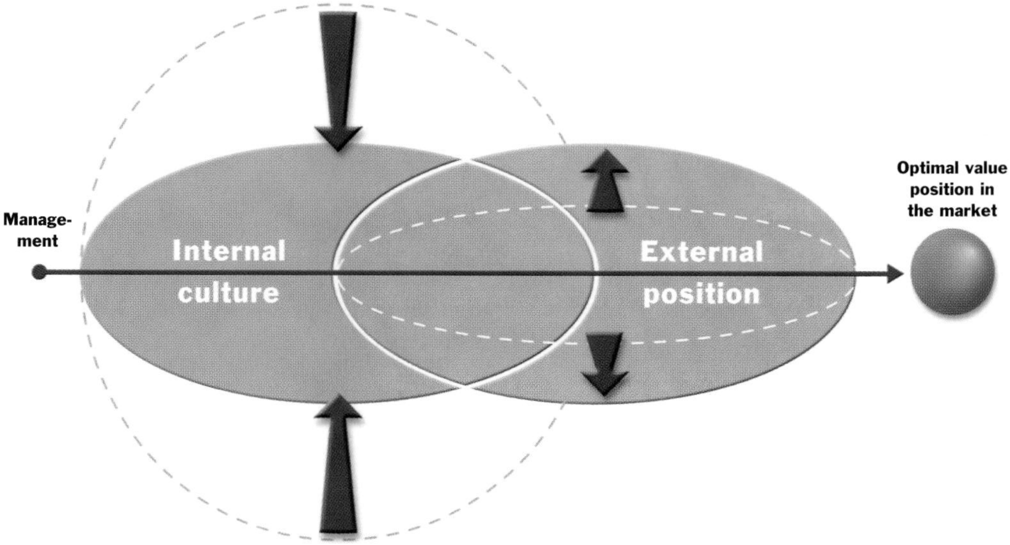

Within the value economy, product fixation must end. This allows resources to be liberated for investment in a stronger external value position. In other words, to optimize your company you must capture the value you aim for.

economy, the scarce resource is mental market access. That is why resources must be spent on being seen, on the involvement of consumers, and on capturing a place in their minds.

Ericsson

A good example of a company that suffered under the weight of product inertia was Sweden's Ericsson. It developed a phone that was proof against small shocks and water. Technologically it was an amazing product. But it was totally irrelevant in the context of the battle that Ericsson is fighting against Nokia and Motorola.

Ericsson should have spent its resources on being the first with handsets that integrate the mobile phone and the Internet. And that is only the beginning. The third generation of mobile phones is coming soon. If competition was tough for Ericsson then, it will be even tougher in the future. Ericsson cannot gain a competitive edge so long as it maintains this focus and fails to control product development in accordance with its brand position. This is a disastrous situation as Ericsson's poor accounts, published in autumn 2000, make clear. But now Ericsson has announced a future co-operation with Sony, and it will be interesting to monitor whether the Swedish product organization can be linked with Sony's high involvement among younger consumers. There is no doubt it's a smart – and vital – move for Ericsson.

Abolish back-stage brands

Figure 18.3 shows how you can think about strategy that will allow your company to make a smooth transition into the value economy. What you need is a complete streamlining of the company. By defining the company as a brand, you can create a corporate brand strategy and gain control over your brand value chain.

Optimizing your brand value chain is key. One way of doing this is a proper allocation of resources, avoiding any one link in the chain dominating the rest. In other words, the company must deliver its value position. The value centrifuge means that the company must gear up to develop mind space in its customers.

Most companies are unique in one way or another but only a few of them are able to articulate and communicate that uniqueness. It is just like people – everyone is unique. If a company does not appear to be unique, it will die in the value economy. This is Darwin's theory – and it has never seemed more relevant. For companies, survival consists of being heard in today's communication society. It is also important that a company is not a feeble, superficial façade with nothing behind it. This can make consumers

2

Delivering the value position must be one company. The company must communicate its uniquness.

Figure 18.3 The brand value chain – optimize your value position in the market

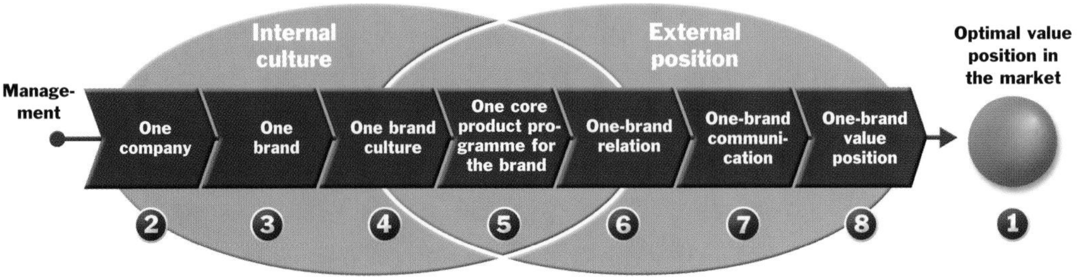

To successfully enter the value economy, the core of corporate strategy must be the optimization of the brand value chain. Only then can it win the best value position in the market. The entire company must be built and shaped according to the brand.

The brand value chain mindset:

1. Defining the value position you want in the market, depicted as a circle to the very right of the figure, is key.
2. At the far left link in the brand value chain it is important to appear as one company. Only one company is in a position to be unique. It has a soul and is a living organism.
3. The company must be built into a brand because the brand mindset is good at gathering and communicating a set of values and attitudes externally and internally.
4. You must develop a brand culture that can hold the brand together globally.
5. It is important to define the product programme on which you focus when building a brand position in the market.
6. You must define the most important target groups for the brand, both those who buy the brand directly and any indirect decisionmakers, who are often the most important carriers of value. Direct connection to these decision makers must be made via a brand relation management system.
7. You need to build a consistent and value-accumulating brand communication that focuses on the brand and not on a lot of different product launches.
8. The brand communication must deliver the brand position in the market, which should equal the value position you wish to capture.

sceptical and insecure, just as we would feel uncomfortable with a person who appears to possess several contradictory personalities.

Employees, too, do not want to work for a company that has a poor environmental record or one that has no proper social policy towards its employees. It is increasingly important for employees that their company has a welfare policy and puts it into practice.

Employees do not want to work for a company that has a poor environmental record or one that has no proper social policy toward its employees. It is increasingly important for employees that their company has a welfare policy and puts it into practice.

A company and a brand that consist of props and a façade will have trouble generating genuine commitment from employees and getting them to say: 'My aim is the optimizing of this chocolate bar and this is one of the most important goals in my life.'

The world is impenetrable without values

So the company must have a life, preferably a good one, and a soul. It also needs a spokesman as its leader. Remember that in the future there will be very close relationships between companies and consumers who buy into the brand wholeheartedly. Companies must try to live up to this kind of idolatry.

The definition of the company must be incorporated into a brand, around which everything is built. This is explained in detail in Part 1. A brand is good at explaining the essence of company values and at conveying them clearly in a way that the market and the internal organization can understand. It is a mission that directs, not a product, which changes all the time anyway.

The value centrifuge means that a brand must be modified to ensure it is capable of communicating a unique value globally. It is worth remembering that a large proportion of major companies were started more than 20 years ago, often much more. When they were created, their main ambition was simply to survive in their domestic

A brand is good at explaining the essence of company values and at conveying them clearly in a way that the market and the internal organization can understand.

market. Consequently, many companies carry a name and a logo that simply don't make it in today's global market.

A brand must mean something to a particular consumer segment across national borders. You must find global common denominators for this customer segment and use these as the basis for constructing the brand. This means that, at some point or other, the company must abandon its national character in order to move on. Unfortunately, this usually happens much too late. Strangely enough, as many cases have demonstrated, customer segments are surprisingly homogeneous across national borders.

You need to define a brand culture (shown in step 4 of Figure 18.2) – a mixture of attitudes and values – as the basis of the company.

In the new value economy it is crucial that a company is driven by a common set of attitudes and values. In other words, a brand culture.

Look at Ericsson. It created networks to convey both fastnet and mobile communication. It was the first to launch fastnet phones, mobile phones, WAP, mp3, communicators, and the mobile Internet.

It must constantly redefine itself in relation to technological advances. This would be impossible were it not driven by attitudes and values that reflect what might or might not happen in the market.

Ericsson would benefit from developing its strategies on the basis of values and basing product development on its view of the world rather than from depending on a product with a minimal life span – such as a mobile phone that can survive a tumble into a puddle.

A company must articulate a brand culture that evolves around what is singular.

A company must articulate a brand culture that evolves around what is singular. This allows everyone to see and understand why it is a unique company. They can see the clear connection between the culture and the external brand position. Try it yourself and relate the value centrifuge to your internal culture – is it unique and can it be communicated globally?

At this point many companies overreact – subsidiaries in different countries must be allowed to live. But of course they should not live their own life – how, then, would the company be able to deliver a homogeneous brand globally? Within the value economy the great challenge for companies is how to increase their capacity for innovation and constantly communicate knowledge throughout the company and across disciplinary boundaries. The Internet can help in technical ways but the real task lies in the development of new ways, and systems to disseminate knowledge. It will certainly not be a house magazine bursting with anniversary mentions, bridge tournament results and sailing sponsorships.

What is required is an extensive, ongoing educational process for the entire company, aimed mainly at optimizing the brand. Top management must understand that employees want to know everything about their company in which they invest their energy and dynamism. Directives and rules won't satisfy them.

At the moment, the highest priority in many companies is the question of how to establish a communication and an educational system that works as a managerial system as well. Meanwhile, everyone talks about acquiring more and more knowledge. But it must be kept under control; otherwise we just end up wasting vast amounts of resources – this time on information rather than on product mania.

What will fashion the company in the future value society is culture in the shape of attitudes and values. The product alone can no longer tie the company together. Companies and their leaders must turn to the value chain now, before it is too late.

What will fashion the company in the future value society is culture in the shape of attitudes and values.

The product must deliver the core of the brand

One thing that each company must decide for itself is whether it wants to be unique. But the more unique you

One core product pro-gramme for the brand

5

Companies must develop one core product programme with unique value that can be communicated globally.

are, the stronger the reaction will be from the outside world.

Uniqueness requires taking a stance. But in the end it is better to have a few highly involved customers than trying to please everyone and ending up by not making anyone happy. On the basis of the brand and your desired position, you must define a range of international core products of which the global brand-culture process is part. This will be hard to achieve since product inertia is so strong. It is very hard to build the discipline and the new routines to ensure a sharp product range that constantly delivers the core of the brand. It is no good moving too far along a product development trail just for the sake of the product. You cannot afford diversity in your brand value chain.

Never forget the soul and the unique

The next field in the brand value chain is brand relation management, that is the systematized relationship between the brand and customers.

Understanding of the concept of customer relationship management is growing in companies, but they should be careful not to make a sudden move from a product-fixated mindset to a customer-fixated mindset. During your efforts to meet the individual demands of consumers, you must not forget the company soul and company uniqueness.

It is better to operate using the concept of brand relation management because you need to focus on the company and the brand as the controllers of the communication that builds up the brand position. In many companies this communication goes via the product and reaches consumers through a long distribution chain. As a result these companies are not really in control of the information the customers get.

One-brand relation

The company and the brand control the communication, which must constantly build up the brand position.

The solution is to separate the physical distribution and the mental distribution of the product. (This is explained further in Chapter 19.)

Another reason for the term brand relation management is that you often find yourself in a situation where you have to enter a dialogue with interested parties other than your actual customers. These will often be indirect value contributors, and it is very important to build close relationships with them. For major pharmaceutical companies, for example, it is very important to be in touch with the key opinion formers within their area. To keep track of all the relationships you use your brand.

Identify the carriers of value

For fashion brands, it is crucial to form relationships with the most important opinion leaders in the market. These could be fashion editors and journalists, trend-setting shop owners, musicians, philosophers, writers and advertising people. Between them, they assist in the acceleration of the brand in the value centrifuge and in the production of global communication.

Fashion brands have systematized their value accumulation by hyping themselves via high-profile fashion shows a couple of times a year, which are transmitted to customers by the world press.

If you wish to build brand value successfully you must identify your future value carriers and systematize the relationships between them and the brand.

If you wish to build brand value successfully you must identify your future value carriers and system-atize the relationships between them and the brand.

Nike has identified its value carriers as international sports stars and has systematized close relations between them and the brand via sponsorship agreements.

Think about it – even if you produce hot-air pumps or harvesters. A value carrier need not be as spectacular as Nike's former athlete Marion Jones to strengthen your brand. Identify your ambassadors and your value carriers and make a business agreement with them.

The biggest problem about value builders or opinion leaders is that it is often hard to see the investment directly reflected in product sales. Most managers can easily understand direct investment in marketing a product. It is a lot harder to spend money on a brand position – and that indirectly. Nevertheless, the largest profits are generated from a credible accumulation of value in your brand. And the highest credibility is found in opinion leaders who talk about your brand. It is similar to classic word of mouth, only now the company and the brand try to control the communication.

In his latest book, *Unleashing the Idea Virus*, (Ideavirus, Seth Godin, Malcom Gladwell, 2001) has tried to illustrate this phenomenon, especially how the Internet can be appropriated for indirect value accumulation. The danger, though, is the absence of control.

Imagine that Michael Jordan, who was Nike's "flagship" throughout the 1990s, had done something wrong and was exposed by the media. He could have pulled the brand down into the same mess because consumers identified Nike's swoosh with Jordan.

Who manipulates who?

Brand communication is the next field in the brand value chain, shown as the seventh link in Figure 18.3. And as with the previous link, it is crucial that you don't just look at the communication of the product but rather at the communication of the entire brand.

Figure 18.4 is an attempt at illustrating what is meant by an integrated brand communication. The communication is incorporated into the company personality model between the internal and the external company.

In the future, we will market both brand and product when we communicate our value positions. Our values strengthen our products – and the products, with their unique properties, strengthen the value position. There are many methods of building value into a brand. It can happen via PR, as in the fashion world, via brand campaigns, such as

Corporate communication must be based on the brand rather than the product. What is needed is an integrated brand communication that works both internally and externally.

Coca-Cola which also sponsors major sporting events, or via product communications, which then build the appropriate position for the brand. How it happens depends on the circumstances and opportunities open to individual companies.

Another aspect is external communication to the public and to investors. Companies cannot simply market products and brands. All major international companies employ PR professionals and communication departments. They are staffed with professionals who are good at handling critical situations. But they have not understood the active role they must play in capturing a value position for the brand in the market. Often they have a misconception of themselves as protectors of objective communication.

Journalists are brought up to believe that the more dirt you can uncover in a large corporation, the better. And, as mentioned before, companies are not best fitted for handling such in-depth scrutiny, either from journalists or consumers.

You will always be able to dig up something in major companies. It is difficult to control all the attitudes and values everyone expects of brands, managers and companies. An important future task of corporate PR professionals will therefore be to create the optimal image of the company in order to support the brand in the market.

An important future task of corporate PR professionals will be to create the optimal image of the company in order to support the brand in the market.

This task will entail managers sitting down and making up their minds about who they are and what they stand for. Another issue is who will carry out this PR work. Most journalists find it difficult to understand the brand way of thinking and also the task of building value because they think it is manipulative. But companies have become such major players in our lives that they contribute to the manipulation of society, just as every news channel manipulates us. All communication is manipulative because it is the outcome of a process of consciously made choices and omissions. Consumers still have the choice of whether or not they buy a brand.

Figure 18.4 Total brand communication

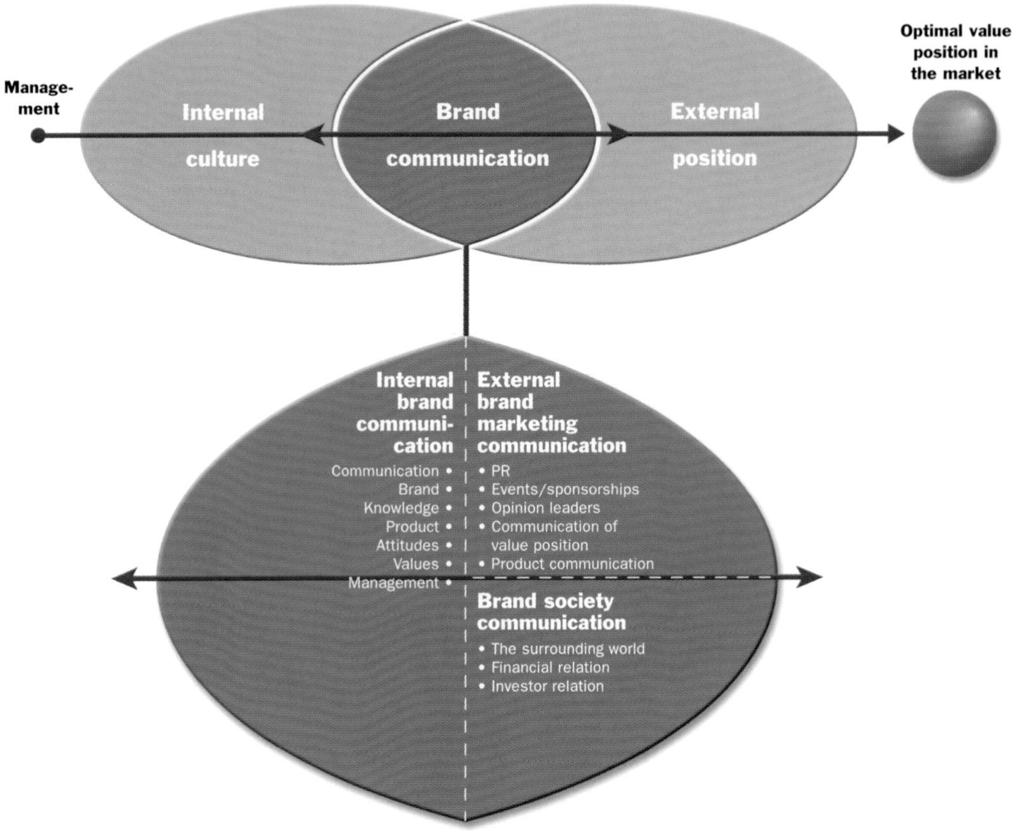

The internal and the external brand communication is the new tool of leadership tying the company together and disseminating information about products and values to the corporation and to the market.

About the creation of internal communication systems

Figure 18.4 also includes the internal communication of the brand. As mentioned in the context of building a strong brand culture, communication is crucial. Only coherent communication externally and internally can enable the brand to accelerate the company into a leading position within the value economy. While systems and directives used to optimize the product value chain, now it is communication that optimizes the value chain.

Traditionally, internal communication has never been seen as a generator of value. Yet there is now a challenge for companies to build an internal communication system that combines brand, knowledge, products, attitudes, values and management, as shown in Figure 18.4. It is no longer a task to be left to a communication department or a corporate secretariat. It is the nerve centre of the entire company.

We are not dealing with communication just for its own sake. You must constantly assess the content and make sure that it really does contribute to value accumulation. And communication is key to the education of the company by constantly distributing focused knowledge, which is the core of the future management of company and brand.

It is an area in which the future top manager will be deeply involved. His or her greatest challenge will be to gather and disseminate knowledge in an appropriate way. In the future there may be internal corporate TV channels or newspapers. Many companies have established intranets and information databases, which is a step in this direction.

Top management must systematize the total brand communication that in future will drive a company. News media all over the world have gained considerable power in society-managers should learn from them.

How do you measure a value position?

The final link in the chain in Figure 18.3 is the value position of the brand, which is the end towards which you constantly work. This was explained in Part 1 and only a few comments are required here.

How are companies going to work on their branding and value positions? How can you become better at determining and evaluating a brand position? How is a top manager going to explain to his or her investors that they

One-brand value position

A brand value position is the end towards which you constantly work.

have just spent millions of dollars on improving a value position – without anyone being able to measure a direct result from the expense?

How does Richard Branson measure whether he has improved his value position 'up against conventions' in the market? He may be able to point to financial results, but the figures might have improved because he was selling parts of the value position and his future business. This happened to Levi's, which increased sales by venturing into very broad distribution channels but lost its opinion leaders and consequently brand value.

It is crucial to determine these issues before you can define your desired value position and steer towards it.

CHAPTER 19

Brand relation management (BRM): redefining the way to market

A company's way to the market will be more differentiated in the value economy. The days when you had one product and distribution handled all your customer relations are gone for ever.

If you want to establish closer relations to your customers – and who would not – then you must make a distinction between the physical and the mental distribution of the brand. In both the industry and the marketing economy, resources used to be tied to the physical distribution system, as shown at the top of Figure 19.1.

Within the value economy, the focus is on all the things consumers receive in addition to the product. That is why investing in a strong value position with customer segments that are profitable to own is vital.

The value economy is not an either-or situation where everything to do with product development and a well-functioning sales system is forgotten. What is new is that the simple physical distribution of products has become a basic competence. The extraordinary competence is the ability to work with values and mental brand distribution.

What is Virgin dealing in?

The Internet is the new bridge between the old economy and the approach of the value economy because it functions both as a communication channel and as an order and sales system. That makes the value economy perfect for both effective physical distribution and potent mental brand distribution. In the value economy, the market is moving in a different way to what we have been used to, which makes it a lot harder to define your place in the market.

**Figure 19.1 A change in the division of resources
– from the old product orientation to the value orientation**

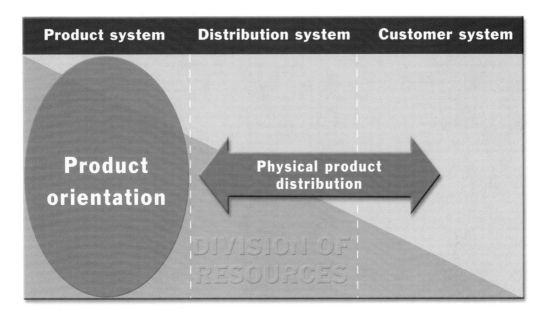

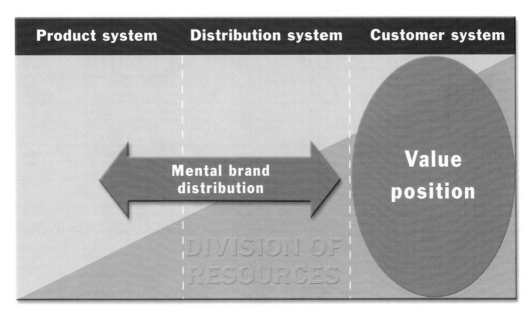

Within the old economy – on top – resources were tied to the physical production and distribution of the product. Within the value economy – below – managers must invest in a strong external value position and in a mental brand distribution and dialogue with consumers.

Which market is Virgin in, for example? Very recently, it used to be enough to implement ERP (Enterprise Resource Planning) systems or ensure efficient control of logistics. Now it is a matter of optimizing relations to your customers and your brand value chain.

The great one-to-one flop

Customer relationship management has already provoked much debate but we should be careful not to get carried away by the CRM way of thinking. It suggests that the customer is always right and that every company should do exactly what Mr or Mrs Consumer tells it to. No way! It must never be customers alone who set the pace and determine the development of the company. That should be the brand.

Take, for example, the hype about the Internet around the turn of the millennium. It was argued then that only individual treatment of consumers could bring competitive advantage. New prophets wrote the new laws in books such as *Cluetrain Manifesto: The End of Business as Usual* by Rick Levine, Christopher Locke, Doc Searls and David Weinberger and *Permission Marketing* by Seth Godin. The customer and individualized communication via the Net was the way forward; everything else was dead and gone.

In Internet jargon this is one-to-one marketing. However, in reality it is little more than a repetition of well-known disciplines.

This sort of thinking assumed the customer was everything and the company was nothing. However, it has long since collapsed. We should remember that consumers have never developed anything, never ventured into new areas and never invented any new products. Renewal comes from companies that push consumers forward.

Consumers find it unusually difficult to see a new direction and they usually reject visionary, groundbreaking concepts that are too far away from what they already know.

Consumers have never developed anything, never ventured into new areas and never invented any new products.

Do not be a creep

Just ask B&O. One of its main values is to introduce groundbreaking products that set new standards. Yet each time it has market tested a new, unique product, the results have been bad. But strangely enough, it is the products that have done worst in these tests that become the greatest successes – once consumers get used to them.

Why we find it so hard to accept the innovative is a paradox, since it is innovations that drive the value economy forward.

But it is certainly wrong to think you should mindlessly follow the consumer. The key – and highly damaging – consequence will be that a company sells out its unique soul. Companies should not be characterless creeps; on the contrary, they should have attitudes and the courage to express them. Consumers buy uniqueness; if we only give them what they say they want, they will lose respect for us.

Companies should not be characterless creeps; on the contrary, they should have attitudes and the courage to express them.

Hot air balloons fall down

It very soon became apparent that going on the Net with a piece of software that was merely playing up to the customers was not enough. What separated the sheep from the goats on the Net was what does so in the non-virtual world – the brand. Consumers want more of everything, particularly substance. They want to be able to visualize the company; lumps of fluffy cotton in cyberspace are much too ephemeral.

Many dot coms thought that they could buy themselves a brand via huge marketing budgets. However, they used traditional media financed by money from a gullible financial world.

The most interesting aspect of this period of Internet hype is that so few could make so many go so wrong. It is a shame really that the Internet got off on a wrong footing. In the right perspective, the Internet is a fabulous techno-

The most interesting aspect of this period of Internet hype is that so few could make so many go so wrong.

logical innovation that plays a huge part in the acceleration of the value centrifuge.

Technologies are not gods

Traditional large corporations have already adopted the Net as a unique channel by which they can fine-tune their business. But there will be many more advanced, interactive means of communication, once broadband, the mobile Internet and digital TV channels are in place. When they are established, we will think of the Internet in the same way that we now think of an ordinary phone.

It is important not to make the old mistake of worshipping technology as some kind of god. Companies and their brands should absorb new possibilities and use them to optimize their businesses. The future can only bring more innovations. That is why companies, if they want to stay in the market for a long period of time, should not base their existence on one innovation alone.

The brand and the value position are the consistent driving forces. They are what helps a company deal with technological innovations.

The value position is sacred

It is often said that B&O is not big enough to keep up with technological developments in its market. That could be correct if B&O's position happened to be to come up with technological innovations. But it isn't. B&O is actually dependent on the technological inventions of others – and the more the better. B&O's mission is to refine the new and add the attitudes and the values of its brand, such as 'clean up the mess' and 'always break the rule'.

B&O contributes with its human touch and design skills to make new technology live up to its own concept of 'a life less ordinary'. B&O is not a slave to the technology race. It owns a value position that its top market segment buys into wholeheartedly. The company constantly redefines both new technologies and itself in relation to the norms of consumers. If B&O cannot buy the product technology it needs to provide 'a life less ordinary', then it develops it itself. For example, it developed small, digital speakers with a high-quality sound. It is important for B&O to be capable of making different and exciting speakers so it developed the appropriate software.

We started from the idea that consumers have the highest priority and that they come before innovation, technology, even the Internet. It is no surprise, as the B&O example shows, that the brand or the value position is more important.

What this is all about is what is your promise to the market, how are you unique, and what are you doing to create high involvement?

This is brand relation management – the relationship between the brand and the consumer, between society and the internal culture and everything around the brand.

Brand relation management

Figure 19.2 is an attempt to illustrate how you should think of your company in the future. You will have to expand the physical distribution of the product to include a mental distribution of the brand.

At the left of Figure 19.2 physical product distribution is at the bottom and mental brand distribution on top. Combining them in the same figure provides a trans-formation model for companies that want to make a transition from the old product-oriented economy to the value economy.

This transformation model is repeated on a larger scale in Figure 19.3, which shows how emphasis was placed on physical product distribution in the old product economy. And this is still important in the value economy. Products

Figure 19.2 Physical product distribution and mental brand distribution

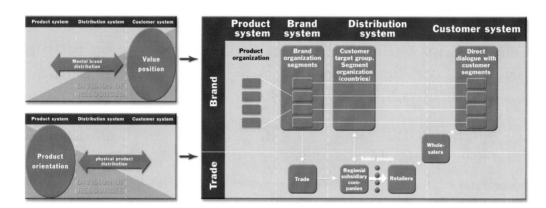

The old economy's focus on physical product distribution will not be enough in the future. In the value economy, mental brand distribution will play a crucial role. In reality, you have two distributions running simultaneously – the physical (below to the right) and the mental (on top to the right).

do need to be physically distributed – a detail that the dot coms forgot at first.

But along with physical product distribution, you must build a mental brand distribution to be safe in the value economy, as illustrated at the top of Figure 19.3. You must aim for the mental distribution of the brand to be as direct a dialogue with consumers as possible. Try to take your point of departure in the customer target group or groups and move from the right towards the left in the figure so that customers, and not the product, become the starting point.

In the other part, you focus on optimizing a physical distribution system, as shown in the lower part of Figure 19.3, which follow the laws of the old economy. Products still need to be moved from A to B.

The point of departure for the brand relation management model is the brand position in the customer system to the far right of the figure. You define the customer segments with which you want to enter into a direct dialogue, aiming to win a dominant position with them. Then you draw a direct line into the company by forming a brand organization in which you concentrate all brand contact with the world. In the value economy this is too risky to leave to product departments. The central brand organization can be duplicated in places where it may be necessary to have a local representation for language or other reasons. This is shown in the top part of the distribution box. You should then establish a distribution in a trade organization, which specializes in the physical distribution of products and services. This could be an existing distribution system, the

Figure 19.3 Brand relation management

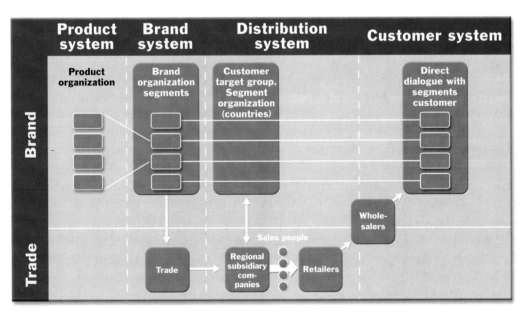

A company's way to market in the future consists of both a traditional product distribution, illustrated in the lower part of the figure, and a mental brand distribution, built on top of the traditional product distribution, at the top of the figure. The starting point is the customer system to the right and a definition of target customers with which you create a direct dialogue.

difference being that you now make sure that it is a professional brand organization that understands brand relation management and the crucial building of value in the market.

Brand relations in B2B

Previously, the trade organization would also have dealt with brand distribution, which meant that only the physical product was distributed. In product-heavy business-to-business (B2B) companies, the product usually serves as the communicator, assisted by a product brochure if any effort has been made. This works badly as the knowledge content of products increases.

At the core of this type of company it usually turns out that it has left it to its distributors to enter a dialogue with customers.

The biggest problem for business-to-business companies that want to work with brand relation management is that their distribution system will not give up ownership of customers. Hardly surprising, since this is their greatest asset.

Find a better way to the market

As far as business-to-consumer (B2C) companies are concerned, many larger brand corporations would think that Figure 19.3 reflects the way in which they already structure their organizations and operate. They have established a brand organization with a marketing department, product managers and marketing managers, and they have a trade organization with a key account function that deals with sales to major retail chains. In other words, they have divided the company organization into a brand communication department and a sales department.

However, what is new in the brand relation management model in Figure 19.3 is the way in which companies could further develop their brand communication.

Most major brand corporations are divided into many

The biggest problem for business-to-business companies that want to work with brand relation management is that their distribution system will not give up ownership of customers. Hardly surprising, since this is their greatest asset.

different product areas, each controlling their own brand and marketing functions. These corporations could benefit from reducing the number of product brands and instead concentrating on a few major superbrands, which can provide much better market penetration and much closer dialogue with core customers.

Ordinary consumer brands mainly use mass communication in their brand construction because it is the only financially manageable way of getting in contact with consumers. However, on the Internet, for example, you will find new options that make it possible, even for very wide brands, to establish a closer dialogue with core customers.

You can look at Figure 19.3 as a way in which several brands are grouped in one major superbrand within one major brand organization, where each customer segment can be integrated via a brand system, as explained in Part 2. You can then use the Internet to establish a closer dialogue with different customer segments.

The advantage of this way of thinking is that you will achieve increased penetration and a much stronger brand, which can serve different market segments. The individual company will always have to decide what is the best way. However, the main idea of brand relation management is that, as a company manager, you redefine your idea of the best way to market in the future and that you incorporate a mental distribution of the brand on top of the physical distribution of the product.

Most major brand corporations are divided into many different product areas, each controlling their own brand and marketing functions.

CHAPTER 20

Redefining the organization

In the future, brands will not be able to remain static. They will have to run faster just to maintain their positions. Those that do not put on their running shoes will disappear.

The law of inertia says that a body at rest will remain at rest unless it is exposed to action. A body in movement will remain in movement unless it is exposed to action. It is the first part of this definition that interests us. Semi-fossilized organizations must get used to the idea of major changes as the company prepares to make a transition to the value economy.

The second part of the definition applies when a company has become used to the new era and the speed of change of the value centrifuge. Then constant movement is essential.

At the moment, corporate management is too static. Despite leading management gurus insisting that a company should be managed according to its value position, most are still stuck in the old mindset of optimizing the product value chain.

Despite leading management gurus insisting that a company should be managed according to its value position, most are still stuck in the old mindset of optimizing the product value chain.

Design your future

The major international management consultants continue to talk about optimizing product value chains, probably because this is their area of knowledge and competence. But they tell us nothing about managing a company with values and attitudes. They do not talk about articulating your company either. However, as Edward de Bono writes in *New Thinking for the New Millennium*: 'You can analyze the past, but you have to design the future.'

Figure 20.1 The traditional product value chain

Production	Product marketing	Logistic distribution	Administration/ economy	Human resource	Marketing	Sales

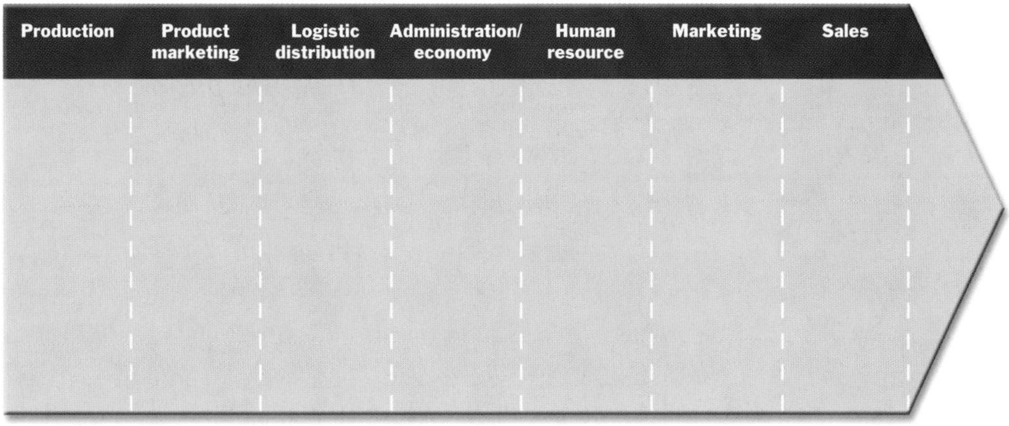

In the traditional product value chain, you optimize the product's progress through various organizational departments.

Professor Michael Porter of Harvard Business School, who developed the concept of the company value chain, divided into primary activities, such as production, logistics, marketing and sales. Across these there are support activities such as human resources, technological research and development. In Porter's model of the product value chain, his main message is that, in terms of strategy, the company's position is the key issue (Figure 20.1).

Invest in mind space

Defining your value position gives you something to aim for. But then companies continue along the old track, because they know no other way. The old way of thinking must be abandoned if the company is to move on. The brand must be made supreme. It is the brand that can define and explain the position externally and internally.

Your corporate mindset must be aligned with the brand value chain, though of course it must be adapted to the individual company.

Figure 18.1 illustrates the unstable situation of companies that are overladen with product features and totally indifferent to brand position and profits. These companies must be brought back in balance via a reallocation of resources that allows larger budgets for capturing consumer mind space.

Fire at the managing director

This way of thinking is illustrated in Figure 20.2, which has traditional corporate functions along the horizontal axis. But it also incorporates the brand value chain as the driving force.

In future the emphasis must be on upgrading the company in its entirety rather than sub-optimizing the different functional areas and departments. Companies are being eaten up from within by a state-within-a-state praxis and by sub-optimizations.

Companies are being eaten up from within by a state-within-a-state praxis and by sub-optimizations.

One response could be to tackle each department or function individually. But it is better to start directly with top management. You cannot achieve a holistic optimization if no one understands what your goal is. As soon as management is able to communicate the goal to each individual within the company, a new era has begun.

This is rarely done. There is no objection to spending lots of money on communicating with consumers but no one spends a penny on explaining the external efforts internally.

Say things the way they are

Today's highly developed knowledge workforce can no longer be treated in the traditional command-and-control way. They must be involved in the company's goals and understand how they fit into the organization as a whole. If this is done properly, they will be able to contribute to the whole, rather than just optimizing their own part. That is why brand communication is a crucial parameter of future company management. The arrows in Figure 20.2

Figure 20.2 The brand value chain organization

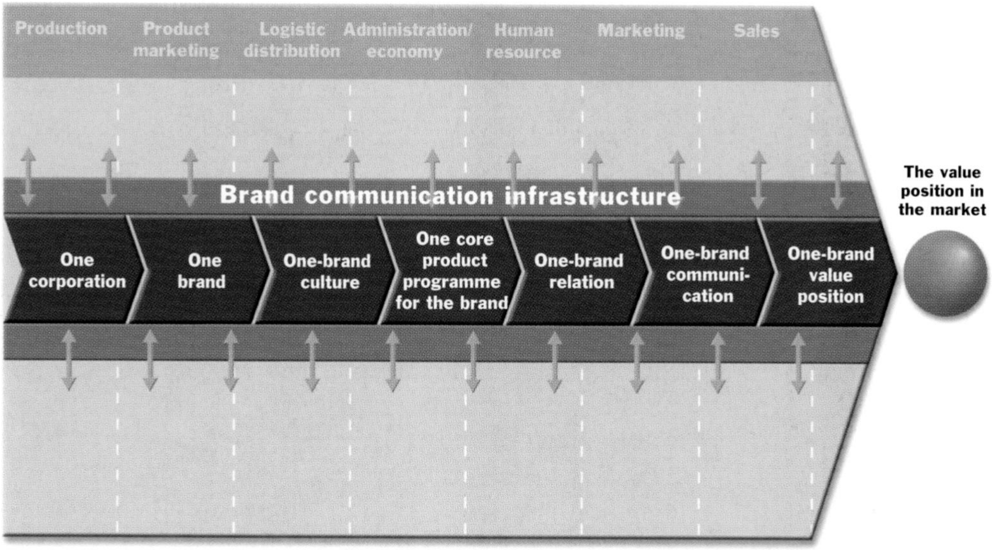

In the future, the value position in the market will be what the entire organization works towards. The brand value chain contributes to managing and optimizing the company. This is done by establishing and defining a brand communication infrastructure, which must be the leading brand communication throughout the company.

illustrate how product knowledge, customer knowledge and management knowledge flow from the brand value chain throughout the organization.

Directing a knowledge workforce in horizontal organizations means involving more people in the management task. What ties it all together is the brand communication, both internal and external, in the brand value chain. A brand communication infrastructure is not a traditional IT structure, but rather an editing of the messages in a brand-controlled infrastructure. This will be crucial for efficiency and innovation in the future. Every company must constantly redefine itself, which requires a fast and efficient accumulation of technological progress, and then articulate an attitude to these that you communicate to your employees.

Simplifying clarity

In Figure 20.2, the brand communication infrastructure is shown as a band that ties your brand value chain together and makes sure that communication is disseminated from management to the various functional areas of the company and back again. It is fundamentally a matter of being able to provide a satisfying answer to the question 'Who are we?'.

At this point, it might be appropriate to reread the passage in Chapter 7 about different forms of intelligence.

The CEO, Louis Gerstner was very clear about what was involved in turning round IBM. His internal book *One Voice*, which set out what IBM was good at, what it was not so good at, and how Gerstner saw its future, was sent to every employee to avoid any communication breakdown at middle management level. Middle managers assume they have power because they possess information. In fact it is the other way round: people who are able to accumulate and pass on the right information are not just sitting on power, they are using it creatively and intelligently.

People who are able to accumulate and pass on the right information are not just sitting on power, they are using it creatively and intelligently.

Gerstner reduced the number of employees in IBM from 400,000 to 200,000 by removing the middle layer, which is superfluous in a modern company because the need for formal administrative control is gone.

Knock over the pyramid

The same kind of clarity is apparent in Virgin. There is no need for a disciplinary schoolmaster-like regime in this context. Clarity is the way forward.

The biggest problem companies face today is that as they grow, the various functions and departments begin to de-focus. This is not deliberate; they are merely trying to create their own identity on which to base their work.

In the past there was simply not enough awareness of the importance of creating an identity for the whole company and that it is this identity that unites people – not control and direction. Control and direction work against the intelligence of employees. They have long since worked out what they are doing in the organization. Companies must look at themselves differently. They are not pyramids. In pyramids things have a tendency to get stuck at the top. But what about the rest of the corporation, that part of it that meets customers and lives the brand?

Use information efficiently

As shown to the left of Figure 20.3, you must force yourself to view the organization as a box that contains many branches in a criss-cross pattern free from direction from above. This creates a much more level organization. The place for management is to the right, at the brand value chain arrow, where ongoing brand communication is the most important tool.

The brand organization is an internal nerve centre, a corporate backbone with nerve ends sending impulses to and from individual departments. All input reaches the central nerve, which handles the information and returns it to employees.

The difference is that the brand is incorporated into every part of the organization. Controlling the brand is no longer a task just for the marketing department. All departments must understand the brand and actively take part in delivering it.

All departments must understand the brand and actively take part in delivering it.

The new nerve centre

The challenge of the future is to transform a top-down giant into a more horizontal, dynamic company by moving everyone closer together. This doesn't necessarily mean in a physical sense but rather via new IT options such as the Internet. This principle is illustrated to the right of Figure 20.3. The vertical lines represent different departments and knowledge centres and whatever else it takes to deliver

Figure 20.3 Future organization structure

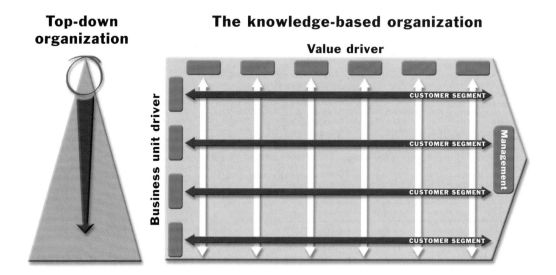

The traditional top-down management of companies is outdated. In the future it will be crucial to channel and exploit the huge amounts of knowledge organizations accumulate. This can only happen in a knowledge-based organization where knowledge is channelled vertically through the matrix and where business units based on customer segments carry the brand horizontally to the market. The most important management task is an ongoing articulation of the company.

the brand. The horizontal lines represent communication from the company to consumers, which could be illustrated by the brand relation management model in Figure 19.3. Management of the company is handled from a nerve centre, whose most important tasks will be to run the brand value chain and to control the brand communication infrastructure.

Centralizing is no solution

Many companies are likely to go bust because they will be unable to respond quickly and efficiently to global change. They do not possess systems that allow them to read market signals and interpret and respond to them. Only companies that manage themselves through a brand value chain and an efficient brand communication will be competitive in the market.

Organizational diagrams often give the impression that companies are well-structured entities. But in reality most of them are fragmented. Combine this fragmentation with increased amounts of knowledge within companies and the picture will be as described in Figure 20.4.

Above a certain size, few companies are as tightly structured as their organizational diagrams suggest. Physically, they will be divided into units, often miles apart, and many employees may never actually see each other. Departments that are very interdependent are located far away from each other and never really talk.

Figure 20.4 The nerve centre organization

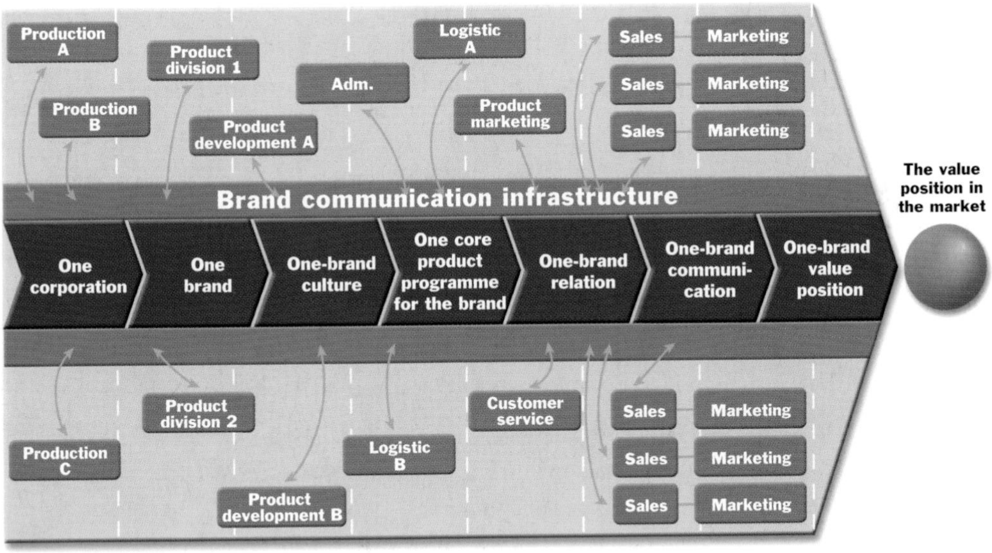

The organization of the future can be seen as a nerve centre receiving input. The various departments and units of global companies are geographically scattered and do not hang together as simply as organizational diagrams suggest. It is therefore important that they are tied together by a brand value chain mindset and a brand communication infrastructure.

The illustration in Figure 20.4 should really be even more chaotic. You might wonder how companies manage to operate so efficiently and hang together globally, as many do. It's rather like the bumblebee, which should not be able to fly but does anyway. The reason why companies have functioned anyway is that the same physical product has been moved around globally and kept the organization together. But in the value economy of the future, the brand will be what is moved around globally.

The ultimate challenge for companies is to control a brand globally. The brand must have unique values and be delivered in a homogeneous way everywhere. The only way to deliver unique value is by creating a unique global company culture. Products alone cannot do this. The foundation of a unique, global company culture is the unique idea, the unique product, the unique attitude and the unique values communicated by a unique brand. Brands are about to create a new world order and you have to understand what is going on if you want to be involved. Have you got something to contribute to the world or not? Have you got something to offer to those who offer their work or not?

This challenge, illustrated in Figure 20.4, is a major task for the future. Companies must build new organizational systems that are not just ways of moving physical products around but are also a virtual system transporting communication, knowledge, attitudes and values – in brief, the brand.

At the moment, companies are building extensive IT infrastructure systems because they are essential for global competition and for tying the organization together globally. But they are focusing on hardware, which is not worth much without the right kind of software. What matters is developing a brand communication infrastructure that can disseminate the brand. Then you can determine the content that is to control the brand and, more importantly, how you get it out through the company, who is in control of it, and how you deliver the brand value in the market.

In the past, systems were designed to allow an organization to deliver a physical product to the market. In the future, you will have to design your organization to run via communication and to accumulate information about products, customers, culture and management from scattered units in different countries. The system must, in particular, be capable of extracting the essence of the information flow and disseminating it around the brand value chain. Everyone talks about knowledge management, but is knowledge controllable? In the future, the information gatekeepers – people who are good at collecting and disseminating relevant knowledge – will be important assets for a company.

In the future, you will have to design your organization to run via communication.

There will be two systems running simultaneously in companies; one that controls the production and logistics and another that develops knowledge and competitive power. It will probably take a mini-revolution to get traditional hierarchies to accept this. But top-down management won't add any value whatever to the company.

There will be two systems running simultaneously in companies; one that controls the production and logistics and another that develops knowledge and competitive power.

In the future, mastering communication will be a priority and it will be the only way of managing a company. Organizations that can combine and optimize scattered knowledge departments, that can deal with markets across the world, and that can disseminate a common culture within a brand communication infrastructure will be the winners in the value economy.

Many now realize that companies must organize themselves around a common idea and culture, that they must be made smaller. Most have realized that major hierarchies with many layers make no sense any more and that you need to share management.

The decentralized brand communication infrastructure

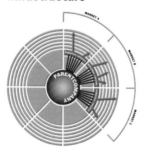

In old-fashioned companies, where communication to the market is controlled by a decentralized organization, markets experience many different positions, which is damaging to the company.

The centralized brand communication infrastructure

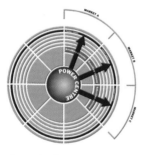

Instead, the company should be managed according to centrally articulated values and attitudes to achieve a unified position in all markets.

Here are two examples of leaders of major international companies who have tried to restructure their organizations as an entity.

Henrik Håkonsson from Brüel og Kjær, one of the world's leading corporations making acoustic measuring equipment, has acknowledged that he has to unite the corporation around a mission to move it onwards. He has also realized that it is necessary to have the entire corporation with him.

As Brüel og Kjær is a very global corporation, Håkonsson spends more than 160 days a year travelling and personally getting everyone to join in the same mission, direction and values. In three years he succeeded in turning round a huge deficit with a no-nonsense managerial style. It is very demanding to manage an international corporation this way, which is an approach most people will be able to handle only for a short period of time.

The other example is Jacob Schram, managing director of one of Norway's largest corporations, Statoil's Norwegian Retail organization. He realized that the many different departments within the organization were working independently of each other and all had their own values and attitudes. His task was to create a common spirit and he did this in a rather direct manner. His theory was that you simply had to gather together the various departments physically to get them to understand each other and work in the same direction. He identified the most essential people in promoting the brand – 130 individuals.

Direct communication was established throughout the organization so that no information was lost on its way from the top to other parts of the organization. Schram tried to reunite the corporation around a common mission and idea, and he made sure that it reached all the vital parts of the company and that it was implemented. This allowed him to turn the unit from deficit to profit. He restructured the management from traditional functional

Figure 20.5 Global communication infrastructure

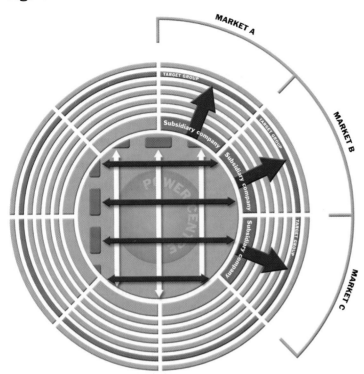

It is crucial for success that market communication is centralized and controlled by the knowledge-based organization of the future. With new information technology and a brand communication infrastructure, you can tie the global organization together into one major, unified entity.

managers to a much larger group of those who atually took the brand out into the market.

These two examples illustrate different ways of solving the problem facing all brands at the moment: how you group the company organization around a common idea and restructure it into an entity that works as a strong, dynamic force in the market.

It is crucial to group the company organization around a common idea and restructure it into an entity that works as a strong, dynamic force in the market.

The challenge of the future lies in being able to exploit the new technologies that become available – the Internet, the mobile Internet, the new broadband Net, and interactive TV. All can help tie the company closer together through lively and direct communication. However, this requires managers to understand the possibilities and the need for a constant articulation and communication of the company and the brand within the organization. Doing so will create a sense of belonging.

Figure 20.5 illustrates how you can make international organizations more open via a communication infrastructure. It is the internal, knowledge-based organization that is the central point of all communication and building value in the market.

While it is a matter of tying the organization together with communication technology, it also requires management to take their task as editorial board and communicator very seriously. This means editing all the communication that flows within the organization. This is an entirely new managerial task.

CHAPTER 21

Redefining leadership

When the brand, rather than one or more products, directs, the company managers have to change their self-perception. What used to be considered sensible leadership will not be enough in the value economy.

A good manager must understand the fundamental difference between the expansive value perception of the brand way of thinking and a narrow product perception. The manager must also be quite clear about the fundamental definition of the corporation as a brand (see the models in Chapter 6 and/or *Corporate Religion*).

A manager must be part of the very roots of the company to fully understand the brand. Old virtues, such as being a good administrator, won't work in the value economy. The prerequisite for knowing something about how the company has come to own a unique position in the market is being able to really live your brand. Otherwise you cannot be at the head of the company and its brand communication infrastructure.

Anybody can administer

So, the leader must decide how to decode new trends and technologies and be able to transform these into redefinitions of the brand. Quite a difference to going through accounts and attending board meetings tailed by your financial manager. And it gets better.

First and foremost, the manager must be able to articulate and to communicate the brand to the external market and to the internal organization – in other words, he or she must be a good communicator.

First and foremost, the manager must be able to articulate and to communicate the brand to the external market and to the internal organization – in other words, he or she must be a good communicator. Today, administration of a company is basic stuff, a qualification you just have. In the same manner, you just know how to develop products and distribute them physically in the market.

Because these two departments have lacked power within organizations as top management have focused on production, finances and administrative control. What is needed now is a personal stance. The brand must move upwards in the organization, as shown in Figure 8.2.

Only the few express the future clearly

Begin by getting familiar with the rules of the value economy game and focus on innovation. Working actively with innovation will seem even stranger to the typical administrative manager than to the technical manager. But if the manager makes an effort to understand developments and spends time cultivating new trends in relation to the brand and the brand position, he or she will succeed in creating an innovation culture within the company.

Another major change for the manager is that the nature of management will be radically transformed. The future of management is a team game of several highly qualified employees who have agreed to join forces around a particular task. Seen in this light, the articulation of the brand position you are aiming to capture is important. This is communication leadership.

In the value economy you do not manage via directives and rules, which make little sense to highly educated employees. They can only be directed via articulations of the brand values and the brand direction. In the past, the most important tasks of top management were administrative, financial and control tasks. Now their task is the mental understanding of attitudes and values and the articulation of the direction in which the company is going. In the future, when markets and technologies will change faster than ever, innovation will be essential. The manager will have

The future of management is a team game of several highly qualified employees who have agreed to join forces around a particular task.

to be on the cutting edge of the market-place if he or she wants to stand a chance of understanding what is going on, be able to articulate it, and to guide the company forward. The only way of handling the accelerating flow of information is by sticking to a firm set of values. Otherwise there will be too many loose ends. The manager will get nowhere by shouting orders. Direction must be based on a mutual understanding of where the company is going and how fast. Companies need to be like personalities. The same thing goes for their leaders. In other words: be unique.

Within the new value economy, choices must be made. You need to have the courage to believe in something and to pursue it. The manager cannot make do with merely administrating. You are more than just a leader in name; you must also demonstrate leadership in all areas. The company needs a strong personality to succeed in the value economy, and the same thing goes for the leader. But what if you haven't got great charisma? Then you must bring something else very strong and powerful to the table.

We are back to the days of tribal cultures, where the person who was stronger, smarter or had some other competence became the chief. He became the chief because he had something special; otherwise power was shared between a group of people. Leaders of tomorrow must possess the same kind of skills, as there will be fewer machines and physical assets to manage but more highly educated people. This requires proper leadership, as in the old tribal cultures. Employees need a leader whom they can follow, respect and relate to.

We are facing a paradox. The reliance on knowledge means more independent employees, who are harder to manage within old management systems. At the same time, the market is demanding unique value in the brand, which must be delivered consistently every time. These two things are opposites and mean that new ways of managing companies in the future will have to be found.

In Chapter 7, I mentioned the concepts of IQ and EQ, which were the normal and the emotional intelligence quotient, and above these the SQ to control them. The successful leader of the future can deliver SQ to the company in the form of an understanding of where the company is located on a larger scale.

The leaders of tomorrow must possess the same skills as the ancient chiefs of tribal cultures – competence, faith and substance. Using spiritual intelligence (SQ) the leader must provide an understanding of where the company is located on a larger scale.

Most important is an understanding of who the company is, how it is related to the market and competitors, and how it fits into a large and chaotic globalized world. By being able to articulate and constantly communicate this complicated context, you become a real leader. The leader contributes a higher level of understanding to his or her highly productive and knowledgeable employees.

It is no longer possible to hide behind closed doors and sheets of figures. The manager must get out on the floor, where he or she can be seen, and must be able to perform if people are to follow. The cleverest employees are going to places that have a mission and which are run by proper leaders.

Good leaders are usually the ones who are extremely good at communicating, or who can get someone to help them with it. Without insulting anyone, it is safe to say that Bill Gates is not the world's best communicator. But he has still managed to build an empire by communicating his attitudes via the media and by taking the leading role in his field.

Is he a manager or does he believe in it?

There is a tremendous difference between a person who is running a company and someone who believes in a company. If the leader is strong in his or her belief and deeply involved in the company, it cannot but rub off on everyone else.

We see more and more examples of great company leaders being headhunted to manage large corporations. But more and more often this tends to end in failure. Most people find an explanation in the way that financial markets control companies. But the truth lies elsewhere. When leaders are headhunted, they are assessed according to old virtues, such as their skills in company administration, and not by whether they believe in the companies and what they are doing.

Leaders can be divided into two categories – those who live with and for their company and those who are happy just administering the company.

Leaders can be divided into two categories: Those who live with and for their company and whose passion rubs off on the entire organization – these are also very giving leaders, who are in great demand to work for and with – and those who are happy just administering the company. It is obvious that they are bored – they are physically present but not mentally. People notice this and it spreads rapidly throughout the organization. How is the company to have faith if its leader has none?

In the value economy, companies must contribute a unique value. This requires a leader who has the courage to make decisions and who can communicate them to the entire company. Communicating figures via systems won't suffice. What really creates involvement is passion. Not only internally but also externally, the leader must articulate values and culture in order to attract people of the same belief.

Not only internally but also externally, the leader must articulate values and culture in order to attract people of the same belief.

Management via the brand

The brand is what accumulates and articulates company values, both internally and externally, which is why one of the most important tasks of the manager is ensure that everyone delivers the brand. The manager is in charge of employees' efforts to optimize the brand, which means that the brand is no longer just a marketing function. Leaders must make radical changes within their companies if they are to succeed in redefining them to operate in the value economy.

The company must be streamlined via the brand value chain mindset, that is according to the brand and the value position it wants to capture. If the leader used to be the control expert, now he or she is out and about educating all areas in the company identity and the ways in which they can contribute to value accumulation. It isn't enough for the IT department, for example, just to deliver IT. The leader must determine how IT contributes to the optimizing of the brand communication through the development of a brand communication infrastructure. The product

If the leader used to be the control expert, now he or she is out and about educating all areas in the company identity and the ways in which they can contribute to value accumulation.

development department is not just making products. It should develop products that constantly reinforce the brand position.

It is the task of the leader to make sure that all links within the company work closely together around the brand. In the product economy companies grew and branched in all directions so that any overview disappeared. All this now needs clearing up so that the essence of the company can be articulated.

This requires one thing: that the leader has the courage to find something to believe in.

CHAPTER 22

Redefining market boundaries

Companies once defined their markets in terms of products. In the value economy, market boundaries are fuzzier. Markets must be understood in terms of the value they provide in the consumer's mind. Mind space is the new frontier, and one where boundaries are metaphysical.

Companies have always put a lot of effort into strengthening their market position – and keeping up with competitors. Within the industry economy, this was manageable. You had a clear idea of which companies made the same types of product as you; the challenge was making better products to safeguard your future.

But there was also a battle between production and sales, where the latter made persistent attempts to gain control over customers. This way, the distribution link could turn into just as much of a competitor as other companies. In the value economy, competition will again increase because the concept of market boundaries is going to be radically different.

In the past, market boundaries have been defined by products. There were markets for washing powder, air travel, bank services, packaging, bridal wear, water pipes, furniture, socks, lemonade and insurance. Companies had very well-defined product areas to relate to. Within these you built brands with precise positions.

This will be challenged in the value economy, especially if the product is inferior. Now what matters is the mind space a brand's values can capture in consumers' heads

Figure 22.1 Market boundaries are multi-dimensional within the value economy

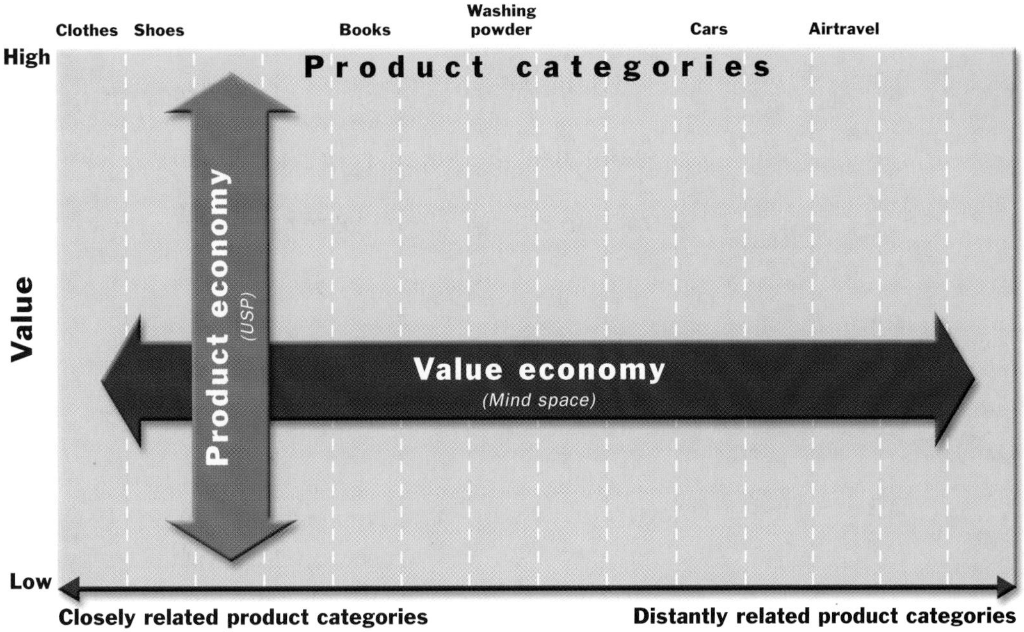

In the product orientation mindset, market boundaries are made up of product categories. However, if you understand the value economy, you can spread your brand across a large number of categories and fields. Consequently, it will be harder to see where new competitors emerge, radically altering the rules of the game.

– they take products for granted. The value economy means that only intangible value positions have financial value. These ideas are illustrated in Figure 22.1. The value economy is a paradigm shift in thinking about companies and markets. Before, you could relate to a particular market defined by product; in the future, it will be much more difficult because competition will moves across boundaries, as shown in the figure. A brand with a strong value position can appear from an entirely different area and capture large market shares. The value economy makes it much harder to manage a company because the market is going to be multi-dimensional. But rather than seeing this as a problem, you could also see it as an opportunity. What it needs is to develop the company itself into a strong brand capable of moving across markets (see Figure 22.1). It takes a strong belief and great courage.

Show fight against a virginal bank

In most companies, market boundaries are viewed traditionally – that is, product oriented. If, however, you were aware of the value position that you own – or could own – in the market, you would find out how easily you can expand into several different product categories. What differentiates companies from each other is their value positions and their brands. Virgin's value position, 'up against conventions', is so powerful that it creates a whole new market area across the usual product boundaries. Virgin ventures into air travel, the bridalwear market, the bank market, the insurance market, and so on.

This places higher demands on, for example, traditional banks because the reasons for choosing Virgin bank are completely different to those that consumers usually have for choosing a bank. The cult around the Richard Branson personality is hard to match if you are a dull financial expert.

Virgin has spread its value position 'up against conventions' into a large number of areas.

Virgin's approach is the same for the air travel market, and British Airways cannot contain it. It tried with the discount brand GO, but its original brand is powerless. Virgin, on the contrary, accumulates its brand and value position from many other places rather than one specific product category.

Create involvement or get driven out of business

Nike has done a similar thing. It now has such a firm grip on the youth market that youngsters steer clear of ordinary shoe shops. Not many years ago, no one in the traditional shoe business would have thought that a sports shoe label would be their biggest competitor. Thanks to its all-encompassing value position, Nike will also, with time, be able to expand its product stretch considerably.

Figure 22.2 Levi's redefinition of the market

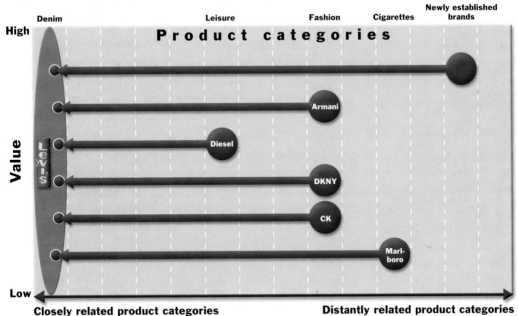

By the end of the last century Levi Strauss jeans was challenged by a number of brands, which conquered a part of the denim market with value positions gained in other product categories.

Levi's experienced just how severely you can be attacked from completely different product segments by brands with strong value positions, as shown in Figure 22.2. Levi's owned the denim segment – and it still does really – yet it lost both sales and customers. Levi's did everything right according to the basic rules of the industry and the marketing economy. It had a strong product and a strong brand, which was superior within the product category. However, slowly but surely, the major fashion brands built brand positions based on emotional values that created strong consumer involvement.

Calvin Klein once said to a magazine that he would not dream of wearing a pair of CK jeans because, to him, jeans are Levi's. However, Calvin Klein, Giorgio Armani (Armani Jeans), DKNY and others all sell jeans made from denim and other comfortable materials. Diesel does the same and so do Benetton, Sisley, Banana Republic and Gap. The original jeans, with their roots in the Californian gold rush, were undermined by the fashion business.

How much brand power have you got?

Levi's was not beaten by a company selling a better product, which would have been the rule in the old economy. Many would even say that it was entirely new products that replaced the classic denim jeans. But that is not the most important point. The main reason why fashion brands stole the customers was brand power, the ownership of a particular customer group who buy into a value position.

The right kind of value position can take over a market and completely redefine market boundaries.

A traditional approach would have been for Levi's to try to make its denim trouser even better, which in fact would have made no difference whatsoever in this situation. The battle was fought in a new and intangible place – the universe of value positions and brand power.

Levi's was challenged by brands, which possessed more brand power.

Brand surveys still place Levi's as one of the most powerful youth brands. However, these surveys are performed according to old ways of assessing brands, which shows how difficult it is going to be in future to measure and monitor your brand position. The Levi's brand has maintained its power of penetration but it will still have to renew its relevance to its target group. An identity can no longer be formed from a pair of denim trousers with riveted pockets. Levi's must recover the rebellious, freedom-loving value essence for its brand position. As we saw in Chapter 3, awareness makes no difference to a brand that fails to create involvement for its customers. Awareness in itself sells nothing.

Value positions redefine markets

In the future, companies will be operating along an entirely new axis named value positions in the market. When trying to find out who your future competitors might be, you must draw a broader picture than you might be used to in order to account for all threats and opportunities.

As Figure 22.3 shows, it is obviously appealing to create an entirely new market based on a patented product innovation. But even those companies that launch major new products and should be able to consolidate a new market as a first mover increasingly fail to profit from it. Why? The answer is simple: they have neither the brand nor the power to penetrate the market.

A good example of the conflict between product orientation and value orientation is the telecommunications market. This market is becoming very crowded. So here, as in so many other places, it will be brand power that makes the difference.

A packed telecommunications market

Take a look at the development from the point of view of Sweden's Ericsson (now Sony Ericsson), which contributed

Figure 22.3 Create a market

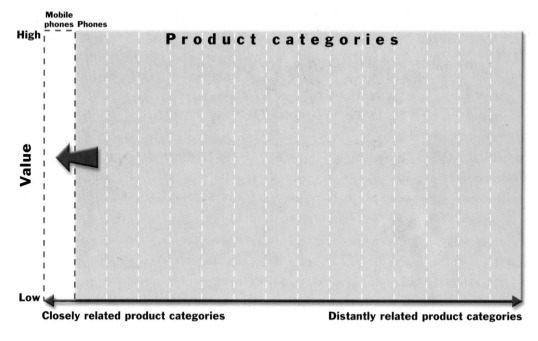

The possibilities of creating and dominating a new market are better with the right value position than with simple product development because nowadays anyone can make anything.

to a redefining of the telecoms market with its mobile phones. Sony Ericsson's immediate competitors are Finland's Nokia and America's Motorola, though it is also battling with Holland's Philips and Germany's Siemens.

Soon high-speed UMTS (Universal Mobile Tele-communication System) – the third generation of mobile phones – will be available. UMTS facilitates the mobile multi-media market of data, photographs and moving images. A large number of providers will be battling to get into this market, as illustrated in Figure 22.4.

The players are, of course, Nokia, Sony Ericsson, Motorola, Philips, Siemens and Panasonic. Who knows, maybe Palm, Compaq, IBM, Apple, Microsoft, and even some fashion brands, may also join in.

Figure 22.4 The value position battle of the new UMTS market (mobile Internet)

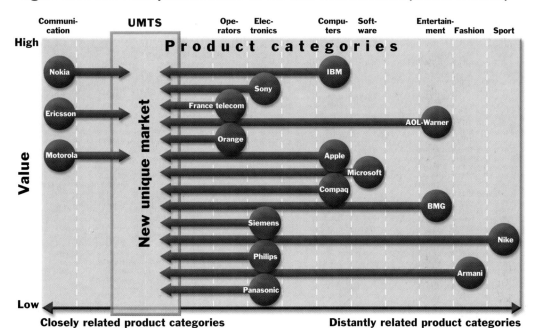

The future UMTS market – the mobile Internet – will, in reality, be captured by many different companies from widely different business areas. The winners will be those that possess the most powerful value positions, which they can transfer into new markets.

Who would want to be pushed over by a superbrand?

Let us, once again, take a look at the situation from the point of view of Ericsson, which has built a position within the fastnet phone market that has been transferred to mobile communication. The brand is very product oriented and has not received any added value, let alone a clear direction. The new situation calls for a clarification of the brand and that Ericsson builds a more distinct value position for the new multi-media market. This the partnering with Sony could help contribute to. Otherwise, it runs the risk of being overtaken by superbrands with strong brand positions and ownership of particular customer groups.

Ericsson is not the only one to lack a position that it can transfer into new markets. Change is taking place so quickly that only a very few business areas will avoid having to redefine themselves for new markets. The sooner a company reacts to the new value economy, the better. Read, for example, the LEGO case study in Chapter 4 again.

The product value chain is pointless

The great challenge for companies will be to develop a brand with a brand position that can direct the organization into the future. This brand position must express the essence of the company and its culture – what it is really good at, according to our definition of a company's corporate religion in Chapter 6. It is crucial that companies define themselves and articulate which value positions they want to capture and then adjust their brand and company culture in relation to this position.

This is an entirely new task for companies, managers and consultants, who are used to planning strategies according to an optimized product value chain. However, this makes no sense if you haven't got a grip on your brand. What matters is that you optimize your brand value chain, as explained in previous chapters.

All this calls for some entirely new fields of competence, which are hard to acquire because they are based on an understanding of values and attitudes and on the ability to communicate knowledge.

See you in the value economy

It cannot be emphasized enough that all companies are facing a major paradigm shift and that the ones that fully come to terms with it will acquire some significant competitive advantages within the value economy.

The inertia of the industry economy means that consultancy businesses basing their services on IT, the product value chain optimizing, global analysis, and so on, will fail to meet the demands for creative strategy development.

The ability to see the uniqueness of a company and really get to its core and describe its qualities is something you cannot do via analysis.

To get by in the value economy, you must deliver unique value. History shows that conservatism tends to prevail; no one dares take a stand for fear of making a mistake. But in the value economy, you have to take a stand.

Figure 22.5 is an attempt at illustrating the new competence areas. Along one axis is IT and along the other the competence fields belonging to the old product economy, where the traditional management consultants will typically be found. Along the third axis are traditional communication agencies. These really ought to arm themselves now because the battle is moving in their direction. Communication has never been more important and it will become even more so in the future.

At the moment, everyone is focusing on the circle in the middle of the figure, which is the establishment of new IT structures relating to the Internet and CRM systems. It is here that the new web agencies are springing up and challenging traditional IT businesses.

Consultants claim to have a monopoly on strategy development. But often what they do is to restructure companies and establish new processes. They are still operating within the old economy and focusing on the product chain. The fact that the Internet has now become a part of the product chain does not legitimize their way of operating in the value economy. The problem with consultants is that their culture is all about analysis and best practice.

What is required is that you have the courage to believe in something and that you accumulate value. You need to channel value into companies by helping them to define themselves, developing values and articulating and communicating them. All of which is far removed from consultants' usual fields of competence. It requires a deeper

Figure 22.5 The new competences of the value economy

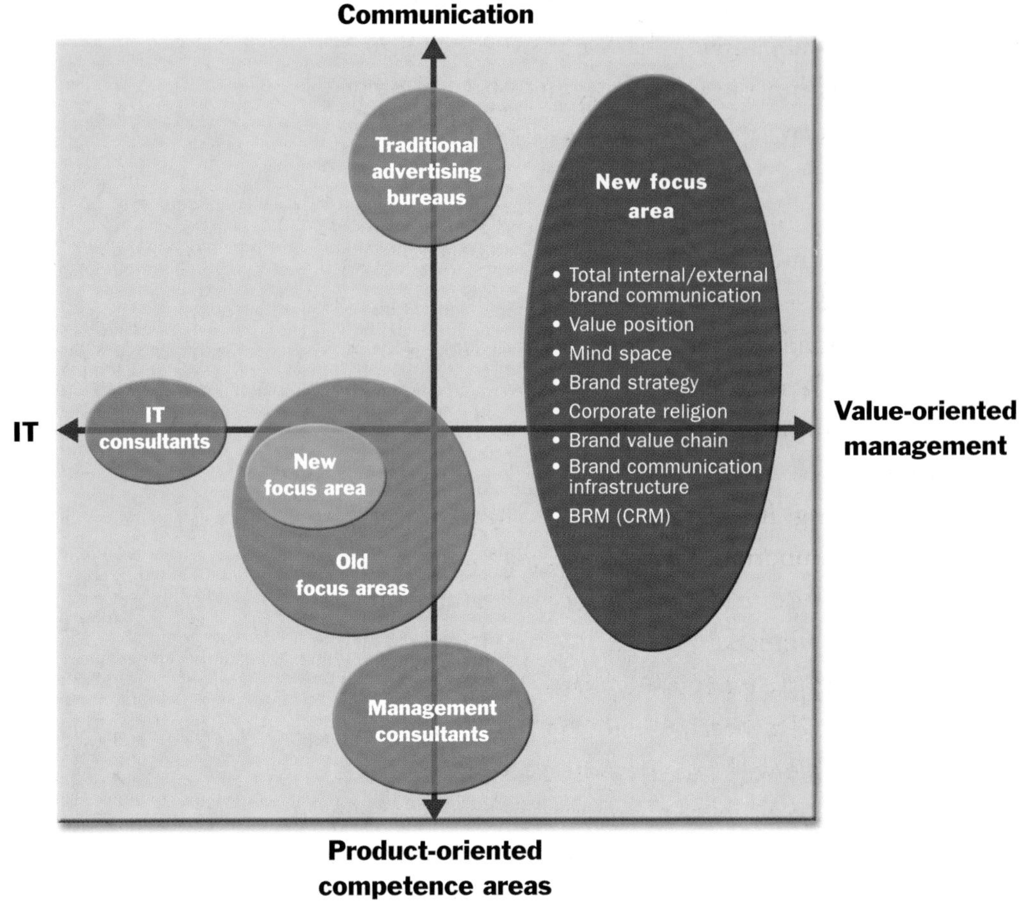

Communication

Traditional advertising bureaus

New focus area

- Total internal/external brand communication
- Value position
- Mind space
- Brand strategy
- Corporate religion
- Brand value chain
- Brand communication infrastructure
- BRM (CRM)

IT

IT consultants

New focus area

Old focus areas

Value-oriented management

Management consultants

Product-oriented competence areas

For the time being the focus is on IT infrastructure. The future value economy demands new competencies which take into account the brand and its value position in the market. These are competencies which the traditional suppliers of strategy development, communication and IT do not possess.

understanding of customer segments, trends, values and a holistic approach that goes deeper than the usual analysis.

Naturally, there is still going to be a demand for people who know how to restructure and optimize processes. But that has nothing to do with strategic work. The capability to develop unique brands with unique value positions is what will separate the goats from the sheep in the value economy.

Figure 22.5 opens a new front on the market of competence – the value economy – illustrated by an oval to the right. This oval contains the concepts that will make the difference within the value economy, though we will also see many new and exciting concepts and areas of competence in the near future.

Managers who attempt to develop unique corporate strategies in the future should focus on the concepts dealt with in this book – mind space, corporate religion, brand value chain, brand communication infrastructure, and BRM (CRM). These are the areas to manage – and focus must be placed on the creation of unique value and value accumulation.

We are facing interesting times. Only those who understand the importance of becoming familiar with the new areas of competence and exploiting the possibilities will come out as winners.

We can anticipate great market battles fought out with values and attitudes because only by living up to the values in a credible way can you hope to win customers. Companies must contribute to the market, which is why managers must give everything they have got. They must have the courage to make decisions and to create something. Within the value economy, the power lies in unique value, and this is going to create a whole new dimension. It is not good enough to simply improve things a bit – you must get out of the closet and have the courage to believe in something so that you have something to offer to consumers and to employees.

Get unique now… or never.

See you in the new value economy.

CORPORATE RELIGION

Jesper Kunde

ISBN   0273 66111 6

Paperback

Size   244x172mm

Extent   304pp

Corporate Religion is the international best-selling predecessor to *Unique Now...or Never*. It explains how to build a strong market position in a world where consumers no longer simply demand the product, but reliable companies and brands. The winners of the future will be those corporations who can handle the consequences of this change and implement strategies revealed in this book. The aim is to unite everything in a Corporate Religion. A religion that brings together the internal company and the external market in a shared, connected flow of understanding.

"I wish I'd written *Corporate Religion*! It is a genuine original in a world full of 'me too' management books. Bottom line: This is a timely, brilliant, eadable, important book."
Tom Peters

Visit our website at
www.business-minds.com

More guru power to your [business-mind]

Even at the end there's more we can learn. If today's idea is tomorrow's task, then we believe there's always value to be found in getting to tomorrow's ideas first. That's why *Business Minds* is more than a book.

For who to read, what to know and where to go in the world of business, visit us at **business-minds.com**.

Here we're creating a place where you can go to connect with new business ideas as they evolve, and engage with the next generation of thought leaders.

Share the latest ideas with the people that can make you and your business more innovative and productive. Each month our e-newsletter, *Business-minds Express*, delivers an infusion of thought leadership, guru interviews, new business practice and reviews of key business resources directly to you. Subscribe for free at

www.business-minds.com/goto/newsletters

If you want to explore some of these ideas further, then at business-minds.com you'll find books by many of the gurus interviewed as well as a wide range of additional books and executive briefings that will help you put these ideas, and many more, to work.

To connect with the gurus and participate in the annual *Thinkers 50* guru ranking survey, go to

www.business-minds.com/goto/gurus

Spreading knowledge is a great way to improve performance and enhance business relationships. If you found this book useful, then so might your colleagues or customers. If you would like to explore corporate purchases or custom editions personalized with your brand or message, then just get in touch at

www.business-minds.com/corporatesales

Visit our website at [**www.business-minds.com**]